The Overrepresentation
African American Childr

Race Matters

in Child Welfare

Edited by Dennette M. Derezotes, MSW, LCSW; John Poertner, DSW; and Mark F. Testa, PhD

CWLA Press • Washington, DC

CWLA Press is an imprint of the Child Welfare League of America. The Child Welfare League of America is the nation's oldest and largest membership-based child welfare organization. We are committed to engaging people everywhere in promoting the well-being of children, youth, and their families, and protecting every child from harm.

CHILD WELFARE LEAGUE OF AMERICA, INC.
HEADQUARTERS
440 First Street, NW, Third Floor, Washington, DC 20001-2085
E-mail: books@cwla.org

CURRENT PRINTING (last digit)
10 9 8 7 6 5 4 3 2 1

Cover and text design by Jennifer R. Geanakos
Edited by Julie Gwin
Printed in the United States of America

ISBN-13: 978-0-87868-874-6
ISBN-10: 0–87868–874–9

Library of Congress Cataloging-in-Publication Data
Race matters in child welfare : the overrepresentation of African American children in the system / edited by Dennette Derezotes, Mark F. Testa, and John Poertner.
p. cm.
ISBN 0-87868-874-9 (alk. paper)
1. Child welfare--United States. 2. Social work with African American children. 3. Social work with minorities--United States. 4. Social service and race relations--United States. 5. Race discrimination--United States. I. Derezotes, Dennette. II. Testa, Mark. III. Poertner, John.
HV741.R26 2005
362.7'089'96073--dc22 2004011299

Contents

Introduction

African American children are significantly overrepresented in America's child welfare system. Some researchers contend that this overrepresentation is a consequence of social vulnerabilities such as poverty, single parenthood, and unemployment, which put African American children at greater risk of maltreatment than white children.

Although research documents higher levels of abuse and neglect among economically vulnerable families, the results of three National Incidence Studies of Child Abuse and Neglect (1980, 1986, and 1993) show no significant differences in overall child maltreatment rates between African Americans and whites. This unexpected finding implies that African American children, although poorer than white children as a whole, are actually at lower risk of maltreatment compared with white children in similar economic circumstances.

Westat, the research firm that conducted the National Incidence Studies, recognized the challenge to conventional wisdom posed by these findings and formed an internal Race Matters Study Group to initiate inquiries into the factors responsible for the disproportionate representation of African American children in the child welfare system. At the same time, the Children and Family Research Center in the School of Social Work, University of Illinois at Urbana-Champaign, focused attention on the overrepresentation of African American children in Illinois's child welfare system.

During 1999, Westat and the center initiated discussions about jointly examining the factors contributing to the overrepresentation of African American children in the child welfare system. With financial support from the Illinois Department of Children and Family Services, Westat and the center organized a forum at which scholars presented papers that addressed various aspects of the overrepresentation issue. The forum offered a platform for sharing research findings and afforded an opportunity to initiate an open discussion with child welfare professionals from across the country. The first Race Matters forum was held in Washington, DC, on January 8–9, 2001. The papers that were presented are reproduced in chapters 2 through 14 in this book. Chapter 1 provides a context for the ongoing discussion, including a summary of research in this area, a discussion of different perspectives on the issues, and a model for examining them.

Soon after the first forum, Casey Family Programs, a private, national operating foundation, joined the collaboration. Casey was examining disproportionality as well as disparities in outcomes for children of color in the child welfare system. Casey was looking for better ways to explain the causes of disproportionality and what could be done through practice, policy, research, and community engagement to mitigate both the disproportionality and disparities. A second Race Matters forum, cosponsored by Casey, the center, and Westat was convened in Chicago, IL, on March 25–26, 2002. This forum broadened the dialogue to examine disproportionality of different racial and ethnic groups and drew a diverse group of child welfare experts representing research, policy, administration, practice, and advocacy interests committed to developing a national agenda for addressing disproportionality in the child welfare system.

Interest in these issues has resulted in the formation of the The Race Matters Consortium, a national, multisystem initiative whose mission is to research and develop policy responses to the phenomenon of racial and ethnic disproportionality in the child welfare system. The Children and Family Research Center administers the consortium with financial support from Casey and the Illinois Department of Children and Family Services. The consortium's goals are to: (a) gain a greater understanding of issues that affect racial disproportionality, (b) create a national awareness of racial and ethnic disproportionality and the resulting disparities in child welfare outcomes, (c) develop and promote policies and practices that address racial and ethnic disproportionality and disparities, and (d) develop and maintain an organizational structure to support the consortium's mission.

What can be done about the disproportionate representation of children of color in the child welfare system? The lessons learned are that disproportionality and disparities arise from the complex interaction of multiple factors at the child, family, community, and policy levels. Underlying conditions of individual risk and family vulnerability can be mitigated by informal supports and formal services that can compensate for the disadvantaged circumstances in which many children of color are raised. Sometimes these agents of informal and formal protection can bring attention to the needs of vulnerable children, which can result in overrepresentation in the formal systems, and at other times, it can shield these same families from formal investigation.

The extent of overrepresentation varies historically and can be magnified or diminished at each stage of the decisionmaking continuum, from child abuse reporting and investigation to foster care and adoption. Formal authorities have the capacity to develop responsive policies and supportive practices that can reduce and sometimes eliminate the disparities in outcomes experienced by children of color. What more can be done to improve child welfare outcomes?

- Researchers should enhance the quality of their studies to identify more completely and adequately the causes of the problem and the specific stages in the child welfare processes (i.e., looking at key decision points along the continuum where disparities continue to exist).

- State administrators of child welfare agencies should enhance the cultural competence of their workers and regularly conduct self-assessments of their strategies to reduce bias at all stages of decisionmaking.

- Federal policymakers should monitor state progress in addressing this problem and provide states with resources to implement effective interventions.

- Organizations involved nationally and locally with child welfare need to make disproportionality a priority for research and action.

- Concerned citizens should mobilize community groups to address the problem and encourage policymakers at all levels of government to develop policies and programs to ameliorate the sources of disproportionality and disparity in the child welfare system.

This book is the first product of the Race Matters Consortium. It provides readers with information to promote the systematic examination of disproportionality and related issues in the child welfare system. It does not answer all questions related to what happens to children and families in their communities or how broad federal policies may affect them, but instead looks specifically at what is going on in the child welfare system and provides readers with a decision-point model with which to look more precisely at what is happening along the child welfare continuum of intervention. We hope you will find this volume valuable in your search to understand racial and ethnic disproportionality and disparities better, as well as the role you can play to improve outcomes for all children in care.

—*The Race Matters Consortium*

CHAPTER 1

Factors Contributing to the Overrepresentation of African American Children in the Child Welfare System

Dennette M. Derezotes and John Poertner

African American children are overrepresented in America's child welfare system. Although African Americans constituted 15% of the child population of the United States in 1999, they accounted for 45% of the children in substitute care (U.S. Bureau of the Census, 2000; U.S. Department of Health and Human Services [DHHS], 1999). In contrast, although white children constituted 60% of the U.S. child population, they constituted only 36% of the children in out-of-home care (Morton, 1999). In addition, several studies show that children of different ethnic or racial backgrounds receive dissimilar treatment by the child welfare system, but little is known about the appropriateness of the treatment (Capellari, Eckenrode, & Powers, 1993; Courtney et al., 1996; Garland & Besinger, 1997; Hampton, 1987; McCabe et al., 1999; Wulczyn, Brunner, & Goerge, 1999).

Why is the path that a child takes through the child welfare system linked to his or her racial background? Do the services best meet the needs of the child from a cultural perspective? Why are African American children overrepresented in out-of-home care? This book examines this social phenomenon by taking a critical look at child welfare policy and practice and the causes of child maltreatment and how each affects the disproportionate representation and outcomes of African American children. This chapter provides a context for the discussion, with an examination of child maltreatment research in the United States, a model for investigating the causes of the disproportionality of African Americans in the child welfare system, and a review of factors affecting the proportion of African Americans in the child welfare system. Chapter 2 provides a comparative look at alternative models for examining the disproportionality phenomenon. Chapters 3 through 14 present research conducted on disproportionality at different decision points in the child welfare system.

An Approach to Discussing Disproportionality in Child Welfare

Current models of child maltreatment suggest that child abuse and neglect result from complex constellations of correlated variables whose influence may increase or decrease during different developmental and historical periods (National Academy of the Sciences, 1993). Within these models, child maltreatment is believed to occur when multiple risk factors outweigh protective, compensatory, and buffering factors (Cicchetti & Carlson, 1989). In addition, these models emphasize the importance of viewing child maltreatment in the context of the family, community, and society, over and above individual parental characteristics or stressors (Belsky, 1980, 1992; Cicchetti & Carlson, 1989; Garbarino, 1977; National Academy of the Sciences, 1993; Parke & Collmer, 1975).

Ongoing debates exist regarding the degree of risk of child abuse or neglect faced by African American children. Some suggest that these children are in fact at greater risk of maltreatment than other children in this country (McCabe et al., 1999). Still others contend that the risk of child abuse and neglect is not larger for African American families and that children from these families are being placed inappropriately in the child welfare system (Hill, 1998; Hill et al., 1993; Roberts, 2002).

Assuming that child maltreatment is linked to risks that exist in the general population, children who live in families and communities that have high levels of risk are more likely to experience abuse or neglect unless factors protect them from harm, compensate for the risk, or buffer them from the risk. To examine the risks of child maltreatment that African American children face and the factors that could mediate those risks, this chapter maps out the potential flow of events related to a child's risk of maltreatment and consequent child welfare system involvement.

Expanding on a model proposed by Barth (Chapter 2, this volume), children could follow two hypothesized paths into the child welfare system, each beginning with a high risk of maltreatment. The first path is one in which high-risk factors exist with the absence of factors that would keep a child safe within a community. This phenomenon would result in a greater incidence of abuse or neglect in the community. As a result, a large number of children from this community would come to the attention of the child welfare system. If the system is operating appropriately, more children from this community would enter the child welfare system than children from communities that do not have high-risk factors.

The second path includes children who have high-risk factors, as in the first path, but their effect is mediated by other factors that reduce the likelihood of maltreatment. The result, on average, is that children with high-risk factors exhibit no greater incidence of child abuse and neglect than children with lower risks. If the communities in which the high-risk children reside and the child welfare agencies serving them react proportionately to the incidence of abuse and neglect, children from these communities will have no greater representation in the child welfare system than children who are at lower risk. On the other hand, if these communities and agencies discriminate in ways that target the underlying risk or need without regard for the mitigating factors that reduce the actual incidence of maltreatment, or the communities do not have adequate resources to meet the needs of the children and families in the communities, the result can be a disproportionately higher rate of substantiation and foster placement that contribute to overrepresentation in the child welfare system.

The overrepresentation of African Americans in the child welfare system mirrors that found in the juvenile justice system, which has faced allegations of discrimination for more than four decades. In January 1989, the National Coalition of Juvenile Justice Advisory Groups produced their 1998 annual report to Congress titled *A Delicate Balance,* which identified problems facing youth of color in the juvenile justice system, as well as their overrepresentation in secure facilities. On receipt of these findings, Congress amended the Juvenile Justice and Delinquency Prevention Act of 1974 (P.L. 93-415) mandating that states address the problems creating this overrepresentation.

This emphasis has produced a line of research that provides a better understanding of how overrepresentation of a minority group in a service system can occur (Pope & Feyerherm, 1992). By examining the influences at each of a system's decision points from the time a criminal act takes place to the time of sentencing, a clearer understanding of the causes of overrepresentation of populations of youth of color in the juvenile justice system has been obtained. The racial disparity in the child welfare system is less well understood and would benefit from the same type of research.

Considering the potential pathways through which children enter the child welfare system (see Figure 2-2, Chapter 2, this volume) in conjunction with an examination of the decisions made as children pass through the child welfare system (see Figure 2-1, Chapter 2, this volume), one can begin to get a picture of the conditions in a child's life that influence the amount of child welfare involvement they have. An investigation of conditions in a child's life that put him or her at risk of child welfare system involvement raises the following questions: Who is at greatest risk of maltreatment? Is it racially or ethnically determined? Are there potential mediating factors that decrease risk for any group? How do agencies and communities respond to identified risks? Are the responses made by agencies and communities appropriate? When and how are reports of abuse or neglect made, investigated and substantiated?[1] What factors explain which children are placed in substitute care? When and how does each child leave the child welfare system? Because there are many factors that may affect children's lives at each point, it is important to investigate each of the potential factors and determine the effect of each both individually and in relationship to the other factors.

Child Welfare System Involvement: Risk Factors for African American Children

What does research tell us about the overrepresentation of African Americans in the child welfare system? Are African American children at greater risk of child maltreatment than other children in this country? What factors influence the risk of maltreatment? Are there any factors that mediate this risk?

Maltreatment Risk in the Community

The National Incidence Studies

Three National Incidence Studies (NIS-1, NIS-2, NIS-3) provide the best estimates and are the only studies available with national figures on the proportion of children who are abused and neglected. The NISs include children who were investigated by child protective service (CPS) agencies, but they also contain data on children who were not reported to CPS, or who were screened out by CPS without investigation but who were seen by community professionals. This means that NIS estimates, resulting from the studies' nationally representative design, provide a more comprehensive measure of the scope of child abuse and neglect known to community professionals, including both abused and neglected children who are in the official statistics and those who are not.

Sedlak and Schultz (Chapter 3, this volume) found no overall differences in the harm standard of maltreatment among races in all but three categories of maltreatment based on the three NISs when the analysis controls for other factors in the model. In fact, they found that African American children had a lower risk of physical abuse, sexual abuse, and physical neglect than white children, according to NIS data (Sedlak & Schultz, Chapter 3, this volume).

However, they also found highly significant differences in four family characteristics that are independently associated with significantly higher risk of maltreatment. African American children are overrepresented among children in low-income families, fami-

[1] A substantiated report is a report of abuse or neglect that has been found to have enough evidence supporting the allegation to be true. These reports may also be described as *indicated* or *founded* in some jurisdictions.

lies of children with unemployed parents, children with parents who are not in the labor force, children with single parents, and children in families with four or more children.

Ards, Chung, and Meyers (1998) conducted an examination of design features of the 1980 NIS-1 sample selection to determine if sample selection bias exists in the method. They found substantial differences in characteristics of African American and white victims by source of report and type of maltreatment, and in each racial group, they found differences between sampled agencies and nonsampled agencies. They found selection bias affected the estimation of child abuse reporting rates by race. In the African American sample, sample selection bias reduced the statistical significance of the effects of the reporting agency, and physical and sexual abuse reporting rates. In the white sample, most significant factors in the basic model remained statistically significant with the correction for sample selection bias. The authors suggest that conclusions about racial differences in child maltreatment be reached cautiously, given the study design.

Community Factors

Are there qualities that communities that are safe for children have that are missing in communities in which children are at greater risk? If so, what are they? A family's first exposure to the child welfare system begins with a report of abuse or neglect to the authorities in the state in which the alleged abuse or neglect occurred. In many states, a central reporting system is set up to initiate investigations throughout the state. In Illinois, agencies take reports of abuse and neglect of African American children at three times the rate of reports of white children (Child and Family Research Center, 2002). Initially, one might assume that statewide institutional racism could be at work. When researchers examined more closely, however, they found that reporting rates differed significantly between counties. These findings suggest that other, more localized factors contribute to the overrepresentation.

Based on a century of research examining social problems in Chicago, Illinois, from an ecological perspective, researchers observed a continuity of communities in which child abuse and neglect occurs despite changes in ethnic and racial background (Garbarino & Kostelny, 1992; Testa & Furstenburg, 2002). When examining these same neighborhoods, other researchers have observed that high rates of delinquency, infant mortality, low birthweight, tuberculosis (Shaw & McKay, 1942), suicide (Cavan, 1928), and mental illness (Faris & Dunham, 1939) existed in them. Although the ethnic and racial composition of neighborhoods plays a part, its relative importance was found to be secondary to economic and family indicators of high-risk neighborhoods.

Testa and Furstenberg (2002) reported a strong correlation between community-level rates of substantiated abuse and neglect in Cook County, Illinois, and demographic and socioeconomic indicators of community context, such as single parenthood and child poverty. In a previous study of these same communities, Garbarino and Kostelny (1992) found a strong relationship between reports of child abuse and neglect and socioeconomic and demographic indicators of community context. They reported that in similar neighborhoods that varied dramatically in terms of rates of child maltreatment, certain community characteristics differentiated communities with high rates of maltreatment from those with lower rates of maltreatment. In neighborhoods in which maltreatment was higher than expected, informants had a difficult time saying anything positive about the community, knew less about what community services and agencies were available, suggested a lack of a formal and informal network or support system, described the physical places where the community programs were located as dark and depressing, and reported that the neighborhood was owned by a prominent local gang. In contrast, where maltreatment was lower than expected, informants reported that the converse was true.

Coleman (1990) contended that the willingness of local residents to intervene for the common good depends in large part on conditions of mutual trust and solidarity among neighbors (Coleman, 1990). Sampson, Raudenbush, and Earls (1997) proposed that the differential ability of neighborhoods to realize the common values of residents and maintain both social cohesion among neighbors and neighbors' willingness to intervene on behalf of the common good is a major source of neighborhood variation in violence. Using the term *collective efficacy* to define this phenomenon, they found three neighborhood characteristics accounted for 70% of the neighborhood variation: concentrated disadvantage, immigrant concentration, and residential stability. Concentrated disadvantage and immigrant concentration were negatively correlated with collective efficacy, and residential stability was positively correlated with it. Sampson, Raudenbush, and Earls contended that the capacity of residents to control group-level processes and visible signs of social disorder is a key mechanism influencing opportunities for interpersonal crime in a neighborhood. In contrast, Fromm (2004) found that collective efficacy and the willingness of neighbors to intervene may have the opposite effect on reporting of child abuse and neglect, bringing suspected cases of child abuse and neglect to official attention more often than communities where these qualities are lacking.

Family Characteristics

Welfare policies, poverty status, level of income, lack of resources, community of residence, and single parenthood all affect the risk of a family's child welfare system involvement. The influence of these factors creates an environment in which African American children are placed at greater risk of entering the child welfare system because African American families represent a large percentage of the U.S. population that have these characteristics. At the same time, African American families often have a composition and qualities that are flexible and different from other cultures in the United States, creating a home environment that can serve to protect children in these homes from maltreatment. Despite these mediating factors, African American children continue to be overrepresented in the child welfare system. The following is a discussion of some of the risk and protective factors of African American families.

Income, Poverty, and Welfare Receipt. Some researchers suggest that poverty and race are so interrelated that the disproportionality of African American children in the child welfare system may be caused by poverty and lack of resources, not race (Courtney et al., 1996; Malson & Williams, 1989; McCabe et al., 1999; Wu, Cernkovich, & Dunn, 1997), as families of color are most likely to be the families with the least income and most likely to be in poverty (U.S. Bureau of the Census, 2000). Other researchers contend that African American children may be more likely to enter into the child welfare and other related systems, regardless of level of income, poverty status, or other factors that may increase risk of entry into the child welfare system (McCabe et al., 1999; Testa, 1992).

According to the U.S. Bureau of the Census and Bureau of Labor Statistics (2000), 33.1% of African American children lived in poverty in 1999, compared with 13.5% of white children. Moreover, a widening of the already-significant income gap between African American and white families developed during the 1970s and 1980s with high unemployment rates (Hill et al., 1993). In 1969, African American families had a median income that was 61% that of white families. In 1999, the real median income of African American families was $29,740, compared with $52,821 for white families (U.S. Bureau of the Census, 2000), or 56% of the income of white families.

The situation is even more dismal for female-headed African American households. The percentage of female-headed African American households rose from 18% in 1940 to 48% in 1994. This number remains near 50% today (U.S. Bureau of the Census, 2000). At the same time, African American female-headed households have an income of slightly more than half of that of other African American households, and slightly less than a third of that of white households (U.S. Bureau of the Census, 2000). The real median income for African American female-headed households in 1999 was $17,316 compared with $29,740 for all African American families—32% of white families' median incomes and 58% of all African American families' median incomes.

In studies on the relationship between welfare receipt and child welfare system involvement, families receiving welfare benefits were more likely to have child welfare system activity. Goerge and Lee (Chapter 10, this volume) found that the receipt of welfare benefits (Aid to Dependent Families, Temporary Assistance to Needy Families) doubles the risk of substantiation of abuse or neglect. In addition, Barth (Chapter 2, this volume) found that receiving public assistance also has a positive relationship with increased overrepresentation of African Americans in out-of-home placements.

African American Family Factors That Mediate Risk of Abuse and Neglect

Family Structure

The preponderance of historical studies of African American families has examined family functioning from a nuclear family approach, although anthropological research of family patterns among West Africans and African Americans reveals that conventional definitions of American families differ markedly from the West African concept of family in the following three dimensions: coresidence (in West African cultures, the concept of family is not limited to individuals living in the same household), formal kinship relations (including networks of related and nonrelated people living in separate households in West African cultures), and nuclear families (the West African nuclear family is but part of a larger unit) (Hill et al., 1993).

African American households often have extended family configurations. In 1980, 28% of African American households were composed of extended family, compared with 11% of white families (Allen & Farley, 1986). By 1990, two out of five African American households were three-generational. Numerous studies have shown that the majority of African Americans live in close proximity to kin and visit them often. In fact, 85% of all African Americans have relatives that live in the same city but in separate households (Hill et al., 1993). Extended family arrangements are recognized to have important economic benefits and are viewed as an effective mechanism for pooling limited economic resources (Taylor, Chatters, Tucker, & Lewis, 1990). They can also provide the opportunity for single parents to pursue educational goals and obtain employment outside of the home (Hogan, Hao, & Parish, 1990).

Hill (1998) defined African American families as constellations of households related by blood or marriage or function that provide basic instrumental and expressive functions of the family to the members of those networks. The extended family is one cultural structure that has enhanced African American families since their days in Africa. In addition, they have provided the strength and support necessary for African Americans to survive through slavery in this country. Acknowledging the uniqueness of African American families requires the awareness that an examination of African American family functioning requires more than a traditional nuclear-family approach.

Strengths of African American Families

African American family strengths have been defined as African-based cultural assets that are handed down from generation to generation, not adaptations or coping responses to racial or economic oppression (McDaniel, 1990; Slaughter & McWorter, 1985). Based on the works of Du Bois, Frazier, Johnson, Lewis, and Billingsley, in *The Strengths of Black Families*, Hill (1971) identified several attributes as functional for the survival, stability, and advancement of African American families: strong achievement, work and educational orientation, flexible family roles, strong kinship bonds, and strong religious orientation. These attributes have been used to describe African American families in studies over time (Hill et al., 1993; McAdoo, 1993).

In their work, Hill (1998) used Rutter's (1990) research on resilience mechanisms as a framework for further understanding family strengths. Rutter defined resilience as a protective mechanism that affects the individual's response to a risk or to a stressful situation. There are four protective mechanisms: (1) the reduction of negative outcomes by altering either the risk or the child's exposure to the risk, (2) the reduction of negative chain reactions following risk exposure, (3) the establishment and maintenance of self-esteem and self-efficacy, and (4) the opening-up of opportunities. Hill proposed that Rutter's protective processes contribute to the enhancement of African American family strengths, and a further examination of the interaction could prove to help our understanding of the functioning of African American families.

Recognizing that these strengths are not unique to African Americans, Hill (1998) stated that these mechanisms operate differently among African Americans because of the unique history of slavery and other racial oppression. He went on to say that any assessment of the family life of African Americans must systematically examine societal, community, family, and individual factors that facilitate or impede African American family strengths. No researcher has yet examined the effect of these strengths on the lives of African Americans, but such an investigation would provide insight into child maltreatment in African American families.

Strong Achievement, Work, and Educational Orientation

It is the dream of many African American parents to improve living conditions for their children. High academic performance and ambitious career goals are values often instilled in their children from early childhood, as an avenue to accomplish this goal (Barnes, 1985; Jordan, 1991). Skills associated with this orientation are responsibility for feelings and bodily functions, making good use of time, and participation in decisionmaking (LeVine & Bartz, 1978). Parents also may exhaust their resources to provide educational foundations to provide entry for their children into the economic and political structure (Ball & Robbins, 1986; Hall & King, 1982).

Flexible Family Roles

African American families manifest much flexibility and fluidity in areas such as household composition, marital relations, division of family roles, the role of women, and child rearing (Hill et al., 1993). For many African American families, households expand or contract in response to external and internal pressures. This includes the informal adoption of children of relatives and friends when parents are unable to provide for their needs. Beginning during the time of slavery, this network still serves as a source of stability and fortitude, functioning to provide day care, foster care, and income support (Boyd-Franklin, 1989). Numerous studies have found that African American women are more likely than white women to be breadwinners, and African American men are more likely than white men to perform household chores (Jackson, 1971; Stone & Schlamp, 1971; Lewis, 1975). Fluid roles also include extended family members and nonrelatives who share in providing emotional nurturance and in carrying out instrumental tasks.

Strong Kinship Bonds

The African concept of family is not confined to relations between formal kin, but includes networks of unrelated as well as related persons living in separate households. Strong kinship bonds can be observed in African American families in the maintenance of extended family ties, the development of fictive kin relationships (Scott & Black, 1989), the carrying out of informal adoptions (Boyd-Franklin, 1989), and the flexibility of parenting roles in times of stress (Boyd-Franklin, 1989; McAdoo, 1988; Scott & Black, 1989).

Strong Religious Orientation

A belief held by most African American families that conditions will improve has been described as unfaltering faith and religious orientation (Hill, 1971). The University of Michigan's National Survey of Black Americans reported that two-thirds of all African Americans were church members (Taylor, 1988). Among them, 40% attended church weekly and another 31% attended church several times per month.

Religious orientation for African Americans goes beyond church attendance and pervades the life of individuals who may not attend formal religious institutions. It is an awareness of and commitment to a spiritual lifestyle that provides a sense of power and purpose greater than self. The African sense of spirituality is woven into the fabric of society and is a central characteristic of the African psyche. Individuals who grow up in traditional African American communities are equipped with a system of core beliefs, particularly spiritual beliefs that are rooted in the traditions of African religions (Mitchell & Lewter, 1986). This system of core beliefs is the foundation of their inner strength (Boyd-Franklin, 1989). It offers both support and opportunities for growth, providing comfort in the face of oppression, social and economic support, and opportunities for self-expression, leadership, and community participation (Barnes, 1985; Scott & Black, 1989).

Additional Factors that May Affect Child Welfare System Involvement

Institutional Racism

Some suggest that institutional racism negates the strengths of black families and explains the overrepresentation of black children in the child welfare system. Unintentional institutional discrimination refers to societal forces or policies that have adverse effects on racial and ethnic minorities, although these actions were not designed to be discriminatory (Hill et al., 1993). One important form of institutional racism and structural discrimination refers to the disparate adverse effects of societal forces or policies on racial and ethnic groups, even if those forces or policies are not consciously or intentionally discriminatory. Such racially disparate policies often rely on nonracial proxies (such as income, residence, family structure, or education) that are strongly correlated with race (Hill, 1998).

Several researchers claim discrimination and racial oppression have become institutionalized through welfare polices originating with the inception of the Aid to Families with Dependent Children program in the 1930s (Abramovitz, 1988; Gordon, 1990; Mink, 1996; Quadagno, 1988; Skocpol, 1995). These researchers identify biases against African Americans and single parents that have created ongoing dependence on the welfare system and brought intrusive monitoring into recipients' lives, which often results in the children from these families entering the child welfare system. Recognizing that nearly 50% of African American households are single-parent households, the risk of bias is multiplied for African Americans.

The Effect of Human Decisionmaking

Human decisionmaking has the potential to affect outcomes at each point of action. The factors that workers consider in making assessments vary, as do factors in the assessments of the severity of risk and the level of intervention indicated (Williams, 1997). Stein and Rzepnicki (1984) found that decisions are more likely to be made based on deficits in available resources, accepted agency practice, worker values, and biases. In a review of the literature on decisionmaking in placement decisions, Harris and Poertner (2000) identified five categories of decisionmaking factors considered in the decision to place a child: safety, child characteristics, parent characteristics, family characteristics, and child welfare system characteristics. Studies using placement decision as the dependent variable, although not conclusive, have found relationships between three types of independent variables: caseworker, client, and availability of resources (DePanfilis & Scannapieco, 1994).

Tatora (1989) reported that caseworkers have usually relied on intuition, experience, and interview engagement skills to ascertain future risk. In addition, several researchers have suggested that caseworker characteristics and perceptions of their clients influence their final decisions (Billingsley & Giovannoni, 1972; Boehm, 1962, 1968; Meyer, 1972; Wolock, 1982). Conversely, others have found no association between caseworker characteristics and placement decision (Fanshel & Shinn, 1978). In addition, Rossi, Schuerman, and Budde (1999) found that decisions were not consistently based on case characteristics, resulting in two errors: unnecessary removal of children, and failure to remove children from their families when it is called for.

Researchers who have looked specifically at racial bias have found that the race of the family being investigated affects workers' decisions. This research, however, does not predict the way in which race influences decisions. Sometimes, assessments of African American families lead to more intrusive interventions; other times, they normalize unacceptable behavior. Future research efforts should give attention to the effect of race on decisions regarding the existence of maltreatment, whether children stay at home, what level and kind of effort is necessary to help families, and what level of effort is called for to achieve permanence for children (Williams, 1997).

Several researchers have asserted that African American children are overrepresented in the child welfare system due to biased decisionmaking by child welfare workers (Capellari et al., 1993; Hampton, 1987; Spearly & Lauderdale, 1983). Research provides evidence of a powerful racial disparity at the point of the original report of abuse or neglect. To better understand this phenomenon, it is critical to closely examine decisions and how they are made.

Reporting and Screening in for Investigation

Child welfare system entry is initiated by a call to the hotline, where a screener makes a decision about whether to accept a report for investigation. Individuals in many fields are mandated by law to report, however, any concerned party can make hotline calls. Considerations in decisionmaking at this juncture include decisions by the individuals calling the hotline to make a call or the screening process conducted by the person receiving the call regarding whether to accept the call for further investigation.

Gryzlak, Wells, and Johnson (Chapter 4, this volume) found nonwhite workers screened in reports at higher rates than white workers (65% vs 50%). When controlling for the color of the child, nearly half of the cases in which the worker and the child were of color (46.2%) or both worker and child were white (49.1%) were screened in. When workers of color made screening decisions for white children, 76.6% were screened in for investigation.

According to three NISs (1980, 1986, 1993), calls to the hotline regarding African American children are accepted for investigation disproportionately more than for whites and other minorities. Although a reanalysis of NIS-III did not find that race alone had any effect on the decision to execute investigations, it did find strong interactions between race and severity of injury and type of maltreatment, such as children who were emotionally maltreated, who suffered serious or fatal injuries, when reports came from a mental health or social service professional, or when the parent was a substance abuser (Sedlak & Schultz, Chapter 5, this volume).

Although several studies indicate that African Americans are more likely reported for maltreatment than whites, most research suggests a strong correlation between social class and child abuse and neglect reporting, meaning that child maltreatment is more likely to be reported for low-income than for middle- and upper-income families (Sedlak & Schultz, Chapter 5, this volume). This does not mean that the numbers are not disproportional by race, but that it is not race alone that creates the disproportional representation at this stage. Factors known to increase risk of maltreatment include income, employment, single parenthood, and number of children in the home (Sedlak & Schultz, Chapter 3, this volume). In fact, Sedlak and Schultz (Chapter 3, this volume) found differences in reporting rates for African American and white children only in the lowest income group studied. In this group, African American children are represented at much higher rates than white children (45.7% vs. 19.1%). In this group, they found that white children were emotionally maltreated marginally more often than African American children and physically neglected significantly more than African American children. When controlling for parental employment, they found that otherwise marginal racial differences are especially pronounced among children whose parents are not in the labor force, where white children are physically abused at a much higher rate than African American children. They also found that 6% of white children living in households with four or more children experienced maltreatment compared with 3% of African American children.

Once reported, allegations of abuse and neglect go through a process of investigation to determine the validity of the report. To determine racial differences in CPS investigations of abused and neglected children, Sedlak and Schultz (Chapter 5, this volume) analyzed the NIS-3 data. They found a greater likelihood of investigations of African American families than white families when the allegations include emotional maltreatment, physical neglect, fatal or serious injury, harm, or perpetrator alcohol or drug involvement. They also found that African American families are more likely to be investigated when the reports come from mental health or social service agencies. White families are at a higher risk of investigation if the parents are not in the workforce, or if the perpetrator is not a parent or parent substitute.

Substantiation

Several studies have concluded that African Americans are overrepresented in the rate of substantiation of abuse or neglect (Capellari et al., 1993; Hampton, 1987). Other studies, however, contradict these findings. Goerge and Lee (Chapter 10, this volume) found that African Americans are less likely to have an allegation of abuse or neglect substantiated. Baird (Chapter 7, this volume) found that reports made on African American families are no more likely to be substantiated following a report of abuse or neglect, and whites had a slightly higher overall risk profile. When looking at abuse and neglect scales, African Americans scored higher than whites on neglect scales, whereas whites scored higher than African Americans on abuse scales. Gryzlak, Wells, and Johnson (Chapter 4, this volume) found a relationship among race, ethnicity, and office location. Their research suggests site of the investigator is the best predictor of overrepresentation.

Ards, Chung, and Myers (1999) completed an analysis of 1993, 1994, and 1995 National Child Abuse and Neglect Data System data to study the relationship between the proportion of African Americans in the state and the proportion of cases substantiated. They hypothesized that if the cases of African Americans are more likely to be substantiated than those of whites, their substantiation rates would be higher in states with large proportions of African American children reported as being abused or neglected. What they found instead was a trend toward an inverse relationship, indicating that a higher proportion of African American children reported as maltreated is associated with lower substantiation rates. They also found no difference in substantiation rates for African Americans and whites in cases that the investigator rated as very probable or judged on information that was determined insufficient. This exercise was undertaken to examine the hypothesis that more African American cases would have been substantiated even if there were not sufficient data to support it. On completion of these analyses, Ards and colleagues (1998) concluded that the results of their study provided data contrary to Morton's hypothesis that African American child maltreatment cases were disproportionally substantiated.

Rolock and Testa (Chapter 6, this volume) looked at the effect of the investigator's race on the substantiation rate of allegations. They found that children in African American families are more likely to have an indicated (substantiated) report of abuse or neglect regardless of the race of the investigator, and that white investigators are more likely to indicate a report of abuse or neglect, regardless of family race. Racial differences in the propensity of investigators to substantiate a report appear to be related to the type of allegation and the community in which the investigation was conducted.

Some studies show that other factors correlated with race affect child welfare involvement. The receipt of welfare benefits (Aid to Families with Dependent Children, Temporary Assistance to Needy Families) doubles the risk of entry into foster care (Goerge & Lee, Chapter 10, this volume). Barth (Chapter 2, this volume) also found that a greater percentage of African American children receiving public assistance has a positive relationship with increased overrepresentation of African Americans in placements.

Single-caregiver families had an 87% greater risk of substantiation of physical neglect than those of two-caregiver families, and 52% of African American families versus 18% of white families had a single female caregiver present in the study (Baird, Chapter 7, this volume). Several other studies support this finding (Barth, Chapter 2, this volume). California data showed that whites are more likely than African Americans to have additional maltreatment allegations substantiated within two years of the first substantiation (Baird, Chapter 7, this volume).

Through an analysis of data used by the National Council on Crime and Delinquency, the California Department of Social Services used data from 2,198 substantiated cases of child maltreatment in seven California counties and found that white children have slightly higher item, subscale, and overall scores on the Family Risk Assessment than African American children (Johnson, Chapter 8, this volume). They also found that items, subscales, and overall scores are statistically related to the recurrence of maltreatment, regardless of race or ethnicity. Based on this information, Johnson (Chapter 8, this volume) concluded that the California Family Risk Assessment was not racially biased in its assessment of risk for child maltreatment and gave some indication of the level of services needed to prevent further maltreatment.

The Decision to Place

Once children come to the attention of the child welfare system, public policy mandates that "reasonable efforts" be made to prevent the placement of children into foster care. Numerous studies over the years have identified race as predictive of the decision to place. An early report from Phillips, Haring, and Shyne (1972) found that children from homes in which an African American father was present were far more likely to be placed in foster care in contrast to homes in which a white father was present. There was no significant difference when the race of the mother was considered. Looking at the race of the child, Groeneveld and Giovannoni (1977) found that neglected nonwhite children were more likely to be removed from their homes than neglected white children. More recently, DHHS (1999) reported that nationally, the majority of African American children (56%) were placed in foster care, whereas the majority of white children (72%) received in-home services.

Because child's race is correlated with risk factors that are also predictive of placement, such as poverty and single parenthood, studies attempt to adjust statistically for the differences in risk profiles to assess whether the racial disparity remains significant after the risk factors are controlled. Two such studies undertaken with a retrospective cross-sectional design showed race to be significant when considered alone but not significant when other risk factors were included in the analysis (Harris & Poertner, 1999; Harris, Tittle, & Poertner, Chapter 9, this volume). Other studies have reached similar conclusions (Katz, Hampton, Newberger, Bowles & Snyder, 1986; Runyan, Gould, Trost, & Loda, 1982).

The chapters in this volume also report that the bivariate effect of race is reduced in multivariate models, but in contrast to the above studies, most find that the child's race still remains a significant predictor of placement (Barth, Chapter 2, this volume; Goerge & Lee, Chapter 10, this volume; Hill, Chapter 11, this volume). Goerge and Lee (Chapter 10, this volume) attempted to control for racial differences in poverty and public assistance receipt by limiting their analysis to white and African American families in Illinois who received either AFDC or TANF from 1991 to 1998. They found that the odds of placement for African American children were twice as large as for white children, but that this difference was cut in half after taking into account mother's education, continued receipt of public assistance, and concentrated community poverty. Similarly, Hill (Chapter 11, this volume) found that substance abuse problems, allegations of abuse or neglect, and child's disability mediated the effects of race on foster placement.

More refined analyses of the influence of race find that placement decisions differ depending on placement reason and placement destination. Lindsay (1994) found that in dependency cases, African American children were twice as likely to be placed in foster care as were white children. When placement was due to environmental factors, African American children were again at a higher risk of placement. But the results changed when parental condition (e.g., illness, mental disorder, addiction) was the major reason for placement. In this circumstance, white children were 10% more likely to be placed than African American children. If neglect were the precipitating condition, white and African American children had equal rates of placement.

The recent incorporation of relative foster parents into the formal foster care system also modifies the influence of race on the decision to place. Since the mid-1980s, African American children have been placed increasingly with kin rather than into unrelated foster homes. Goerge and Lee (Chapter 10, this volume) found that the effect of race is substantially stronger when the placement destination if the foster home is one of a relative rather than a nonrelative: The odds of placement with kin for African American children in Illinois were 113% larger than the odds for white children whereas the odds of placement with nonkin for African American children were only 28% larger. The interaction of race and kinship foster care raises the possibility that the overrepresentation of African American children in foster care may arise, in part, from the increased recruitment of extended family members, who formerly were denied or discouraged by state and local policies from becoming licensed or approved foster parents (Testa, 1997).

Permanency Options/Length of Time in Care

Once in care, African American children have longer lengths of stay than white children (Close, 1983). In addition, they appear to be at a disadvantage in terms of the range, quantity, and quality of services provided; the type of agency to which they are referred; the efficiency with which their cases are handled; and the support their families receive (Close, 1983; Courtney & Wong, 1996; Maluccio & Fein, 1989).

An analysis of administrative data from the Multi-State Data Archive (Wulczyn et al., 1999) found that African American children tended to stay in care longer than white children in all 11 states that contributed data to the archive. The likelihood of exiting foster care via reunification with birthfamilies or adoption was consistently lower for African American children than white children. Barth (1997) reported similar results in California: African American children were 37% less likely to be reunified and 80% less likely to be adopted than white children. McMurtry and Lie (1992) found similar results in Arizona: African American children were half as likely to return home to his or her family as white children. In the Multi-State Archive, overall, African American children were about half as likely to be adopted as white children (Wulczyn et al., 1999).

Many reasons could explain the longer lengths of stay of African Americans in care and their lesser opportunities for reunification or adoption. These include geographical location, the ages of the children at placement, and the type of care into which children of different races are placed (Barth, Chapter 2, this volume). In a study by Wulczyn et al. (1999), the likelihood of African American children exiting care to adoption or to their birthfamily was shown to be dependent on location. In urban counties, adoptions of African American children were 40% lower and exit to their birthfamilies was 25% lower than in nonurban counties.

In a study of kinship foster care in California, children remained much longer in care if they were in Title IV-E–funded kinship care than in nonrelated foster care (Berrick & Needell, 1996). Similarly, Courtney and Wong (1996) found that reunification rates were lower for African American children than white children, and that the disparity became greater for children placed with kin.

Because African American children are more likely to be placed in foster care with kin than white children (Goerge & Lee, Chapter 10, this volume), the racial disparity in length of stay may reflect the influences of kinship foster care. Some consider the longer lengths of stay of African American children in kinship foster care acceptable, making the argument that kinship care is a culturally appropriate approach to serving African American children and families (Everett, 1995) that meets the needs of African American children more than adoption by kin (Thornton, 1991) or by non–African American families (McRoy, Oglesby, & Grape, 1997).

Recent trends in permanency planning suggest that many of the historical barriers to adoption and other permanency options for African American families may finally be falling. Examining adoption patterns in the Multi-State Archive over a lengthy time period, Wulczyn (2003) found that even though adoptions of African American children took longer to complete than those of white children, ultimately African American children were more likely to be adopted than white children. Moreover, the data point to a significant increase in the relative rate of adoption among African American children from urban areas who had been placed with kin.

Testa (Chapter 14, this volume) examined some of the program and policy factors in Illinois that figured prominently in narrowing the gap between the rate of exit from foster care for African American children compared with white children. He found that by offering subsidized guardianship under a federal Title IV-E waiver and by aligning contractual incentives with permanency plans that built on the cultural traditions of informal adoption among African Americans, Illinois was able to diminish racial disparities in permanency rates and transform kinship from an obstacle into a positive advantage for the timely achievement of permanence. Whereas children who entered kinship foster care in the early 1990s in Illinois were 43% less likely than children in nonrelated foster care to find permanent homes with their caregivers, children who entered kinship foster care in the late 1990s were 57% *more* likely to be adopted or taken into private guardianship by their caregivers.

Risk of Reentry into the Child Welfare System

Analysis of six states in MSDA showed that longer lengths of stay in foster care for African American children had only a very small net benefit in lower re-entry rates into foster care (Wulczyn et al., 1999). Reentry rates for both African American and white children in Oklahoma were similar; 37% of them reenter the system within three and a half years (Terling, 1999).

What We Know About Disproportionality

African American children continue to be represented in the child welfare system at higher rates than they are represented in the general population throughout the country. Through examination of this phenomenon by decision point, we can better understand where disproportional representation occurs and the factors that contribute to it. The following chapters provide information about what happens at several decision points in the child welfare system to result in these outcomes, the types of policy and practice changes that could potentially assist in addressing these issues, and the further research that could help us better understand this phenomenon.

References

Abramovitz, M. (1988). *Regulating the lives of women: Social welfare policy from colonial times to the present.* Madison WI: University of Wisconsin Press.

Adoption Assistance and Child Welfare Act of 1980, Pub. L. No. 96-272,H.R. 343 4, 94 Stat. 500 (June 17, 1980).

Allen, W. R., & Farley, R. (1986). The shifting social and economic tides of black America, 1950–1980. *American Sociological Review, 12,* 277–306.

Ards, S., Chung, C., & Myers, S. L. (1998). The effects of sample selection bias on racial differences in child abuse reporting. *Child Abuse & Neglect, 22,* 103–115.

Ards, S., Chung, C., & Myers, S. L. (1999). Letter to the editor. *Child Abuse & Neglect, 23,* 103–115.

Ball, R. E., & Robbins, L. (1986). Marital status and life satisfaction among black Americans. *Journal of Marriage and the Family, 48,* 389–394.

Barnes, A. S. (1985). *The black middle class family.* Bristol, IN: Wyndham Hall.

Barth, R. P. (1997). Effects of age and race on the odds of adoption versus remaining in long-term out-of-home care. *Child Welfare, 76,* 285–308.

Barth, R. P., & Courtney, M. E. (1994). Timing is everything: An analysis of the time to adoption and legalization. *Social Work Research, 18*(3), 139–148.

Barth, R. P., Webster, D., & Lee, S. (2000). *Adoption of American Indian children in California.* Unpublished manuscript. (Available from the author at University of North Carolina, Chapel Hill, School of Social Work, 301 Pittsboro Street, CB #3550, Chapel Hill, NC 27599-3550).

Belsky, J. (1980). Child maltreatment: An ecological integration. *American Psychologist, 35,* 320–335.

Belsky, J. (1992). *The etiology of child maltreatment: An ecological-contextual analysis.* Paper presented at the Panel on Research on Child Abuse and Neglect, Washington, DC.

Berrick, J. D., & Needell, B. (1996). *Kinship care in California.* Berkeley, CA: Child Welfare Research Center.

Billingsley, A., & Giovannoni, J. M. (1972). *Children of the storm: Black children and American child welfare.* New York: Harcourt Brace and Jovanovich.

Boehm, B. (1962). The community and the social agency define neglect. *Child Welfare, 41,* 10–16.

Boehm, B. (1968). Protective services for neglected children. *Proceedings of the National Conference on Social Welfare, 95th Annual Forum.* New York: Columbia University Press.

Boyd-Franklin, N. (1989). *Black families in therapy.* New York: Guilford.

Brissett-Chapman, S., & Issacs-Shockley, M. (1997). *Children in social peril: A community vision for preserving family care of African American children and youths.* Washington, DC: CWLA Press.

Capellari, J. C., Eckenrode, J., & Powers, J. L. (1993). The epidemiology of child abuse: Findings from the Second National Incidence and Prevalence Study of Child Abuse and Neglect. *American Journal of Public Health, 83,* 1622–1624.

Cavan, R. S. (1928). *Suicide.* Chicago: University of Chicago Press.

Children and Family Research Center. (2002). [Child protective services reporting rates by Illinois county]. Unpublished raw data.

Cicchetti, D., & Carlson, V. (1989). *Child maltreatment: Theory and research on the causes and consequences of child abuse and neglect.* New York: Cambridge University Press.

Close, M. M. (1983). Child welfare and people of color: Denial of equal access. *Social Work Research and Abstracts, 19*(4), 13–20.

Coleman, J. (1990). *Foundations of social theory*. Cambridge, MA: Harvard University Press.

Courtney, M. E. (1999). Reentry to foster care of children returned to their families. *Social Service Review, 69*, 226–241.

Courtney, M. E., Barth, R. P., Berrick, J. D., Brooks, D., Needell, B., & Park, L. (1996). Race and child welfare services: Past research and future directions. *Child Welfare, 75*, 99–137.

Courtney, M. E., & Wong, Y. L. I. (1996). Comparing the timing of exits from substitute care. *Children and Youth Services Review, 18*, 307–334.

DePanfilis, D., & Scannapieco, M. (1994). Assessing the safety of children at risk of maltreatment: Decision-making models. *Child Welfare, 73*, 229–245.

Everett, J. E. (1995). Child foster care. In R. L. Edwards & G. J. Hopps (Eds.), *Encyclopedia of social work* (Vol. 1, pp. 375–389). Washington DC: NASW Press.

Fanshel, D., & Shinn, E. B. (1978). *Children in foster care: A longitudinal investigation*. New York: Columbia University Press.

Faris, R. E. L., & Dunham, H. W. (1939). *Mental disorders in urban areas; An ecological study of schizophrenia and other psychoses*. Chicago: University of Chicago Press.

Fromm, S. (2004). *The processes that moderate the effect of community structural factors on neighborhood child maltreatment rates*. Unpublished disssertation.

Garbarino, J. (1977). The human ecology of child maltreatment: A conceptual model for research. *Journal of Marriage and the Family, 39*, 721–735.

Garbarino, J., & & Kostelny, K. (1992). Child maltreatment as a community problem. *Child Abuse & Neglect, 19*, 455–464.

Garland, A. F., & Besinger, B. A. (1997). Racial/ethnic differences in court referred pathways to mental health services for children in foster care. *Children and Youth Services Review, 19*, 651–666.

Gordon, L. (1990). *Women, the state, and welfare*. Madison, WI: University of Wisconsin Press.

Groeneveld, L. P., & Giovannoni, J. M. (1977). Disposition of child abuse and neglect cases. *Social Work Research and Abstracts, 13*(2), 24–30.

Hall, E. H. & King, G. C. (1982). Working with the strengths of black families. *Child Welfare, 61*, 536–444.

Hampton, R. L. (1987). Race, class, and child maltreatment. *Journal of Comparative Family Studies, 18*(1), 113–126.

Harris, G., & Poertner, J. (1999). *Factors that influence the decision to place a child: Administrative data* (Report #0899I). Urbana, IL: University of Illinois at Urbana-Champaign, Children and Family Research Center.

Harris, G., & Poertner, J. (2000). *Factors that predict the decision to place a child: Administrative data*. Urbana, IL: University of Illinois at Urbana-Champaign, Children and Family Research Center.

Hill, R. B. (1971). *The strengths of black families*. New York: Emerson Hall.

Hill, R. B. (1998). Understanding black family functioning: a holistic perspective. *Journal of Comparative Family Studies, 29*(1), 15–25.

Hill, R. B., Billingsley, A., Engram, E., Malson, M. R., Rubin, R.H., Stack, C. B., et al. (1993). *Research on the African American family: A holistic perspective*. Westport, CT: Auburn House.

Hogan, D., Hao, L., & Parish, W. L. (1990). Race, kin networks and assistance to mother-headed families. *Social Forces, 68*, 797–812.

Jackson, J. J. (1971). But where are the men? *The Black Scholar, 3*(4), 30–41.

Jordan, J. M. (1991). Counseling African American women: Sister-friends. In C. C. Lee & B. L. Richardson (Eds.), *Multicultural issues in counseling: New approaches to diversity.* Alexandria, VA: American Association for Counseling and Development.

Katz, M. H., Hampton, R. L., Newberger, E. H., Bowles, R. T., & Snyder, J. C. (1986). Returning children home: Clinical decisionmaking in cases of child abuse and neglect. *American Journal of Orthopsychiatry, 56*, 253–262.

LeVine, E. S., & Bartz, K. W. (1978). Comparative child-rearing attitudes among Chicano, Anglo, and black parents. *Hispanic Journal of Behavioral Sciences, 1*, 165–178.

Lewis, D. K. (1975). The black family: Socialization and sex roles. *Phylon, 36*, 221–237.

Lindsay, D. (1994). Factors affecting the foster care placement decision: An analysis of national survey data. *American Journal of Orthopsychiatry, 6*, 272–281.

Malson, M., & Williams, C. (1989). *Black children in placement in North Carolina.* Report to the North Carolina Task Force on Permanent Families for Children.

Maluccio, A. N., & Fein, E. (1989). An examination of long-term family foster care for children and youth. In J. Hudson & B. Galaway (Eds.), *The state as parent: International research perspectives on interventions with young persons* (Vol. 53, pp. 387–400). Dordrecht, The Netherlands: Kluwer.

McAdoo, H. (1988). *Black families.* Newbury Park, CA: Sage.

McCabe, K., Yeh, M., Hough, R. L., Landsverk, J., Hurlburt, M. S., Culver, S. W., et al. (1999). Racial ethnic representation across five public sectors of care for youth. *Journal of Emotional and Behavioral Disorders, 7*(2), 72–82.

McDaniel, A. (1990). The power of culture: A review of the idea of Africa's influence on family structure in antebellum America. *Journal of Family History,* 15, 225–238.

McMurtry, S. L., & Lie, G. Y. (1992). Differential exit rates of minority children in foster care. *Social Work Research and Abstracts, 28*(1), 42–48.

McRoy, R. G., Oglesby, G., & Grape, H. (1997). Achieving same-race adoptive placements for African American children: Culturally sensitive practice approaches. *Child Welfare, 76,* 85–104.

Meyer, C. H. (1972). Review of when parents fail. *Children Today, 1,* 28.

Mink, G. (1996). *The wages of motherhood: Inequality in the welfare state.* Ithaca, NY: Cornell University Press.

Mitchell, H., & Lewter, N. (1986). *Soul theology: The heart of American black culture.* San Francisco: Harper & Row.

Morton, T. (1999). Letter to the editor. *Child Abuse & Neglect, 23,* 1209.

National Academy of the Sciences. (1993). Etiology of child maltreatment. *Understanding Child Abuse and Neglect.* Retrieved November 12, 2001, from http://www4.nationalacademies.org/news.nsf/isbn/0309048893?OpenDocument.

National Coalition of Juvenile Justice Advisory Groups. (1988). *A delicate balance. Annual report to Congress.* Washington, DC: Office of Juvenile Justice and Delinquency Prevention.

Needell, B., Webster, D., Cuccaro-Alamin, S., & Armijo, M. (2000). *Performance indicators for child welfare services in California: Caseload updates from CWS/CMS extract through quarter four, 1999.* Retrieved March 2, 2001, from http://cssr21.socwel.berkeley.edu/alan/cwscms/index.html.

Parke, R. D., & Collmer, C. W. (1975). Child abuse: An interdisciplinary analysis. In E. M. Hetherington (Ed.), *Review of child development research 5* (pp. 509–590). Chicago: University of Chicago Press.

Phillips, M. H., Haring, B., & Shyne, A. (1972). *A model for intake decisions in child welfare.* New York: Child Welfare League of America.

Pope, C. E., & Feyerherm, W. (1992). *Minorities and the juvenile justice system* (OJJDP Grant No. 87-JN-CX0014). Washington, DC: U.S. Department of Justice.

Quadagno, J. (1988). From old-age assistance to supplemental security income: The political economy of relief in the South, 1935–1972. In M. Weir, A. S. Orloff, & T. Skocpol (Eds.), *The politics of social policy in the United States.* Princeton, NJ: Princeton University Press.

Roberts, D. (2002). *Shattered bonds: The color of child welfare.* New York: Civitas Books.

Rossi, P. H., Schuerman, J., & Budde, S. J. (1999). Understanding decisions about child maltreatment. *Evaluation Review, 6,* 579–598.

Runyan, D. K., Gould, C. L., Trost, D. C., & Loda, F. A. (1982). Determinants of foster care placement for the maltreated child. *Child Abuse & Neglect, 6,* 343–350.

Sampson, R. J., Raudenbush, S. W., & Earls, F. (1997). Neighborhoods and violent crime: A multilevel study of collective efficacy. *Science, 277,* 918–924.

Saunders, E. J., & Nelson, K. (1993). Racial inequality and child neglect: Findings in a metropolitan area. *Child Welfare, 72,* 341–355.

Scott, J. W., & Black, A. (1989). Deep structures of African American family life: Female and male kin networks. *Western Journal of Black Studies, 13,* 17–24.

Shaw, C. R., & McKay, H. D. (1942). *Juvenile delinquency and urban areas: A study of rates of delinquents in relation to differential characteristics of local communities in American cities.* Chicago: University of Chicago Press.

Skocpol, T. (1995). *Social policy in the United States: Future possibilities in historical perspective.* Princeton, NJ: Princeton University Press.

Slaughter, D. T., & McWorter, G. (1985). Social origins and early features of the scientific study of black American families and children. In M. B. Spencer, G. Brookins, & W. R. Allen (Eds.), *Beginnings: The social affective development of black children* (pp. 5–18). Hillside NJ: Lawrence Erlbaum.

Spearly, J. L., & Lauderdale, M. (1983). Community characteristics and ethnicity in the prediction of child maltreatment rates. *Child Abuse & Neglect, 7,* 91–105.

Stein, S., & Rzepnicki, T. (1984). *Decisionmaking in child welfare services intake and planning.* Boston: Kluwer-Nijhoff.

Stone, R. C., & Schlamp, F. T. (1971). *Welfare and working fathers: Low-income family lifestyles.* Lexington, MA: Lexington Books.

Tatora, T. (1989). *CPS risks assessment survey of status on CPS risk assessment findings.* Washington, DC: American Public Welfare Association.

Taylor, R. J. (1988). Correlates of religious non-involvement among black Americans. *Review of Religious Research, 30,* 126–139.

Taylor, R. J., Chatters, L. M., Tucker, M. D., & Lewis, E. (1990). Developments in research on black families: A decade review. *Journal of Marriage and Family, 52,* 993–1014.

Terling, T. (1999). The efficacy of family reunification practices: reentry rates and correlates of reentry for abused and neglected children reunited with their families. *Child Abuse & Neglect, 23,* 1359–1370.

Testa, M. F. (1992). Conditions of risk for substitute care. *Children and Youth Services Review, 14,* 27–36.

Testa, M. F., & Furstenberg, F. F. (2002). The social ecology of child endangerment. In M. K. Rosenhem, F. E. Zimring, D. S. Tenehaus, & B. Dohrn (Eds.), *A century of juvenile justice* (pp. 237–263). Chicago: University of Chicago Press.

Thornton, J. L. (1991). Permanency planning for children in kinship foster homes. *Child Welfare, 70,* 593–601.

Taylor, R. J., Chatters, L. M., Tucker, M. B., & Lewis, E. (1990). Developments in research on black families: A decade review. *Journal of Marriage and the Family, 52,* 993–1014.

U.S. Bureau of the Census. (1999). *Poverty in the United States 1999, current population reports series* (pp. 60–210). Washington, DC: U.S. Government Printing Office.

U.S. Bureau of the Census. (2000). *Presence of children under 18 years old—Households by total money income in 1999, type of household, race and Hispanic origin of householder.* Retrieved January 21, 2001, from http://www.census.gov/hhes/poverty/poverty97/pv97est1.html.

U.S. Bureau of the Census and Bureau of Labor Statistics. (2000). Age, sex, household relationship, race and Hispanic origin—Poverty status of people by selected characteristics in 1999. In *Annual Demographic Survey, March Supplement.* Retrieved September 14, 2000, from http://ferret.blx.census.gov/macro/032000/pov/new01_005.htm.

U.S. Department of Health and Human Services. (1999, June 18). *How many children entered foster care during the period 10/1/97 through 3/31/98?* Retrieved December 10, 2000, from http://www.acf.dhhs.gov/programs/cb/stats/ar0199.htm.

Williams, C. (1997). Personal reflections on permanency planning and cultural competency. *Journal of Multicultural Social Work, 5*(1/2), 9–18.

Wolock, I. (1982). Community characteristics in child abuse and neglect cases. *Social Work Research and Abstracts, 18*(2), 9–15.

Wu, B., Cernkovich, S., & Dunn, C. S. (1997). Assessing the effects of race and class on juvenile justice processing in Ohio. *Journal of Criminal Justice, 25,* 265–277.

Wulczyn, F. (2003). Closing the gap: Are changing exit patterns recucing the time African American children spend in foster care relative to Caucasian children? *Children and Youth Services Review, 25,* 431–462.

Wulczyn, F., II, Brunner, K., & Goerge, R. M. (1999). *A report from the multistate foster care data archive. Foster care dynamics, 1983–1997.* Chicago: Chapin Hall Center for Children at the University of Chicago.

CHAPTER 2

Child Welfare and Race

Models of Disproportionality

Richard P. Barth

Child welfare services have long struggled with issues of race. A telescoped history of child welfare would find race operating as a centrifugal force in the administration of orphanages, the development of the federal entitlement program to pay for foster care for all children, the placement of children for adoption, and the emergence of kinship foster care. At the current time, many states, including Illinois, North Carolina, and Minnesota, and the federal government are particularly concerned about the overrepresentation of children of color in foster care. Yet the concern about disproportionality of all children of color is too broad a rubric, as the overrepresentation is not proportionately distributed across the Latino or Asian child population but is particularly germane to African American children. This chapter explores the possible reasons for this disparity of representation and offers several explanations as to why this phenomenon might occur.

Understanding Disproportionality

Understanding the ways children of color may become disproportionately involved in child welfare services requires an understanding of the paths into and out of child welfare services. As shown in Figure 2-1, official child welfare services begin with a report of abuse or neglect. Some of these reports are investigated and, of those investigated,

Figure 2–1: Simplified Model of Caseload Flow of Children

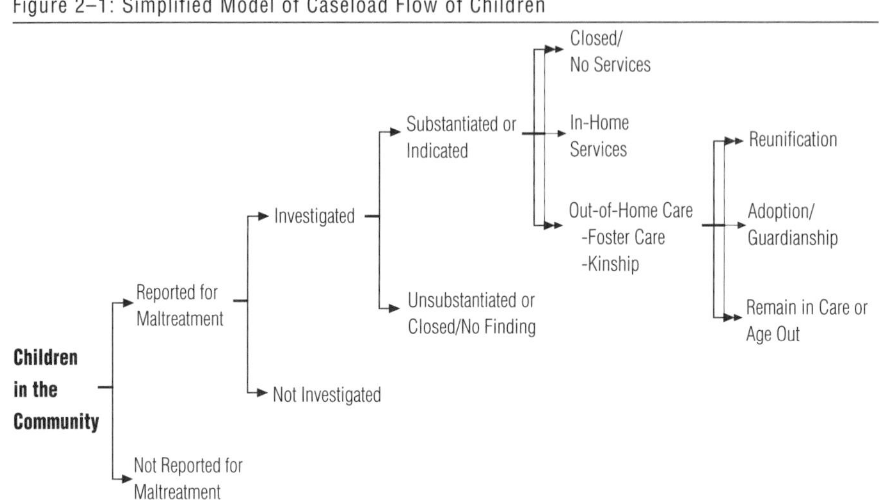

some are substantiated. Among those that are substantiated, some children receive no ongoing services, others receive services at home, and a small proportion of children are placed into foster care for their protection. The majority of all children who enter foster care subsequently return home, others leave for different permanent placements (that is, to guardianship or adoption), and some remain in foster care until adulthood.

Each possible transition point in the child welfare system requires child welfare workers to make choices about services that will affect two different kinds of proportionalities. First, these decisions will affect the proportionate or disproportionate fit between the needs of the children and the services they actually receive. When the services are precisely what a child needs, this can be called *proportionate to need*. Second, child welfare decisions will affect the proportionate or disproportionate fit between the population of children receiving those services and the general population. When children receive services in a precise one-to-one ratio to their proportion in the general population, this can be called *proportionate to population* (Table 2-1).

Race and the Incidence of Abuse and Neglect

Determining what amount of child welfare services is proportionate to need requires estimating the needs of children for these services. This is not easy to do. It is much easier to measure proportionality to population. One way to establish need for child welfare services is to understand the incidence of child abuse and neglect and the severity of abuse and neglect. Although many data sources on child abuse and neglect reports (for example, the National Child Abuse and Neglect Data System [NCANDS]) and

Table 2–1: Disproportionality of Services per Population and Need

	Low Level of Services Provided	**High Level of Services Provided**	**Proportionate Level of Services Provided**
Higher Than Average Need in Subpopulation	Services provided are disproportionately low per need.	Services provided are proportionately low per need.	Services provided are disproportionately high per representation in general population.
Lower Than Average Need in Subpopulation	Services provided are proportionate to need.	Services provided are proportionately high to need.	Services provided are disproportionately low per representation in general population.

Note: Children could also have average need and low, average, or high service receipt. Average service receipt and need are not considered in the table or text to streamline the discussion.

child welfare services receipt (for example, the Adoption and Foster Care Analysis Reporting System) exist, ascertaining the underlying incidence of child abuse and neglect requires a study of reported and unreported child abuse and neglect.

The federal government has funded three National Incidence Studies (NIS-1, NIS-2, NIS-3) to try to determine the incidence of child abuse and neglect. These studies provide the best estimates available about the incidence of child abuse and neglect and are the only studies that have endeavored to provide national figures about the proportion of children who are abused and neglected and, among them, the proportion who ever receive child welfare services. Yet, the challenges of adequately estimating the underlying incidence of private events such as child abuse and neglect remain largely unmet.

NISs have all found no differences in the incidence of child abuse and neglect according to racial group.[1] Among those who have confidence in NISs as an estimate of the incidence of abuse and neglect among racial groups, the findings call for considerable concern. Morton (1999) and Yegidis and Morton (1999) have led the call to use the NIS findings as a basis for reviewing the apparent racial disparities in service provision. Yegidis and Morton wrote:

> States are potentially vulnerable in a number of ways. First, all three National Incidence Studies (NIS) conducted by the Department of Health and Human Services concluded that there are no significant or marginal differences in the incidence of child maltreatment based on race. Since incidence is measured in rates per thousand, this means that all groups should be represented in the child welfare system consistent with their proportion of the population as a whole. If not, then a basis for the presumption of bias exists. (p. 1)

[1] In the NIS, the comparison was made between white, African American, and other children. Latino children were a small percentage of identified cases and grouped with white children. Biracial children were coded as "other."

Yegidis and Morton (1999) also relied on NCANDS data to make their argument. They found that among states reporting NCANDS data in 1995, only one had a ratio below 1.0 of founded allegations of child abuse and neglect involving African American children to African American children as percentage of the state's child population. They reported that all other states reporting had ratios of 1.22 to 6.94 and that the highest reporting state founded allegations of maltreatment involving African American children at a rate almost equal to seven times their proportion of the state's child population. If the NIS-3 estimates are accepted and this interpretation of the NCANDS data was optimal, then a plausible explanation would be that child welfare agencies were largely responsible for the vastly disproportionate rates of child welfare services involvement.

The estimates from NIS cannot be so readily accepted, however. In their analysis of the design of the NIS-1, Ards, Chung, and Myers (1998) found marked differences in the characteristics of African American and white victims by source of report and type of maltreatment. They also found significant differences in each racial group between sampled agencies and nonsampled agencies, so that sample selection biases affected the estimation of both white and African American child abuse reporting rates. The most significant contributor to these biases resulted from the "exclusion of family, friends, and neighbors in the NIS sample design. Such exclusion has the effect of altering the interpretation of the determinants of child abuse reporting among African Americans but not among Caucasians" (p. 103). Ards et al. (1998) concluded that this finding is inconsistent with NIS's findings and raises questions about the validity of NIS to address racial differences in child welfare services.

In response to the conclusion of Morton (1999) that a likely explanation for the disproportionality of African American children in care are their high substantiation rates, Ards, Chung, and Myers (1999) compiled and analyzed data from the 1993, 1994, and 1995 NCANDS. They endeavored to determine if a linear relationship between the proportion of African Americans in the state and the proportion of cases substantiated existed. Their theory was that if cases involving African Americans are more likely to be substantiated than cases involving whites, African Americans' substantiation rates would be higher in states with large proportions of African American children reported. They found no such relationship and found instead a trend toward an inverse relationship (that is, one in which the higher proportion of African American children reported is associated with lower substantiation rates).

Ards et al. (1999) also found no difference between the likelihood that African Americans and whites would have substantiated cases if the likelihood of abuse in their cases had been rated as "very probable" or judged on information that might be "insufficient."

If race had been a major influence, then it might be expected that more cases involving African American children would have been substantiated although an independent rater could not find sufficient information to justify it. That is, workers would be less likely to give maltreators of African American children the benefit of the doubt. Following these analyses, the authors concluded that the results "may rule out Morton's hypothesis that African American child maltreatment cases are disproportionately substantiated" (p. 1212). They argued that the significance of this finding is that we should not look to the child welfare system to explain the differences in proportions of substantiations for children of color, but we must look beyond that to much broader social conditions.

The debate is much larger than an academic exercise and is critical to the way planners design services. "The policy implications of this debate are profound," stated Ards et al. (1999, p. 1212). If children of color are disproportionately represented in the child welfare system because of child welfare practices, this calls for very different responses than if children of color are in the child welfare system primarily because other social and economic forces result in their greater need for services.

A major concern about NIS-3 is that the procedure of recruiting and training professional and paraprofessional "sentinels" who could watch for abuse and neglect that would be otherwise undetected excluded friends and kin. A second concern is that the procedures appeared to break down in urban communities where referrals were low: Sentinel referrals were more typically from suburban communities. Ards and colleagues (1998) reviewed the findings of NIS-1 with regard to the sample selection bias. They concluded that there are at least three reasons why African American children could be overrepresented (per population) in the child welfare system if the NIS findings are true, and Morton (1999) added three additional reasons. These reasons are:

1. African American children are overreported (that is, reported when they do not need to be or reported more often when they do need to be).
2. White children are underreported (that is, not reported when they need to be or reported less often when they do need to be).
3. The types of maltreatment reported for African American children are different than those for white children and more likely to be reported to child protective services (CPS).
4. Racial differences exist in rates of investigation.
5. Racial differences exist in substantiation rates.
6. Racial differences exist in the rates of case openings.

NIS-1 gave some indication of underreporting of African American children, as only 28% of African American victims of child maltreatment were known to the study as compared to 33% of white victims. White maltreated children were more likely than African American children to be reported as suffering from physical abuse (33% vs. 25%), sexual abuse (7% vs. 4%), emotional abuse (24% vs. 9%), and emotional neglect (9% vs. 6%), whereas African American children were more likely to be reported because of educational neglect (46% vs. 24%).

The Westat investigators agreed that there was likely to be an inner-city undercount and argued that NIS gives a minimum estimate (Andrea Sedlak, personal communication, October 29, 1999). They also found no race differences in the type of maltreatment, which is a counterintuitive finding because of the generally higher rates of neglect among poorer families (U.S. Department of Health and Human Services, 1996). This further suggests problems in NIS with regard to its incidence counts.

It is still unclear how all the strong correlates of higher child abuse incidence (for example, poverty, single-parent status, large family size, urbanization) identified by the NIS-3 could be present in high proportions for African American families without any bivariate relationship between race and incidence. If NIS-3 had found a spurious correlation between race and child abuse incidence that researchers later eliminated by controlling for higher risk, this would be plausible, but it found no such relationship.

In a much smaller ($N = 644$) epidemiological study that followed children in upstate New York for 17 years (Brown, Cohen, Johnson, & Salzinger, 1998), researchers largely confirmed risk factors identified in NIS-3. The odds of experiencing any kind of abuse or neglect were elevated by large family size (odds ratio [OR] = 1.83), low income (OR = 3.02), single-parent status (OR = 2.09), and being on welfare (OR = 5.14). The study sample was 91% white and 8% African American. In multivariate analyses that controlled for many familial risk factors and children's temperament, being nonwhite had an OR of 2.63 (95% confidence interval = 1.41–5.00). In analyses of the association between race and different types of abuse, being African American did not show up as an elevated risk in physical abuse or sexual abuse cases, but was strong for neglect. The findings are interesting in another way, as they point to a multiplicative effect of risk factors. For families with no risk factors present, only 3% experienced abuse or neglect; this rose to 4%, 8%, 10%, and 24% for families when one, two, three, or four or more risk factors were present, respectively.

Although neither NIS-3's authors nor Yegidis and Morton (1999) offered an explanation for the lack of association between high risk factors and low incidence of abuse and neglect in NIS-3, one possibility is that these risk factors operate for groups other than for African Americans and are less salient for African Americans. Such an interaction between race and risk factors has been observed in other studies. For example, Needell, Cuccaro-Alamin, Brookhart, and Lee (1999) found that being on welfare was a better predictor of subsequent participation in the child welfare system for white families than it was for African American families. This possibility is also supported by the findings of NIS-1 that children of color may be less maltreated at lower income levels than whites; these findings are not quite statistically significant. Still, a reduction in the magnitude of the effect when compared with whites would not necessarily mean that no direct relationship between poverty and abuse for African Americans exists. Although NIS-3 reports no such interaction between income and race, it is unclear that the study ever tested for it. Still, it is unlikely that the strong and significant main findings of the relationship between risk and child abuse and neglect could be found if this was not true for African American families. Other data on the high levels of child abuse and neglect among the poor suggest that this is not just an artifact of NIS-3 and that it does apply to African American families (Drake & Zuravin, 1998).

Figure 2-2 depicts two versions of the relationships that may exist between risk factors, incidence of abuse and neglect, and disproportionate child welfare services that could reasonably derive from the data described previously. Although the mechanisms by which these relationships would come to exist are certainly multifaceted, Figure 2-2 identifies some of the possible assumptions that have been offered by scholars. Although this report cannot directly test these assumptions, the analysis of secondary data is intended to, in part, clarify the likelihood that these alternative understandings explain how the disproportionality in child welfare services arises.

Previous Research on Disproportionality in Child Welfare

Although to date no comprehensive national study has explicitly examined at race as a factor in the disparity of child welfare services, a number of smaller studies have shown that children of different racial and ethnic backgrounds often have different trajectories through the human service system (Cappellari, Eckenrode, & Powers, 1993; Garland & Besinger, 1997; Hampton, 1987; McCabe et al., 1999; Wulczyn, Brunner, & Goerge, 1999). At times, these differences appear to be less for African American children than for Latino children (for example, with regard to the protective effects of child welfare services [Jonson-Reid & Barth, 2000]), at times they appear to be less for white children than for African American children (for example, in mental health services receipt [McCabe et al., 1999]), and at times they are less for white than Latino children (for example, in

Figure 2–2: Assumption of Analysis of African American Overrepresentation

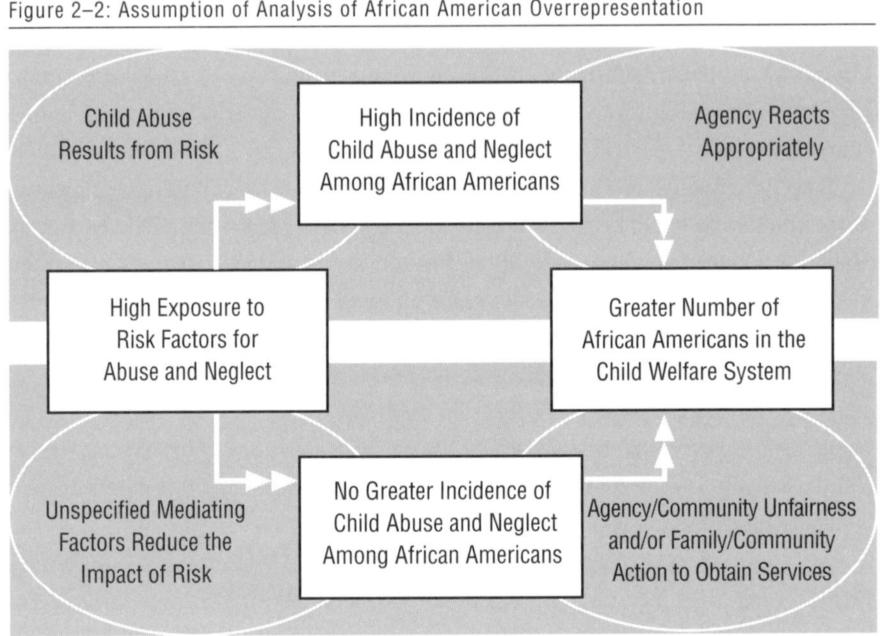

foster care dynamics [Wulczyn et al., 1999]). In the child welfare services system, evidence exists, although it is hardly uniform, of substantial disparities in service receipt for African American children compared with Latino and white children (who have more similar patterns of care). From the African American child's first entrance into the child welfare system at the point of child abuse reporting, to investigation and substantiation of that report, and continuing through the system to out-of-home care, and, most clearly, into adoption, there appears to be differential treatment (Courtney et al., 1996).

Child Protective Services

Decisions about the reporting of a child or further investigation of a child who has been reported depend on many factors. Given the overt practice of racial profiling in some local police offices, and the de facto racial profiling identified in the searching of airline passengers by U.S. Customs agents (U.S. General Accounting Office, 2000), race may be being regarded as a risk factor. Drake and Zuravin (1998) reviewed the literature related to CPS and class and identified four ways that bias may become part of the decisionmaking process. Their analysis was not of race per se, but given the distinct overlap between race and class, their conceptualization is useful in thinking about race.

They noted several types of bias. *Labeling bias* involves looking for maltreatment among the poor because they are labeled as deviant (by virtue of being poor). *Reporting bias* is the tendency to report a case that is suspected with a bias against one group (generally against those in the lower class). *Substantiation bias* occurs when child welfare investigators try to substantiate reported abuse and neglect based on unrelated factors such as socioeconomic status or race. Finally, *visibility bias* is when poor families are reported in excess of what would be proportionate to their behavior because of their greater visibility to potential reporters due to their frequent use of public services. Drake and Zuravin concluded that "there is no significant body of empirical data suggesting that these findings are a product of bias predisposing toward overestimates of child maltreatment among the poor" (p. 295).

Some studies indicate that race has an important role in the handling of abuse and neglect cases. Eckenrode, Powers, Doris, Munsch, and Bolger (1988) found that for physical abuse reports, race was the only demographic characteristic having an effect on substantiation rates, explaining 8% of the variance in substantiation. They were unable to control for abuse severity or other factors that contribute to substantiation (for example, legal considerations [Smith, Sullivan, & Cohen, 1995]).

Other studies have concluded that bias exists in CPS investigations because they found race effects in reports of abuse and neglect among women who had tested positive for substance use during pregnancy (i.e., Chasnoff, Landress, & Barrett, 1990) or who had come to the attention of hospital authorities (Hampton & Newberger, 1987). As detailed elsewhere (Courtney et al., 1996), these results have been overinterpreted because these studies were not able to control for the type or severity of substance abuse or the severity of the abuse of the child. Still, they provide some evidence that underlying inequalities exist in response to child abuse and neglect that might be attributable to the race of the parent.

Risk assessment data are beginning to provide some information about ways that race may operate in CPS decisionmaking (Johnson, 1999). The California Department of Social Services analyzed data used by the National Council on Crime and Delinquency to determine if their instrument, the California Family Risk Assessment, fairly assessed the risk of maltreatment recurrence for white, African American, and Latino children. Using data from 2,198 substantiated cases of child maltreatment (1,103 white, 413 African American, and 682 Latino) in seven California counties, researchers analyzing the California Family Risk Assessment found that white children have slightly higher item, subscale, and overall scores on the Family Risk Assessment than African American or Latino children. In addition, the items, subscales, and overall scores of the Family Risk

Assessment are statistically related to the recurrence of maltreatment, regardless of race or ethnicity. Based on these findings, Johnson (1999) concluded that the California Family Risk Assessment was not racially biased in its assessment of risk for child maltreatment and seemed to fairly indicate what level of services would be needed to prevent recurrence of maltreatment. No evidence is available from this study to indicate whether workers provided the appropriate level of service.

In-Home Services: Family Preservation and Reunification Versus Placement

Children of color appear to receive fewer services than white children once they enter the child welfare system, although evidence about this must be gleaned from a wide variety of small and imperfect studies. Child welfare research consistently finds that children of color are at a disadvantage in terms of the range and quality of services provided, the type of agency to which workers refer them, the efficiency with which workers handle their cases, the support their families receive, and their eventual outcomes (Close, 1983; Courtney et al., 1996; Maluccio & Fein, 1989; Olsen, 1982). Indeed, minority status in itself is considered as a special need, along with learning disabilities, developmental delays, sibling-group membership, and a history of abuse, all of which make a child more difficult to place for adoption (Groze, Young, & Corcran-Rumppe, 1991; Olsen, 1982; Rosenthal, Schmidt, & Conner, 1988).

Children of color appear to experience different placement and treatment options than white children. In an analysis of administrative data in San Diego, researchers showed African American children and adolescents to be overrepresented in child welfare, juvenile justice, mental health, and public school services for children with serious emotional disturbances, even when the researchers controlled for socioeconomic status, compared with the youths' proportion in the population and compared with white children (McCabe et al., 1999).

Disproportionality by Population in Out-of-Home Care

Although the disproportionate involvement of children of color in other parts of the child welfare system is not definitively shown by research, there is no doubt that African American children are disproportionately present in foster care compared with their numbers in the population. Even though African American children comprise only 15% of the U.S. population, they account for 45% of the total number of children in foster care (U.S. Department of Health and Human Services [DHHS], 1999). This disproportionality could be caused by many factors, including:

- disproportionality in events leading up to foster care placement (for example, reports and substantiations of reports),
- different rates in the use of various types of foster care placement (i.e., kinship foster care, treatment foster care, conventional foster care, group care, and residential care),
- interactions between race and types of placements (for example, African American children are more likely to be in kinship foster care),
- different rates with regard to lengths of stay, and
- differential rates of reentry into foster care.

Different lengths of stay for children of different races might be attributable to unequal access to reunification, guardianship, or adoption. Each of these contributors to disproportionality in the numbers of African American children in foster care may be linked to (or may be independent from) disproportionalities in the need for protective care that may result from higher rates of abuse and neglect and mortality among African American children.

Explaining Disproportionality: Four Models

From the review of previous research, the researchers can construct four dominant models that explain why there is racial disproportionality in the population of children: (1) the risk, incidence, and benefit model; (2) the child welfare services decision-making model, (3) the placement dynamics model; and (4) the multiplicative model (Table 2-2).

Risk, Incidence, and Benefit Model

In this model, the disproportionality according to population results from the provision of services that are proportionate to the greater risk of child abuse and the greater incidence of child abuse among poor, single-parent, and larger families, and the greater benefit that seems to accrue to children of color who receive child welfare services. Basically, the source of the disproportionality in the population is the disproportionality of need. Although this model does not easily square with the findings of NIS-3, it does square with the findings that African American families experience the risk factors for child abuse and neglect to a far greater degree than do non–African Americans.

Table 2-2: Four Models that Explain Disproportionality of Population

	Disproportionality of Risk, Need, and Benefit	Child Welfare Agency Response at Case Opening	Differential Placement Dynamics	Multiplicative Causes
Risk factors for abuse and neglect	X		X	X
Incidence of abuse and neglect	X			X
Reports of abuse and neglect	X	X		X
Investigate abuse and neglect		X		X
Case opens into out-of-home care		X		X
Type of out-of-home placement			X	X
Exits from foster care			X	X
Reentry into foster care			X	X
Disproportionate benefit				X

Child Welfare Services Decisionmaking Model

In this model, the disproportionality in the population is primarily attributed to agency characteristics that allow race to affect decisionmaking about children. Such characteristics might include staffing patterns, culturally incompetent staff, institutionalized racism, and inadequate duration or configuration of services.

Over the past several decades, a variety of studies have concluded that children of color, particularly African Americans, are overrepresented in their referral to the child welfare system and in their rate of substantiation of abuse or neglect (Cappellari et al., 1993; Hampton, 1987; Spearly & Lauderdale, 1983). Because families of color are also most likely to be the families with the least income (U.S. Census Bureau, 1999b), researchers need to avoid confounding race with poverty. When these two variables have been separated, however, some investigators argue that African American children may be more likely to enter into child welfare or other related systems, regardless of income level or poverty status (McCabe et al., 1999; Stehno, 1982). Yet, such a conclusion must still be considered to be very tentative because of the difficulty of controlling for a variety of correlates of race. Ards et al. (1998) posited that reporting differentials may exist because of "cultural differences in child-rearing between the reporter and the perpetrator or an unwillingness to report perpetrators with socioeconomic characteristics similar to the reporter's" (p. 105). This appears to be the case particularly for medical authorities, who may be more likely to report children from poor and nonwhite families as abused (Hampton & Newberger, 1987), whereas children from white and upper-class families may be more likely to escape being labeled as maltreated (Ards et al., 1998).

Placement Dynamics Model

In this model, the major causes of the disproportionality of population are differentiated by out-of-home care placement dynamics by race. Once they enter care, African American children have longer lengths of stay than either white or Latino children (Close, 1983; McMurtry & Lie, 1992; Schmidt-Tieszen & McDonald, 1998; Wulczyn et al., 1999). In their work with state administrative data compiled in the Multi-state Foster Care Data Archive, Wulczyn and colleagues (1999) found that white and Latino children were also more likely to return home to their families than African American children were. McMurtry and Lie (1992) found similar results in Arizona, namely that an African American child in foster care was half as likely to be returned home as a white child. And in California, a white child is more than five times as likely to be adopted than an African American child, and about twice as likely as a Latino or American Indian child is (Barth, 1997; Barth, Webster, & Lee, 2000).

The reasons for sharply longer lengths of stay are complex and include, at least, the types of placements that children of different races and cultures go into, the likelihood of reunification (offset by reentry into care), and the likelihood of exiting from care via timely adoption or guardianship. Certainly each of these is also influenced by child welfare decisionmaking and is related to other factors, such as the perceived benefit of keeping children in foster care for longer or shorter times. Race and culture interact with length of stay in various ways. At times, this has been affirmed as acceptable, as voice has been given by child welfare scholars to support the concept that kinship care is a culturally appropriate approach to serving African American children and families (i.e., Everett, 1995; Thornton, 1991), whereas adoption by kin (Thornton, 1991) or by non–African American families (McRoy, Oglesby, & Grape, 1997) is not. From this perspective, the disproportionality that might arise for African American children could be considered a by-product of an approach to child welfare services which is less concerned about length of time in care—and the disproportionalities that result—than in the quality and characteristics of the time spent in out-of-home care. Efforts to tailor the child welfare system to be more culturally competent by allowing children to remain with kin, and to be placed in same-race adoptive homes, even if those were not the first homes available, might then contribute to disproportionality.

Admissions into Foster Care

In a study of six large states (California, Illinois, Michigan, Missouri, New York, and Texas), about 40% of all children entering foster care between 1988 and 1994 were African American, about 18% were Latino, and about 34% were white, with the remainder being from a variety of groups (Wulczyn, Harden, & Goerge, 1997). In some states (for example, California), the proportion of African American new entrants is declining, whereas in other states (Illinois, Michigan, and Missouri, for example) it is growing. In addition, in some states, the Latino share of the child welfare population is growing (for example, California) and in others it is declining (for example, Texas).

Types of Placements

A component of placement dynamics has arisen from the type of placement that children of different races receive. African American children appear to be far more likely than white children and somewhat more likely than Latino children to be placed with kin (Needell, Webster, Cuccaro-Alamin, & Armijo, 2000). More than half (52%) of African American children in foster care in California at the end of the century were in kinship placements, compared with 38% of white children, 49% of Latino children, 38% of Asian children, and 43% of Native American children.

Length of Stay in Foster Care

The length of stay in the first placement in foster care varies by race and by state. Yet in their analysis of data from 11 states, Wulczyn et al. (1999) concluded that African American children tend to stay in care longer than white or Latino children in all 11 states. The duration for Latino children is close to the duration for white children in all 11 states. In their overall proportional hazards analysis of the duration of the first spell in substitute care (covering kinship care, foster care, and group care), the OR for African American children (when compared with 1.0 for white children) was 0.79, and for Latino children the OR was 1.04. This indicates that being African American resulted in a 21% longer stay in foster care than white children, after controlling for other contributors to foster care stays, including calendar year of entry, urban or nonurban region, age at entry, gender, state, and type of care. Latino children went home slightly faster than white children. Children identified as "other" (including Asian and Native American children) had an OR of 0.96.

An updated analysis of the Multi-State Foster Care Data Archive (MSFCDA) explores the adoption of African American, Latino, and white children from foster care (Wulczyn,

2000). Adoptions of children who entered foster care as infants comprised 57% of all adoptions between 1988 and 1993. This suggests that African American children would have a greater likelihood of adoption, because about 50% of all children who enter foster care are African American infants (Berrick, Barth, Needell, & Jonson-Reid, 1998), and in California at least, 40% of all African American children who enter foster care are infants.

Among all children who entered foster care in the MSFCDA states, the likelihood of adoption for African American children is about half (risk ratio [RR] = .53) what it is for white children, but about the same as it is for Latino children. These findings for Latino children are similar to Barth's (1997) findings from an earlier cohort in California, but are more positive than his findings for African American children. RRs for reunification for African American children were 0.63, compared with whites at 1.00 and Latinos at 1.04, indicating that African American children had a 40% lower likelihood of reunification than Latinos, and almost 40% lower chance than whites had. The author conducted further analyses only on African American children and showed that the odds of reunification have not increased since 1988. The RR of exiting to adoption had, however, increased for children entering foster care, from 0.87 in 1988 to 1.28 in 1996 (1990 admissions were used as the standard with an RR of 1.0). African American children from urban counties were 25% less likely to reunify with family than those children in nonurban counties and were 40% less likely to be adopted from an urban county.

The likelihood of leaving foster care is closely linked to age at entry for African American children. Those who entered foster care older than 12 months had twice the likelihood of newborns (children younger than 4 months) of exiting foster care to reunification, but only one-third the likelihood of exiting to adoption. These age-related effects for African American children were similar to the findings for all children, indicating the absence of an interaction between race and age at the time of placement.

State differences should not be ignored, because they indicate the complexity of understanding why states vary so widely. In California, for example, African American children have median lengths of stay of 28 months, whereas whites and Latinos have stays about half as long (about 14 months). In New York, alternately, median stays for white children in foster care (12.6 months) are one-third shorter than those for Latinos (about 22 months), with African American stays remaining the longest (about 32 months). Some of these differences in lengths of stay may be accounted for by the higher rate at which children of color are placed into family homes with relatives. Yet when the researchers accounted for differential uses of kinship care in an overall model, the results were not very different than they had been without accounting for kinship care. Either way, Latino children have stays that are very similar to white children, and African American children have substantially longer stays in care than other children do.

Courtney and Wong (1996) estimated the likelihood of different exits from foster care (reunification, adoption, and running away) and found that children in California who were African American had a much lower likelihoods of reunification (OR = .672; $p < .001$; compared with whites as 1.00) and adoption (OR = .395; $p < .001$), but not a significantly lower likelihood (OR = .755; $p = .054$) of running away. The odds of leaving foster care for non–African American Latino children differed from whites at a significant level only for the outcome of adoption (OR = .764, $p < .005$).

Reentry into Foster Care

Reentry rates for children who leave foster care and then return to foster care range about 20% in the first three years after leaving (Wulczyn et al., 1999); this is a major contributor to the foster care census. If African American children are more likely to reenter foster care, this could substantially contribute to their disproportionate representation. At the same time, this would, provided that the reasons for their reentry are valid, offer some evidence that their placement in foster care is important to their protection.

Although many things contributors to reentry, the most powerful appears to be the length of stay in foster care, with shorter foster care stays and younger ages at entry into foster care associated with higher reentry rates (Wulczyn et al., 1997). Reentry can be broken down into two components, reentry impact and reentry rate. The reentry impact measure is the proportion of all children who enter care who later reenter care. To be part of the impact measure you must, therefore, have left foster care. The reentry rate is the proportion of children who leave foster care who return to foster care (this measure often excludes children who leave foster care for adoption, because they are difficult to track back into foster care). An analysis of foster care data from six states indicates that reentry impact was highest for whites (18%), followed by African Americans (16%), and non–African American Latinos (15%), whereas the reentry rate was highest for African American children (22%), followed by whites (20%), and non–African American Latinos (17%). This indicates that the slower discharge rates for African American children compared with white children are exacerbated by higher reentry rates, which result in only a small net benefit in lower reentry impact rates. Latino children have exit rates that are far higher than they are for African American children, and reentry and impact rates that are lower, indicating a substantial combined advantage in reducing their proportion in the foster care population (when compared with their proportion of children in the population).

Of the children reunited with their families in Oklahoma, 37% reenter the system within three and a half years (Terling, 1999). Correlates of reentry are identified as abuse type, CPS history, parental competence, race, criminal history, substance abuse, and social support. Latino children are less likely to reenter foster care than white children, and no significant differences in reentry rates exist between African American and white children (Terling, 1999).

Exits Via Adoption

The contributions of differential rates of adoptions to disproportionality of African American children in foster care have been relatively well documented, although much debate exists about the reasons for those differences. Most of the studies related to this question have looked at the length of time that children of different racial and ethnic backgrounds required before their adoptions were completed. Barth, Courtney, and Berry (1994) found that adoptions of African American children were much slower to be finalized once placements had been made. Avery (1998) found that African American children who are adopted had lengths of stay in foster care that were nearly twice as long as other children. Much less has been done to understand the differences in the likelihood that children of different ethnic backgrounds would be adopted at all, assuming that they could not go home. Only Barth (1997) and Courtney and Wong (1996) have compared the likelihood of adoption (independent from other outcomes) by ethnicity and have found that African American children have a likelihood that is far lower than other children. California may not, however, be particularly representative of the rest of the nation, given that it had relatively low rates of adoption from foster care.

Benefits of Foster Care

The decision to leave children in foster care may also arise from a belief that this is the safest and most family-like setting available. This view of the benefits of foster care would be based, in part, on the assumption that children who return to their families risk experiencing serious problems. Barth and Jonson-Reid (2000) found that African American children whose parents were investigated for abuse and neglect and not provided ongoing services had twice the likelihood of later entering the California Youth Authority (California's training school system) as African American youth who did receive ongoing child welfare services (who were probably at lower risk). Receipt of child welfare services apparently provides a protective mechanism for African American youth. White youth did not experience this protective effect, and Latino youth received substantial benefit, but not statistically greater than white youth.

In another analysis of the risks attendant with not entering foster care or leaving foster care, Barth and Blackwell (1998) examined the mortality rates for children in foster care and after leaving foster care. African American infants in foster care in California in the mid-1990s had significantly lower mortality rates than African American children in the general population. The rates were 13.04 per 1,000 for African American infants in foster care and 17.49 for those in the general population in California. This was not true for white or Latino children. Children from each ethnic group who had left foster care had higher rates of preventable deaths (accidents, homicides, poisonings, abuse and neglect, fires, and the like) than children in the general population, with African American children having high mortality rates (6 per 10,000) that were nearly twice those of white children (3 per 10,000) but not statistically higher than Latino children (4 per 10,000). Provision of foster care services may reduce the death rate of children—especially African American children.

Multiplicative Model

An alternative explanation for the massive disproportionality by population of African American children in foster care builds on the prior models. The multiplicative model posits that small to medium increases exist in the disproportionate representation of African American children at different points throughout the child welfare system, which eventually result in a substantial difference in their representation in the child welfare system compared with their representation in the general population. This is the model that we believe best organizes the available research by other investigators. This model would argue that

- substantially greater risks of child abuse and neglect exist for African American children and families;
- slightly less substantial differences in incidence rate exist because of some mediating effects;
- small differences exist in the way that African American children are treated in the decisionmaking process, although we are unclear if these differences consistently reflect a tendency of the child welfare system to overintervene or underintervene proportion to the risk of the child; and
- substantial differences exist in the likelihood that African American children will experience long stays in foster care.

When taken together, the base of children who are exposed to each new factor continues to grow until the disproportionality to population at the end of the service system is massive. The research provides us with no compelling reason to assume that this disproportionality is not, generally, in the best interests of the children served.

Summary

Child welfare services are provided to children of color, particularly African American children, in ways that result in different service patterns than for white children. This chapter presents a variety of models that could help to explain how this disparity could occur. The authors have little concrete evidence, however, to determine the amount of this disproportionality that is attributable to personal and social conditions and the proportion that is attributable to agency organization and practice. It may only be safe to say that there are likely to be contributions from both sides and that if we attribute all of the cause to agency practice, as has been done by others (Downs, Costin, & McFadden, 1996; Yegidis & Morton, 1999), we are at risk of overlooking real risks to African American children and diminishing their opportunities for safe and successful futures.

Yet this is also a partially testable question. By identifying nonagency conditions that might explain outcomes, researchers can begin to determine whether the race of the child is the primary contributor to such decisions and whether to substantiate cases or place children in foster care. In its simplest form, if the race of the child is a strong and primary factor in decisionmaking, then we would expect that the contribution of other parts of the model would be substantially less significant. In such a case, family characteristics, the community risk factors, case characteristics other than race, and even the agency context would not have a substantial influence on case outcomes. Of course, a more likely scenario is that the result would involve an interaction between characteristics of the child (including race), the family, the community, and services.

References

Ards, S., Chung, C., & Myers, S. L. (1998). The effects of sample selection bias on racial differences in child abuse reporting. *Child Abuse & Neglect, 22*, 103–115.

Ards, S., Chung, C., & Myers, S. L. (1999). Letter to the editor. *Child Abuse & Neglect, 23*, 1211–1215.

Avery, R. (1998). *Public agency adoption in New York State: Phase I report. Foster care histories of children freed for adoption in New York State: 1980–1993.* Ithaca, NY: Cornell University.

Barth, R. P. (1997). Effects of age and race on the odds of adoption versus remaining in long-term out-of-home care. *Child Welfare, 76*, 285–308.

Barth, R. P., & Blackwell, D. L. (1998). Death rates among California's foster care and former care populations. *Children and Youth Services Review, 20*, 577–604.

Barth, R. P., Courtney, M., & Berry, M. (1994). Timing is everything: An analysis of the time to adoption and legalization. *Social Work Research, 18*(3), 139–148.

Barth, R. P., & Jonson-Reid, M. (2001). Outcomes after child welfare services: Implications for the design of performance measures. *Children and Youth Services Review, 22*, 787–810.

Barth, R. P., Webster, D., & Lee, S. (2000). *Adoption of American Indian children in California*. Unpublished manuscript. (Available from the author at the University of North Carolina, Chapel Hill, School of Social Work, 301 Pittsboro Street, Chapel Hill, NC 27599-3550).

Berrick, J. D., Barth, R. P., Needell, B., & Jonson-Reid, M. (1998). *The tender years: Toward developmentally-sensitive child welfare services for very young children*. New York: Oxford.

Brown, J., Cohen, P., Johnson, J. G., & Salzinger, S. (1998). A longitudinal analysis of risk factors for child maltreatment: Findings of a 17-year prospective study of officially recorded and self-reported child abuse and neglect. *Child Abuse & Neglect, 22*, 1065–1078.

Cappellari, J. C., Eckenrode, J., & Powers, J. L. (1993). The epidemiology of child abuse: Findings from the Second National Incidence and Prevalence Study of Child Abuse and Neglect. *American Journal of Public Health, 83*, 1622–1624.

Chasnoff, I. J., Landress, H. J., & Barrett, M. E. (1990). The prevalence of illicit-drug or alcohol use during pregnancy and discrepancies in mandatory reporting in Pinellas County, Florida. *New England Journal of Medicine, 322*, 1202–1206.

Close, M. M. (1983). Child welfare and people of color: Denial of equal access. *Social Work Research and Abstracts, 19*(4), 13–20.

Courtney, M. E., Barth, R. P., Berrick, J. D., Brooks, D., Needell, B., & Park, L. (1996). Race and child welfare services: Past research and future directions. *Child Welfare, 75*, 99–137.

Courtney, M. E., & Wong, Y. L. I. (1996). Comparing the timing of exits from substitute care. *Children and Youth Services Review, 18*, 307–334.

Downs, S. W., Costin, L. B., & McFadden, E. J. (1996). *Child welfare and family services: Policies and practice* (5th ed.). White Plains, NY: Longman.

Drake, B., & Zuravin, S. (1998). Bias in child maltreatment reporting: Revisiting the myth of classlessness. *American Journal of Orthopsychiatry, 68*, 295–304.

Eckenrode, J., Powers, J., Doris, J., Munsch, J., & Bolger, N. (1988). Substantiation of child abuse and neglect reports. *Journal of Consulting and Clinical Psychology, 56*(1), 9–16.

Everett, J. E. (1995). Child foster care. In R. L. Edwards & J. G. Hopps (Eds.), *Encyclopedia of social work* (Vol. 1, pp. 375–389). Washington, DC: NASW Press.

Garland, A. F., & Besinger, B. A. (1997). Racial/ethnic differences in court referred pathways to mental health services for children in foster care. *Children and Youth Services Review, 19*, 651–666.

Groze, V., Young, J., & Corcran-Rumppe, K. (1991). *Post Adoption Resources for Training, Networking and Evaluation Services (PARTNERS): Working with special needs adoptive families in stress*. Washington, DC: U.S. Department of Health and Human Services, Adoption Opportunities.

Hampton, R. L. (1987). Race, class, and child maltreatment. *Journal of Comparative Family Studies, 18*(1), 113–126.

Hampton, R. L., & Newberger, E. H. (1987). Child abuse incidence and reporting by hospitals: Significance of severity, class, and race. *American Journal of Public Health, 75*(1), 56–60.

Johnson, W. (1999, June). *Panel on race and bias in risk assessment and decision making*. Paper presented at the Thirteenth National Roundtable on Child Protective Services, San Francisco.

Jonson-Reid, M., & Barth, R. P. (2000). From maltreatment report to juvenile incarceration: The role of child welfare services. *Child Abuse & Neglect, 24*, 505–520.

Maluccio, A. N., & Fein, E. (1989). An examination of long term foster family care for children and youth. In J. Hudson & B. Galaway (Eds.), *The state as parent: International research perspectives on interventions with young persons* (Vol. 53, pp. 387–400). Dordrecht, The Netherlands: Kluwer.

McCabe, K., Yeh, M., Hough, R. L., Landsverk, J., Hurlburt, M. S., Culver, S. W., et al. (1999). Racial ethnic representation across five public sectors of care for youth. *Journal of Emotional and Behavioral Disorders, 7*(2), 72–82.

McMurtry, S. L., & Lie, G. Y. (1992). Differential exit rates of minority children in foster care. *Social Work Research & Abstracts, 28*(1), 42–48.

McRoy, R. G., Oglesby, Z., & Grape, H. (1997). Achieving same-race adoptive placements for African American children: Culturally sensitive practice approaches. *Child Welfare, 76*, 85–104.

Morton, T. (1999). Letter to the editor. *Child Abuse & Neglect, 23*, 1209.

Needell, B., Cuccaro-Alamin, S., Brookhart, A., & Lee, S. (1999). Transitions from AFDC to child welfare in California. *Children and Youth Services Review, 21*, 815–841.

Needell, B., Webster, D., Cuccaro-Alamin, S., & Armijo, M. (2000). *Performance indicators for child welfare services in California: Caseload updates from CWS/CMS extract through quarter four, 1999.* Retrieved March 25, 2000, from http://cssr21.socwel.berkeley.edu/alan/cwscms/index.html.

Olsen, L. (1982). Services for minority children in out-of-home care. *Social Service Review, 56*, 572–585.

Rosenthal, J. A., Schmidt, D. M., & Conner, J. (1988). Predictors of special needs adoption disruption: An exploratory study. *Children and Youth Services Review, 10*, 101–117.

Schmidt-Tieszen, A., & McDonald, T. P. (1998). Children who wait: Long-term foster care or adoption? *Children and Youth Services Review, 20*(1–2), 13–28.

Smith, S. L., Sullivan, Q. E., & Cohen, A. H. (1995). Factors associated with the indication of child abuse reports. *Journal of Social Services Research, 21*, 15–34.

Spearly, J. L., & Lauderdale, M. (1983). Community characteristics and ethnicity in the prediction of child maltreatment rates. *Child Abuse & Neglect, 7*, 91–105.

Stehno, S. M. (1982). Differential treatment of minority children in service systems. *Social Work, 27*, 39–45.

Terling, T. (1999). The efficacy of family reunification practices: Reentry rates and correlates of reentry for abused and neglected children reunited with their families. *Child Abuse & Neglect, 23*, 1359–1370.

Thornton, J. L. (1991). Permanency planning for children in kinship foster homes. *Child Welfare, 70*, 593–601.

U.S. Bureau of the Census. (1999a, February 3). *Poverty 1997: Poverty estimates by selected characteristics.* Retrieved September 11, 1999, from http://www.census.gov/hhes/poverty/poverty97/pv97est1.html.

U.S. Bureau of the Census. (1999b, October 29). *Resident population estimates of the United States by sex, race, and Hispanic origin: April 1, 1990 to September 1, 1999.* Retrieved from http://www.census.gov/population/estimates/nation/intfile3-1.txt.

U.S. Department of Health and Human Services. (1996). *Executive summary of the third national incidence study of child abuse and neglect.* Washington, DC: Westat, Inc.

U.S. Department of Health and Human Services. (1999, June 18). *How many children entered foster care during the period 10/1/97 through 3/31/98?* Retrieved September 11, 1999, from http://www.acf.dhhs.gov/programs/cb/stats/ar0199.htm.

U.S. General Accounting Office. (2000). *US Customs Services: Better targeting of airline passengers for personal searches could produce better results* (GAO/GGGD-00-38). Washington, DC: U.S. Government Printing Office.

Wulczyn, F. (2000). *Adoption dynamics: A report from the Multistate Foster Care Data Archive.* Paper presented at the David and Lucille Packard Foundation Meeting on the Adoption and Safe Families Act of 1997, Santa Cruz, CA.

Wulczyn, F. H., Brunner, K., & Goerge, R. M. (1999). *A report from the multistate foster care data archive. Foster care dynamics, 1983–1997.* Chicago: Chapin Hall Center for Children at the University of Chicago.

Wulczyn, F. H., Harden, A. W., & Goerge, R. M. (1997). *An update from the multistate foster care data archive.* Chicago: Chapin Hall Center for Children at the University of Chicago.

Yegidis, B., & Morton, T. D. (1999). *Ideas in action: Item bias and CPS assessments.* Atlanta, GA: Child Welfare Institute.

CHAPTER 3

Race Differences in Risk of Maltreatment in the General Child Population

Andrea J. Sedlak and Dana Schultz

Background and Purpose

The National Incidence Study of Child Abuse and Neglect (NIS) is a periodic federal effort that provides estimates of the number of children who are abused and neglected in the United States. NIS gathers data through two principal sources: (1) child protective service (CPS) agencies submit information about the cases they investigate, and (2) community professionals in a variety of agencies (e.g., police, schools, hospitals, etc.) serve as sentinels for the study and provide information about all abused and neglected children they encounter. NIS integrates the cases obtained from these two sources, generating estimates of the numbers of abused and neglected children that include both those who receive the attention of CPS agencies and those who do not (Sedlak & Broadhurst, 1996).

NIS has been implemented three times to date: NIS-1 provided annual estimates for children abused or neglected in 1980 (National Center on Child Abuse and Neglect, 1981), the NIS-2 gave estimates for 1986 (Sedlak, 1991), and NIS-3 estimates reflected the number of children maltreated in 1993 (Sedlak & Broadhurst, 1996). NIS has consistently found no significant racial differences in the incidence of abuse and neglect. At the same time, low income has consistently emerged in NIS as a strong risk factor for all forms of maltreatment.

The conjunction of these findings has been puzzling, in light of the differential distribution of people of color at lower income levels in the general population. That is, if low income is a risk marker for abuse and neglect, and families of color are more likely to have low incomes, then one would expect children of color to be at a higher risk of abuse and neglect. The NIS findings are also perplexing in view of the fact that children of color are overrepresented within the child welfare system, well beyond their relative representation in the general child population. The strong nonwhite presence in the child welfare system has been a matter of discussion and concern (e.g., Morton, 1996). It would seem plausible to assume that the situation reflects higher rates of abuse and neglect in the nonwhite population, stemming from minorities' differential experience of risk factors such as low income. The NIS findings of no overall racial differences in risk contradict this assumption, however.

The study reported here attempted to clarify the NIS findings by examining racial differences in the occurrence of abuse and neglect while controlling for notable demographic risk factors. By combining the NIS data with data from the U.S. Bureau of the Census on the general population, the researchers constructed a special database that included nationally representative data on both maltreated and nonmaltreated children. Using this database, the researchers developed multivariate logistic models to account for the occurrence of abuse and neglect in the general population, examining the effects of race in the context of demographic risk factors, such as family income.

Method

Sources

The analyses reported here used a special analysis database that combined two sources: (1) the NIS-3 nationally representative data on children who experienced countable maltreatment in 1993 and (2) the Current Population Survey from the U.S. Bureau of the Census on children in the general population. NIS-3 data included the records on all children who were classified as maltreated under the standardized study definitions of abuse and neglect.[1] Researchers collected these NIS data during the fall of 1993. Only the March supplement of the Current Population Survey provides information on pa-

[1] All children submitted to the National Incidence Study (NIS) as maltreated are evaluated according to standard study definitions of abuse and neglect, and researchers only considered those who fit the standards maltreated and used them to generate the national estimates. NIS-3 simultaneously implemented two different definitional standards—the Harm Standard and the Endangerment Standard. The Endangerment Standard is the more lenient of the two. It includes all the children who qualify under the Harm Standard as well as others who were considered endangered but not yet harmed by abusive or neglectful acts or omissions of their caregivers. To provide the option for analyses pertaining to risk of either Harm Standard or Endangerment Standard maltreatment, the researchers included NIS-3 children who met either of these standards in the synthetic database.

rental employment, so this was the preferred source for general population information. To provide general population data for as comparable a time period as possible, the study consolidated the two March Current Population Surveys that straddled the NIS-3 data period. Specifically, the March 1993 supplement, comprising 42,814 child-level records, was combined with the March 1994 supplement, which included 42,281 child-level records. In joining these two databases, the weights on their cases were halved, to ensure that their union would provide appropriate national estimates regarding children in the general population.

Equivalent Variables

To combine the NIS data with the Census survey data, it was necessary to translate comparable variables into an equivalent classification scheme. This task required derivations across several variables in both databases. In addition, although the NIS-3 database already provided all variables at the child-level of analysis, it was necessary to integrate information across both person and household levels in the Census database. For instance, to extract child-level information from the Census about parental employment, it was necessary to (a) determine from the person-level data which records corresponded to dependent children living in households, then (b) for each of these children, locate the associated record for their household to identify the person codes of the parents, and finally (c) locate the person records for the identified parents to determine their employment status.

It was possible to develop common codes across NIS and the Census for seven demographic characteristics. Table 3-1 lists these seven variables, showing their classification categories in the synthetic database.

Imputation

Because the next step in developing the synthetic database as described here required all children to be fully classified on the seven common variables, it was necessary to impute values for those variables that would enter into the unified database. In imputing values for missing data on countable children in NIS, the researchers made special efforts to preserve the covariance structure of the data. They defined strata using variables with known or potential relationships to the variable being imputed, so that the imputed values would retain the same relationship to the stratification variables as exhibited by the known cases. For certain combinations of variables, the variables were "linked" during the imputation process by imputing unknown values on the combined variables simultaneously, using "donors" with known values on both variables. Appen-

Table 3–1: Variables in the Synthetic Database

Variables	Categories
Child's age (6 levels)	Age: birth to 2, 3–5, 6–8, 9–11, 12–14, 15–17
Child's gender (2 levels)	Male, female
Child's race (4 levels)	White, African American, Hispanic, other
Number of children in household (3 levels)	One child; 2–3 children; ≥4 children
Family structure (3 levels)	Two parents/parent substitutes; only mother or mother/ substitute; only father or father/substitute
Parental employment (3 levels)	Employed full- or part-time[a]; unemployed (unemployed and looking for work and no parent employed); not in the labor force (retired, disabled, or on Aid to Families with Dependent Children)
Annual household income (3 levels)	<\$15,000, \$15,000–29,999; ≥\$30,000

[a] The employed category was more finely differentiated and consisted of two distinct levels during imputation and synthetic database construction. The researchers combined these in all subsequent analyses.

dix 3-A provides details on the imputations, indicating which variables were linked during imputation, what other variables were used to define the strata when imputing values for cases missing information, and what percentage of the NIS sample of countable children required imputation. The Census Current Population Survey data had very few cases with missing values on the critical variables, so imputation followed a simple proportional procedure, with no variable linking or stratification strategies.

Unification in a Synthetic Database

Using the seven equivalent variables listed in Table 3-1, the researchers entered both the Census and NIS data into the full seven-way cross-classification matrix defined by the equivalent variables. The resulting matrix consisted of 4,320 cells.[2] Within each cell, the researchers developed two estimates: (1) from the Census data, an estimate of the number of children in the general population with the combination of characteristics defined by the cell, and (2) from the NIS, an estimate of the total number of children with those characteristics who experienced countable maltreatment. The researchers derived an estimate of the number of nonmaltreated children in each cell by subtracting the maltreated total from the general population total in the cell. The researchers omitted those cells in which both the Census and NIS estimates were zero ($n = 863$) and cells in which the NIS estimate was greater than the Census estimate of the total number of

[2] As noted in connection with Table 3-1, the parent-employment variable had four levels at this stage. When combined with the three levels of the family structure variable, only 10 cells were logically defined (i.e., two cells in the cross-classification matrix of these two variables could not exist, by definition). As a result, the full cross-classification matrix comprised the 4,320 cells defined by Age (6) X Income (3) X Number of Children (3) X Sex (2) X Race (4) X Family Structure and Parental Employment (10).

population children (n = 133) from further consideration, leaving 3,324 cells with a positive estimate for the number of nonmaltreated children. They constructed synthetic records for these cells, with each record assigned a weight equivalent to the estimated total of nonmaltreated children in the cell. They then combined these nonmaltreated synthetic child records with the 5,427 NIS records on countable children to provide a unified database of maltreated and nonmaltreated children that could support logistic regressions to explore multivariate models predicting risk of maltreatment, using the variables available in the conjoined database. The resulting database comprised 8,751 child-level records, representing a weighted total of 68,464,688 children nationwide.

Like many large national surveys, NIS-3 used a multistage sample design (i.e., sentinels were sampled in agencies, agencies in counties, and counties in the United States). When studies use multistage samples, the data have a considerable degree of positive covariance. To accurately assess variances (or standard errors) and for significance tests to yield meaningful results, one must take special measures (Lee, Forthofer, & Lorimor, 1989). NIS provides for computing standard errors of estimates using a replication approach, the jackknife. This process produced 21 replicate weights in NIS-3 (Sedlak, Broadhurst et al., 1997; Sedlak, Hantman, & Schultz, 1997). To support the planned analyses, it was necessary to provide replicate weights for all records in the unified database, so the researchers used the NIS-3 replicate weights to replicate the subtraction process, thereby providing replicate weights for the nonmaltreated child records that coordinated with the 21 replicate weights on NIS-3 maltreated children.

Data Extract of White and African American Children

Preliminary analyses revealed a number of complex and confusing race effects when they included all children, including those of Hispanic and "other" racial origins. To simplify and focus the analyses reported here, the researchers focused solely on uncovering the dynamics of maltreatment risk among white and African American children. The synthetic database was, therefore, reduced to this subset of children. This extraction database comprised 5,879 synthetic child-level records (including 3,684 white children and 2,195 African American children), which represented a weighted total of 56,940,689 children nationwide (46,085,618 white children and 10,855,071 African American children).

Analyses

Three additional strategies guided the analyses reported here. First, these analyses focused on risk of maltreatment that met the NIS Harm Standard criteria. Most previous

Table 3-2: National Distribution of White and African American Children on Demographic Characteristics

	Total	% White	% African American	Significance of χ^2
All White and African American Children	56,940,689	80.9	19.1	
Child's Gender				ns
Male	29,182,777	81.1	18.9	
Female	27,757,912	80.7	19.3	
Child's Age				ns
Birth to 2	9,836,313	80.1	19.9	
3–5	9,862,266	80.3	19.7	
6–8	9,476,425	81.3	18.7	
9–11	9,632,634	81.4	18.6	
12–14	9,357,233	81.3	18.7	
15–17	8,775,818	81.2	18.8	
Family Income				$p < .001$
<$15,000	10,498,202	54.3	45.7	
$15,000–$29,999	11,611,618	76.7	23.3	
≥$30,000	34,830,869	90.4	9.6	
Parental Employment				$p < .001$
Employed	48,216,965	85.8	14.2	
Unemployed	2,244,464	60.6	39.4	
Not in labor force	6,479,260	51.4	48.6	
Family Structure				$p < .001$
Both parents	41,026,867	90.0	10.0	
Single parent	15,913,822	57.6	42.4	
Number of Children in Household				$p < .001$
1	12,827,162	82.4	17.6	
2–3	36,362,410	83.6	16.4	
≥4	7,751,117	65.9	34.1	

analyses have preferred Harm Standard maltreatment because it relies on more objective criteria. The Harm Standard generally requires that evidence of demonstrable harm from abuse or neglect exist to consider children maltreated. In contrast, the Endangerment Standard includes children considered maltreated on the basis of subjective judgments about whether they were endangered by the acts or omissions of their caregivers.

Second, because the goal of these analyses was to control for the influence of potentially confounding factors when examining the risk associated with race, the first step was to localize those factors that are associated with race. Table 3-2 provides the distributions of African American and white children on the equivalent variables in the synthetic extraction database, indicating the significance of the observed differences.

No racial differences existed in distributions by child's age or child's sex, but the remaining four family characteristics evidenced highly significant differences. African

Table 3-3: Single-Factor Logistic Models Predicting Risk of Any Harm Standard Maltreatment as a Function of Four Family Characteristics

Predictor	Model *F*	*p* Value of Model *F*	R^2	Estrella Likelihood Ratio
Family income	201.135	<.001	.140	.032
Family structure	64.377	<.001	.021	.005
Parent labor force status	30.130	<.001	.006	.001
Number of children in household	17.770	<.001	.006	.001

American children are overrepresented among children in low-income families (with incomes less than $15,000 a year) compared with their prevalence in the composite population of African American and white children (45.7% vs. 19.1%). African American children are also overrepresented among children with unemployed parents (39.4%), children with parents who are not in the labor force (48.6%), children with single parents (42.4%), and children in families with four or more children (34.1%).

All four of these family characteristics are also independently associated with significantly higher risk of maltreatment, as shown in Table 3-3. Because of this, these characteristics may confound assessments of race differences in risk. Moreover, these characteristics also evidence correlations with each other, as given in Table 3-4. Thus, the authors were especially concerned about taking them into account simultaneously, to the extent possible, in the analyses reported here.

Third, because the 21 replicate weights (see previous) restrict the total degrees of freedom of any test to 21, model building had to follow a forward-stepwise process. At the same time, because the interest of these analyses was very specific—to identify the variance in risk of maltreatment in relation to race—the model building was topically focused. The authors began with race as the sole predictor of maltreatment and then examined each of the family characteristics independently as expansions of this basic model, both alone and in interaction with race. At each stage of model building, the authors preferred the expansion that maximally revealed race-related patterns in risk.

Findings

Table 3-5 shows the parameter estimates, their significance levels, and the model-fit information for the final composite models that predicted the occurrence of Harm Standard maltreatment, including any Harm Standard maltreatment and four specific categories of maltreatment—physical abuse, sexual abuse, emotional maltreatment, and physical neglect. Each model predicted the occurrence of the category of maltreatment

Table 3-4: Associations Among Four Family Characteristics as Indexed by Pearson Chi-Square

Predictor	Family Income	Family Structure	Parent Labor Force Status	Number of Children in Household
Family income				
Family structure	1960.9****			
Parent labor force status	1987.1****	1777.0****		
Number of children in household	170.4****	20.9****	185.5****	

****$p < .001$.

in question, contrasting children who had experienced maltreatment in the category with those who had not, regardless of whether those in the latter group had experienced any other type of maltreatment, or were entirely nonmaltreated children.

As Table 3-5 indicates, there was a significant overall effect of race on the risk of sexual abuse and physical neglect and a marginal race main effect on the risk of physical abuse. These main effects cannot be interpreted directly from the model parameters, however, because of interaction terms involving race. In fact, race interacted with two of the factors in the overall model and in the models for three of the four more-specific categories of maltreatment. The meaning of these findings is presented in the following sections, which detail the complex patterns of race-related differences that emerged.

Overall Racial Differences in Maltreatment Risk

The findings for "any maltreatment" in Table 3-5 reveal that white and African American children evidence no overall difference in their risk of harm standard maltreatment when the analysis controls for other factors in the model. An overall racial difference did emerge in the models for three of the specific categories of maltreatment, however. Controlling for the other factors in the respective models, white children were at a higher risk of physical abuse, sexual abuse, and physical neglect. These differences are graphed in Figure 3-1, which depicts the average percentage of children who are maltreated across the different cells specified by the model in question.

Racial Differences in Maltreatment Risk Modified by Family Income

Table 3-5 indicates that race and income interact in determining the overall risk of maltreatment. Figure 3-2 shows that the difference between white and African American children in rates of any form of Harm Standard maltreatment appears in the lowest income group. About 10% of white children whose families are in the lowest income group (annual incomes less than $15,000) were maltreated, compared with 6% of Afri-

Table 3-5: Parameter Estimates and Overall Fit of Final Multiple Factor Logistic Regression Models to Predict Harm Standard Maltreatment

Parameter	Any Maltreatment	Physical Abuse	Sexual Abuse	Emotional Maltreatment	Physical Neglect
Intercept	-5.88****	-6.84****	-7.45****	-7.01****	-8.45****
African American (AA)	0.80	-0.28*	-1.19***	0.10	2.71****
Income					
<$15,000	3.72****	3.04****	3.45****	3.51****	4.37****
$15,000–$29,999	2.66****	2.15****	2.03****	2.72****	3.25****
≤$15,000 X AA	-1.04*	NA	NA	-1.56*	-2.35****
$15,000–$29,999 X AA	-1.03**	NA	NA	-1.34*	-2.87****
Children in Household					
2–3	-0.08	NA	NA	NA	0.12
≥4	0.51**	NA	.50	NA	0.99**
2–3 X AA	-0.38*	NA	NA	NA	-0.95***
≥4 X AA	-0.54*	NA	.81	NA	-1.57***
Parental Employment					
Unemployed	NA	0.75***	NA	-0.22	NA
Not in labor force	-0.64****	-0.51**	-.90**	-0.63***	NA
Unemployed X AA	NA	-0.08	NA	0.59	NA
Not in labor force X AA	NA	-0.81***	NA	0.74	NA
Model *F* value	59.51****	31.11****	40.83****	26.03****	37.41****
R^2	.16	.12	.13	.12	.15

Note: NA = not included in model.
*.10 ≥ p > .05. **p ≤ .05. ***p ≤ .01. ****p < .001.

can American children. In the two higher income groups, the difference between white and African American children disappears.

This same race and income interaction pattern was statistically significant in accounting for the occurrence of emotional maltreatment and physical neglect, as shown in Figures 3-3 and 3-4. White children in the lowest income group were emotionally maltreated marginally more often than African American children. The same pattern is seen with physical neglect—white children in the lowest income group were physically neglected significantly more often than African American children.

Race Differences in Maltreatment Risk Modified by Parental Employment

Only the final model for physical abuse included significant interaction terms for parental employment and child's race. In this model, all three categories of parental employment were included—employed, unemployed, and not in the labor force.[3] The pattern can be seen in Figure 3-5. The logistic model indicates that the otherwise marginal racial difference is especially pronounced among children whose parents are not in the

[3] Throughout these models, unspecified categories are by default included in the intercept. Thus, the employed category is in the intercept in this model.

Figure 3–1: Risk of Different Forms of Maltreatment by Race (Controlling for Other Factors in the Model)

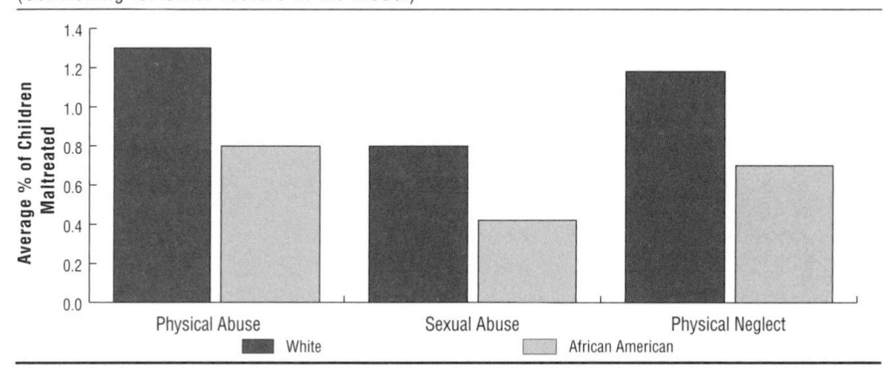

Figure 3–2: Risk of Maltreatment by Income and Child's Race (Controlling for Parental Employment and Number of Children)

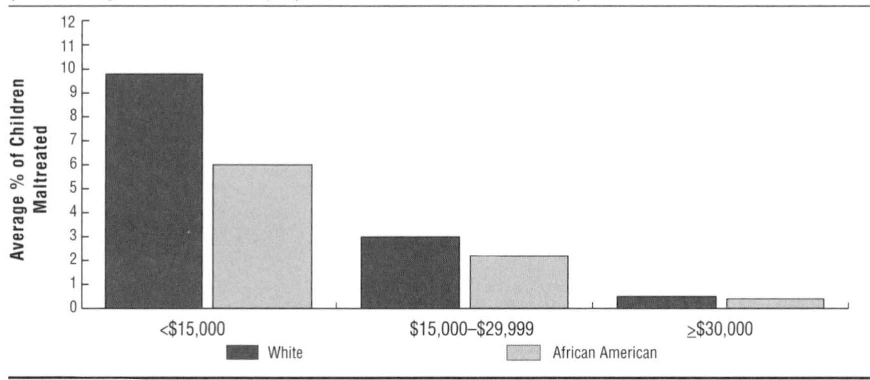

Figure 3–3: Risk of Emotional Maltreatment by Income and Child's Race (Controlling for Parental Employment)

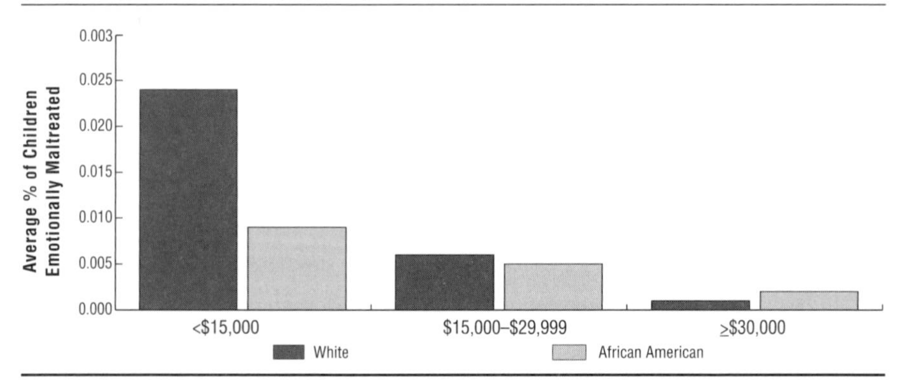

Figure 3–4: Risk of Physical Neglect by Income and Child's Race (Controlling for Number of Children)

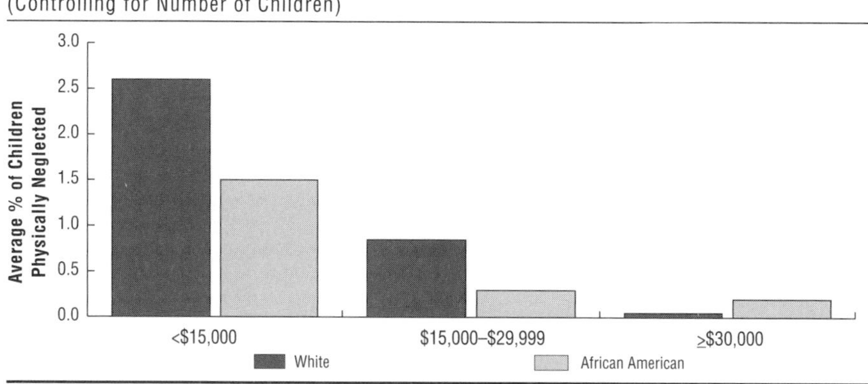

labor force, of whom white children are physically abused at a much higher rate than African American children.

Racial Differences in Maltreatment Risk by Number of Children

The composite models for any Harm Standard maltreatment and for physical neglect revealed that the interaction between the child's race and the number of children in the household affected the risk of maltreatment. Figure 3-6 shows that, among children living in households with four or more children, white children were more likely to be maltreated. Six percent of white children living in these larger households experienced Harm Standard maltreatment, compared with 3% of African American children.

The risk of physical neglect was similarly differentially affected by the child's race when there were four or more children in the household. Figure 3-7 displays the pattern for this maltreatment category. White children in these larger households were physically neglected much more often than African American children.

Conclusion and Next Steps

The findings reported here clarify what has, until now, been an anomaly in NIS—why no significant racial differences exist in it. Because African American children are more likely to be in larger, single-parent families with low incomes and parents who are not in the labor force, and because all of these characteristics are associated with a higher risk of maltreatment, one would expect to find substantial racial differences in the NIS data. The analyses here show that when these disadvantaging characteristics are simultaneously taken into account, African American children in fact have a *lower* risk of being maltreated than white children. Thus, the overall finding of no racial differences actu-

Figure 3–5: Risk of Physical Abuse by Parental Employment and Child's Race (Controlling for Income)

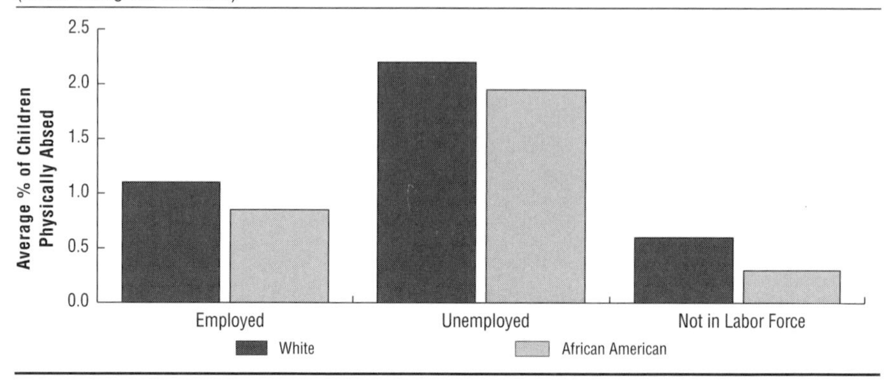

Figure 3–6: Risk of Maltreatment by Number of Children and Child's Race (Controlling for Income and Parental Employment)

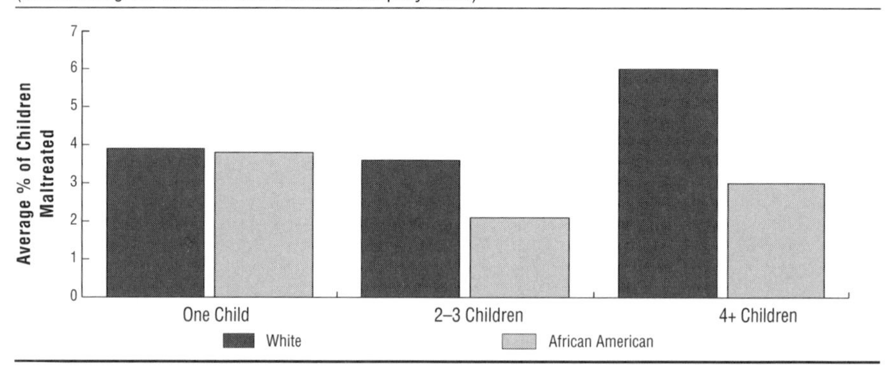

Figure 3–7: Risk of Physical Neglect by Number of Children and Child's Race (Controlling for Income)

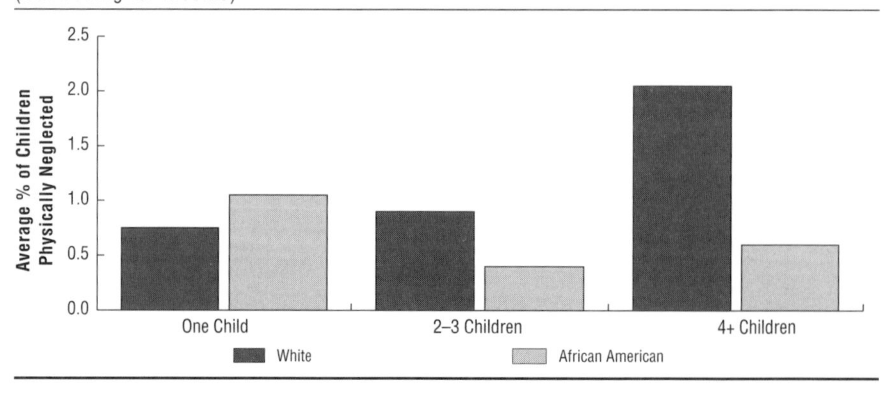

ally reflects the summative result of countervailing forces—the lower risk of African American children is obviated in the overall pattern precisely because of the influences of their several disadvantaging characteristics. The characteristics of low family income, single-parent family structure, parents not in the labor force, and large households all contribute as risk factors, but their effect is to raise the otherwise lower African American maltreatment rates to approximate the level of white maltreatment rates.

Although these results account for the apparent anomaly in the NIS data, they cannot help explain the current overrepresentation of African American children in the child welfare system. In fact, they are exactly the opposite of the risk distributions that could provide a simple explanation for the overrepresentation of African American children in the child welfare system. Toward that end, the companion analyses of the NIS-3 data, reported in Sedlack and Schultz (Chapter 5, this volume), have examined another stage in the entry into child welfare: CPS investigation, considering whether there are circumstances in which African American children's maltreatment is more likely to be investigated by CPS.

Appendix 3-A

Imputation of Missing Data

Table 3-A indicates which variables were linked during imputation of missing values on the NIS countable children, what other variables were used to define the strata when imputing values for the missing value cases, and what percentages of the NIS sample required imputation on the variables in question. Imputation was carried out in the order described by the rows in Table 3-6, with each row awaiting the completion of the preceding rows. Thus, the imputations in the later rows were shaped by the information provided by the earlier imputations.

Note that, except for the last two rows of Table 3-6, few cases had missing values and required imputation. A substantial minority of cases required imputation for mother's employment status (29%), and substantial data were missing on income (40%), however, the authors could not omit these factors from the analyses. As discussed previously, income has reliably emerged as a powerful predictor of maltreatment risk. Moreover, both variables are of central importance to the purpose of the present study regarding racial differences in the underlying risk of maltreatment when other risk indicators are taken into account. Thus, both of these variables were included here, and the analysis imputed their missing values using highly refined stratification structures, as shown in Table 3-6. These stratification structures ensured that the imputed values would retain the complex interrelationships with the other stratification variables as evidenced

Table 3–A: Imputation of Missing Values for National Incidence Studies Children

Variables Imputed	Stratification Variables	Percentages Imputed	
Race and number of children	Census region County metrostatus	Neither missing Race missing Number of children missing Both variables missing	90% 3% 7% <0.1%
Age and gender	Maltreatment category	Neither missing Age missing Gender missing Both variables missing	98% 1% 0.4% 1%
Family structure	AFDC status Race Number of children Age	Not missing Family structure missing	99% 1%
Mother's and father's employment	Family structure AFDC status Race Number of children	Neither missing Only mother's missing Only father's missing Both variables missing	49% 29% 6% 15%
Income	AFDC status Maltreatment category Parents' employment Race Number of children	Not missing Income missing	60% 40%

Note: AFDC = Aid to Families with Dependent Children.

in the known-value cases. Because the analyses in the present study were to be limited to these variables, this approach ensured that the resultant findings would not be distorted by the imputation process used to include missing-value cases.

Very few cases had missing information on the critical data items in the Census data. Only 671 of 85,095 cases (0.8%) were missing values for family structure. Only 676 of the 85,095 cases (0.8%) were missing data on parental employment. The researchers used a simple (nonstratified, nonlinked) hotdeck procedure to impute these missing values.

References

Lee, E. S., Forthofer, R. N., & Lorimor, R. J. (1989). *Analyzing complex survey data*. Newbury Park, CA: Sage.

Morton, T. D. (1999). The increasing colorization of America's child welfare system: The overrepresentation of African American children. *Policy & Practice*, 23–30.

National Center on Child Abuse and Neglect, Children's Bureau. (1981). *Study findings: National study of the incidence and severity of child abuse and neglect* (DHHS Publication No. [OHDS] 81-30325). Washington, DC: U.S. Department of Health and Human Services.

Sedlak, A. J. (1991). *National incidence and prevalence of child abuse and neglect: 1988 (revised report)*. Rockville, MD: Westat.

Sedlak, A. J., & Broadhurst, D. D. (1996). *Third National Incidence Study of Child Abuse and Neglect: Final report.* Washington, DC: U.S. Department of Health and Human Services.

Sedlak, A. J., Broadhurst, D., Shapiro, G., Kalton, G., Goksel, H., Burke, J., et al. (1997). *Third National Incidence Study of Child Abuse and Neglect: Analysis report.* Rockville, MD: Westat.

Sedlak, A. J., Hantman, I., & Schultz, D. (1997). *Third National Incidence Study of Child Abuse and Neglect (NIS-3): Public use files manual.* Washington, DC: National Center on Child Abuse and Neglect, U.S. Department of Health and Human Services.

CHAPTER 4

The Role of Race in Child Protective Services Screening Decisions

Brian M. Gryzlak, Susan J. Wells, and Michelle A. Johnson

CPS agencies are designated to receive reports of alleged child maltreatment, to investigate as they deem appropriate. *Screening* refers to the first step in this process, the decision to investigate. As significant differences in CPS agencies exist both between and within states, screening policies and practices are varied and wide ranging (Costin, Karger, & Stoesz, 1996; Wells, 1985).

The media often highly publicizes instances of CPS agencies failing at their duty to protect children. At the same time, people criticize CPS agencies for being overly intrusive in family life when no intervention is warranted (Costin et al., 1996; Schorr, 1997). In the 1980s, the tension between these often competing goals rose when agencies were forced to handle a burgeoning number of reports in the context of inadequate and diminishing funding. CPS agencies increasingly turned to screening cases to eliminate some of them prior to investigation. Also during this period, the potential for racial disparities in determining which families were reported and which of those workers investigated commanded increasing attention (for example, Gelles, 1982; Hampton &

Authors' Note: The present analysis, conducted for the Symposium on Race Matters (Washington, DC, January 8–9, 2001), builds on previous work conducted on screening decisions in child protective services (CPS). These studies were funded by the U.S. Department of Health and Human Services Children's Bureau, Grant #90-CA-1265 and #90-CA-1407. They were conducted by the American Bar Association Center on Children and the Law with the American Humane Association in consultation with C. Hendricks Brown of the Johns Hopkins University School of Hygiene and Public Health Biostatistics Department and Ted Stein of the State University of New York Albany School of Social Welfare.

Newberger, 1985). Researchers conducted the studies on which this chapter is based to address a lack of knowledge regarding child welfare agencies' intake and investigation of reports of child maltreatment.

Background

From 1981 to 1985, reports of child maltreatment to CPS increased 55% nationally from roughly 1,211,000 to 1,876,000 (U.S. House of Representatives, 1987, p. 3). During this time, states—including those facing the greatest increases in reports—experienced inadequate and diminishing federal, state, and local funding for CPS (U.S. House of Representatives, 1987).

In the context of fiscal pressures, and given the sheer number of reports, CPS agencies found themselves screening out reports of child maltreatment that they previously would have investigated (Schorr, 1997). Many became concerned that children in need of protection were falling through the cracks.

Analyses show that reports to CPS increased by 809,000 from 1989 to 1999. Whereas people reported roughly 2,435,000 children to CPS in 1989, estimates suggest that CPS agencies received 3.2 million reports of child maltreatment in 1999 (Peddle & Wang, 2001). According to a 1996 survey of 50 states conducted by the Urban Institute, in states that provided such information, agencies screened out a median of 36% of cases reported to CPS prior to investigation (Tumlin & Geen, 2000).

Results from the Third National Incidence Study of Child Abuse and Neglect (NIS-3) reveal that of those cases in which children were known by professionals in the community to be abused or neglected, CPS only investigated 28% (Sedlak & Broadhurst, 1996). Agencies investigated known incidents of maltreatment in NIS-3 (data collected in 1993) 16% less frequently than in NIS-2 (data collected in 1986). In addition, there was an 18% decrease between the NIS-2 and NIS-3 in CPS investigations of incidents in which children were endangered (for example, locked in a closet, bound, or threatened with a knife or a gun); CPS only investigated 33% of such cases. Furthermore, among incidents in which community professionals participating in NIS-3 identified children as being severely maltreated, CPS only investigated 25% (Sedlak & Broadhurst, 1996).

Although NIS-3's findings do not differentiate between allegations not reported and those reported but not investigated, they do provide a sense of the degree to which CPS agencies are investigating cases of maltreatment known to community professionals. The NIS-3 findings show that although the number of children recognized as maltreated increased and the percentage of incidents of maltreatment that were investigated declined, the actual number of incidents of maltreatment investigated by CPS remained relatively constant. Thus, as the authors point out, "this picture suggests that the CPS system has reached its capacity to respond to the maltreated child population" (Sedlack & Broadhurst, 1996, p. 9). NIS-3 findings demonstrate the need for further examination of which types of reports agencies screen in for investigation and what other factors are associated with such decisions (for example, report and worker characteristics, geographic location of agency, or population served).

Factors Influencing the Decision to Investigate a Report

Research that has explored factors associated with CPS decisionmaking at report intake has revealed patterns in the decision to investigate. Johnson and Wells (2000) reviewed 13 studies that examined CPS screening practices. The studies varied by the focus of the research, method of analysis, variables examined, and data collection period. Still, all studies examined variables associated with CPS decisionmaking, and several common findings emerged from their review. Wells, Fluke, Downing, and Brown (1989) found that the CPS site where the allegation was made often was associated with decisions to investigate reports of maltreatment. Also, reports to CPS in which reporters described injuries as severe or alleged sexual abuse and reports in which younger children were involved were more likely to be screened in for investigation. In addition, some studies found that reports were more likely to be investigated by CPS in cases of domestic violence or when the family had previous CPS contact. Reports made by mandated reporters or neighbors were also more likely to be investigated. When identified parental problems involved custody disputes or lack of supervision, reports were more likely to be assigned an alternative response to investigation (i.e., assessment, voluntary services) or simply not investigated. In addition, reports in which disclosed parental problems involved inadequate supervision of children were more likely to be referred for a differential response and not investigated.

Johnson and Wells (2000) reviewed studies that examined the explanations workers gave for deciding not to screen in a report for investigation. Again, the studies employed a range of methods (for example, interviews with workers vs. workers completing report form); however, sufficient similarities existed so that Johnson and Wells could make cross-study comparisons. Several studies found that CPS workers' decisions not to refer reports for investigation were based on the workers' assessment that the reports were not appropriate for CPS, were outside the legal definition of maltreatment, or were outside CPS's jurisdiction. Other reasons for not investigating reports included that the victim was not a child or the perpetrator was not a caregiver.

Worker perceptions may also affect screening decisions, however, according to Johnson and Wells's (2000) review. One study found that intimidation of CPS workers by "threatening adults" was a factor in worker decisions not to investigate reports. In four of the studies reviewed, workers did not investigate some cases because they identified a report as false or malicious. Interestingly, two studies reviewed reported discrepancies between the explanations workers offered for not investigating and the particular characteristics of the reports. For example, Gilbert, Karski, and Frame (1997) found that caseworkers screened out 20% of reports that contained allegations of sexual abuse for reasons including insufficient evidence and failure to satisfy legal definitions. Of these reports, they found that 65% contained specific allegations of sexual abuse. In addition, Wells et al. (1989) found that among reports screened out for investigation by workers who cited "no specific act alleged," specific incidents of maltreatment were recorded by workers on report forms.

The Effect of Race on Screening Decisions

Children of color are clearly overrepresented in the child welfare system (see Garland, Ellis-MacLeod, Landsverk, Ganger, & Johnson, 1998; Morton, 1999). For example, 41% of children receiving services in 1994 were African American, whereas African American children comprised only 15% of the general population (U.S. Department of Health and Human Services, 1997). In comparison, although white children made up 69% of the general population, they comprised only 46% of children receiving services.

Because methods and identification of different populations vary among studies, this review will use the terminology and classification identified by each author cited. Johnson and Wells (2000), in their review of 13 CPS screening studies, found that race of the child played a role in the disposition of the report in two studies. In the first study, English and Aubin (1991) examined report disposition in and between sites to identify potential differences in cases referred for CPS investigation and those referred for an alternative response (such as assessment and voluntary services) in Washington State. In Washington, caseworkers screen out reports when they have no way to identify the child, when the reporter makes no specific allegations, or when no immediate risk to the child exists. They assign accepted reports a level of risk from 1 (no risk) to 5 (high risk) and refer them to one of two responses: CPS investigation or an alternative response. Generally, workers referred lower risk cases for an alternative response and investigated higher risk cases. English and Aubin found that among children physically neglected, children of color were more likely to be identified as high risk. In another analysis, English and Aubin looked at site differences between those physical abuse cases referred to an alternative response site and those referred to a CPS site. Compared with the CPS site, significantly more children of color were classified as low risk in the alternative response site.

Johnson and Wells (2000) also identified a study by Siegel and Loman (1997) in which race was associated with the decision to investigate. In Missouri's dual-track response system, workers assign reports either for CPS investigation or to community-based services, with more severe cases assigned for investigation. Analyses of report disposition revealed a significant difference for African American children. Specifically, reports involving African American children were more likely to be investigated rather than referred for community-based assessment or services.

More recent analyses suggest that race, when examined as a function of other factors, is associated with the decision to investigate reports of child maltreatment. Sedlak and Schultz (2001) used NIS-3 data to examine the role of race in explaining which incidents of maltreatment known to community professionals CPS would investigate. Using logistic regression, they created models using race and selected variables (they introduced both individual variables and interaction terms in the models) as independent variables and using whether CPS investigated the case as the dependent variable. Several significant models and associations emerged. In a model examining race as a function of parental employment, they found that workers were less likely to investigate reports to CPS of African American children whose parents were not in the labor force than corresponding reports about white children ($p = 0.016$).

Another model explored race as a function of maltreatment type. The overall model was significant at the 0.01 level, and two significant findings emerged. CPS was more likely to investigate reports of African American children who were emotionally maltreated ($p < .05$) or physically neglected ($p < .01$) than reports of their white counterparts. Among African American children emotionally maltreated, workers investigated 25% of such incidents, compared with 11% of known incidents concerning white children. Although CPS only investigated 11% of physically neglected white children, they investigated 35% of physically neglected African American children.

Another significant finding surfaced when Sedlak and Schultz (2001) examined race as a factor of perpetrator alcohol or drug involvement. Specifically, workers were much more likely to investigate reports to CPS for African American children when the named perpetrator was recorded as involved with alcohol or drugs ($p < .05$). Although CPS investigated 78% of such reports, they only investigated 41% of reports concerning white children for whom the perpetrator was involved with alcohol or drugs.

These findings suggest that race does play a role in screening decisions, although other factors may mediate such an influence. This analysis builds on previous work conducted on the role of race in screening decisions.

Purpose

The U.S. Department of Health and Human Services (DHHS), Administration for Children and Families, Children's Bureau funded the screening study and a follow-up secondary analysis project to better understand what happens to reports once they are referred to CPS. These studies concluded in 1991 but the information collected at that time has continued to be instructive due to the depth and breadth of the work made possible by DHHS, as well as the extraordinary cost of replicating this effort.

Researchers conducted the analyses reported in this chapter to further examine the role of race and ethnicity in decisionmaking at the time a report is made. Earlier analyses using this data generally examined the entire data set or subsets based on case characteristics, such as nature of the report. The findings of the original analysis were that race and site were so highly related that when site was taken into consideration, race was not a factor in the decisionmaking process, even when controlling for all other variables. For this chapter, the researchers examined each site separately to determine whether there were within-site differences in screening activities associated with the race of the reported child.

Using the data from the screening study and the secondary analysis project, this study addresses the following research questions:

- What are the between-site differences with regard to which factors influence the decision to investigate?
- Does the race or ethnicity of the child reported to CPS have any effect on the decision to screen when examined as a two-way interaction variable (for example, the effect of Race/Ethnicity X Source of report on the decision to screen)?
- Does the decision to investigate a case depend on the race or ethnicity of the CPS worker, and if so, does this finding vary based on the race or ethnicity of the child?

Method

The screening projects consisted of a number of substudies of laws, policies, supervisory practices, and worker decisionmaking. This chapter is based on one of these studies. For the subject study, the researchers collected case-level data from workers in 12 local child welfare agencies (sites) from five states on 2,504 unduplicated referrals.

Site Selection

Originally, the researchers purposively selected 10 local offices from five states to represent a broad range of screening policies, geographic distribution, and sociodemographic and economic levels. Sites represented local protective service catchment areas and may have been composed of a city, a county, or a region of several townships or rural counties. In one state, the researchers added an extra site to the study during data collection because the required number of cases did not materialize as expected. In another, they divided one rural region consisting of several counties into two separate sites after examination of the data yielded two different and distinct patterns of decisionmaking that varied by county. Table 4-1 represents the characteristics of the original 12 sites, generalized to protect the identity of the local offices and states. It was necessary to take these precautions due to the administrators' concerns at the time regarding potential liability with respect to federal legal requirements to investigate every report received. They feared at the time that federal reviewers would regard any screening activity as contrary to federal policy.

Recording Case and Contact Information

The workers who were designated to receive reports in each site completed a separate data collection instrument for every contact received during the study period that concerned the welfare of a child. For ease of reference in this chapter, these contacts may be referred to as *reports* or *allegations*. As noted previously, however, it is important to recognize that in some sites the use of the words *report* or *allegation* signified a legal status requiring that an investigation be conducted. For the purposes of the screening study, it was necessary to record every contact regarding concern for a child's welfare, whether or not the local office would label it as an official report or allegation. Hence, the contacts concerning a child's welfare that are described here should not automatically be thought of as valid reports under the state's laws and policies. In fact, the issue of the study was to determine how agency personnel decide which contacts would be investigated and which would not.

The data collected for each contact included report characteristics (date and time of report, source of report, number of prior reports on child or perpetrator, maltreatment alleged, injuries alleged, other problems reported, completeness of report, perpetrator's relationship to child), child characteristics (age, race or ethnicity, gender), type of household (child living with single parent, etc.), the decision made by the worker, and the reasons given for the decision. In addition to collecting information on the reports that workers received, the researchers conducted surveys of the workers who made the case disposition decisions, their supervisors, and the characteristics of each CPS agency's relationships with allied professional agencies and organizations such as schools, hospitals, and

Table 4-1: Site Sociodemographics

Site	Population[a] Nearest 100,000	Percentage Population Change 1980–1986	Percentage Nonwhite	Urban	Unemployment Rate	Number of Families w/ Children < Age 18	Household Median Income	Number of Families in Poverty	Annual Report Rate per 100 Families
A	200,000	<-10	>50	Urban	<10	20,000	<15,000	<10	8
B	100,000	<10	>10	Urban	<10	10,000	<15,000	>10	9
C	200,000	>20	>10	Suburban	<10	30,000	>15,000	<10	2
D	400,000	>20	<10	Suburban	<10	60,000	>15,000	<10	6
E	300,000	10–19	<10	Suburban	<10	50,000	>15,000	<10	7
F	200,000	<10	<10	Urban	<10	20,000	>15,000	<10	8
G	100,000	<10	<10	Urban	<10	10,000	>15,000	<10	6
H	100,000	<10	<10	Urban	>10	10,000	>15,000	>10	6
I	200,000	<10	<10	Rural	>10	40,000	<15,000	>10	6
J	100,000	<10	<10	Rural	>10	20,000	<15,000	>10	9
K	>1,000,000	>20	<10	Urban	>10	200,000	>15,000	<10	5
L	600,000	10–19	<10	Urban	<10	80,000	>15,000	<10	8
United States	241,078,000	6.4	14.9	—	7.0	[b]	16,841	9.6	[b]

Note: All numbers in this chart have been rounded such that the meaning and relative magnitude of the figures will be preserved but the exact figures have been obscured. Data were derived from U.S. Census data 1980 through 1986.

[a] Population data have been rounded to the nearest hundred-thousand.

[b] Not available for 1986.

law enforcement. The instruments used to record the contact and allegation were simple checklists of largely closed-ended items, much like an agency case registry form.

The data collection periods varied by the rate and volume of contacts per month. The goal was to collect a minimum of 100 reports per site. In some cases, the researchers collected 300 reports in two weeks' time. In others, it was necessary to collect data over two months to approach 100 reports. Prior to data collection, the authors trained workers and their supervisors in form completion, including all workers screening cases at the time of the study. During the data collection period, the researchers visited each site at least twice, and as often as necessary to ensure that workers completed data forms accurately and questions or concerns received a prompt response. During the visits, the researchers reviewed every form for completeness and logical edits. If a question arose, the researchers consulted the original worker or the case information to complete the forms accurately.

The original data collection yielded 2,556 contacts, which included some duplicate complaints (multiple calls about the same incident) and re-reports (calls received more than 24 hours after the first call, thus suggesting a continuing problem). The authors retained re-reports for the study, and these averaged 1% to 10% per site. The authors dropped duplicate reports from the file, resulting in a final sample of 2,504. Of these contacts, 1,789 included specific allegations of maltreatment or injury to a child. Other contacts might have involved generalized concerns, such as "She's not taking care of them right." Unless these concerns also included some description of maltreatment or injury such as denial of food, hitting, or observed bruises, however, they were not identified as specific allegations. For the purposes of this study, only the specific allegations of maltreatment or injury were retained.

Analyses

A consideration in this analysis was selecting only those sites in which some variation existed in the screening decision as well as the race or ethnicity of the children reported. To this end, the authors applied three criteria in selecting sites for analysis. They excluded sites that contained less than 100 cases and sites in which 94% or more of the cases were screened in from the analyses. They also omitted sites in which information on the race or ethnicity of the child was missing or unknown for 90% or more of the contacts. Thus, they retained 960 cases from five sites in four states that contained sufficient variability with regard to the race or ethnicity of the child and screening decisions for analysis (Sites C, E, F, K, and L). Table 4-2 illustrates the racial and ethnic composition and screening activity in the 12 original sites. The cases included in this table are only those with specific allegations of maltreatment or injury.

Table 4–2: Percentage of Contacts Screened In or Out by Race/Ethnicity and Site

Site	Race/Ethnicity	*N*	Screened Out	Screened In
A	African American	88	3	97
	Missing	16	19	81
	Other	4	10	100
	Unknown	2	6	100
	White	30	—	90
	Total	140	—	94
B	African American	84	0	100
	Missing	0	—	—
	Other	9	0	100
	Unknown	6	0	100
	White	31	0	100
	Total	130	0	100
C	African American	10	10	90
	Missing	18	56	44
	Other	4	25	75
	Unknown	89	39	61
	White	44	41	59
	Total	165	39	61
D	African American	3	67	33
	Missing	0	—	—
	Other	4	50	50
	Unknown	188	38	62
	White	8	50	50
	Total	203	39	61
E	African American	6	0	100
	Missing	1	0	100
	Other	19	25	75
	Unknown	95	20	80
	White	41	27	73
	Total	162	19	81
F	African American	3	67	33
	Missing	14	71	29
	Other	33	21	79
	Unknown	24	38	63
	White	48	46	54
	Total	122	41	59
G	African American	2	0	100
	Missing	0	—	—
	Other	10	30	70
	Unknown	3	67	33
	White	46	26	74
	Total	61	28	72
H	African American	4	0	100
	Missing	0	—	—
	Other	2	0	100
	Unknown	34	6	94
	White	41	24	76
	Total	81	15	85

Table 4–2: Percentage of Contacts Screened In or Out by Race/Ethnicity and Site (continued)

Site	Race/Ethnicity	*N*	Screened Out	Screened In
I	African American	2	0	100
	Missing	3	0	100
	Other	1	0	100
	Unknown	16	6	94
	White	137	6	94
	Total	159	6	94
J	African American	5	20	80
	Missing	3	0	100
	Other	2	0	100
	Unknown	3	0	100
	White	42	0	100
	Total	55	2	98
K	African American	21	52	48
	Missing	7	100	0
	Other	55	65	35
	Unknown	12	92	8
	White	171	63	37
	Total	266	65	35
L	African American	4	75	25
	Missing	5	40	60
	Other	35	63	37
	Unknown	170	65	35
	White	31	55	45
	Total	245	63	37
Total	African American	232	10	90
	Missing	86	41	59
	Other	168	42	58
	Unknown	633	41	59
	White	670	32	68
	Total	1789	34	66

For a large number of cases, race and ethnicity is either missing or unknown. In this study, "missing" indicates that the worker did not complete the item. "Unknown" signifies that the worker completed the reporting form but did not know the information at the time of the contact. For those cases in which workers did not collect race or ethnicity, it seems likely that agencies did not systematically attempt to capture and record this information. It may be that during the screening decisionmaking process, workers focus more on gathering information that is critical to knowing whether the contact actually constitutes a report that must be investigated. Other information, unless it is required for completing the report, may remain unknown or missing from the recording form.

The number of contacts known to concern children of color is relatively small. Likewise, people of color generally comprise a relatively small proportion of the general population in the sites selected for analysis. For comparison, Table 4-3 illustrates the distri-

Table 4-3: Distribution of Race in Intake and Population by Site

Site	Percentage Nonwhite in Population	Percentage Nonwhite Contacts
A	>50	66
B	>10	69
C	>10	7
D	<10	3
E	<10	8
F	<10	4
G	<10	3
H	<10	7
I	<10	2
J	<10	13
K	<10	12
L	<10	8

bution of people of color at intake and in the population by site. This table is based on 1986 census definitions (U.S. Bureau of the Census, 1988). The authors rounded the percentages of people of color in the population to protect the identity of CPS sites.

The U.S. Bureau of the Census does not provide data on what percentage of the population Hispanic people comprise. Thus, Hispanic people are not included in the Census's or our tabulations as white or nonwhite (Table 4-3), as they may be either, based on the Census's operational definition of Hispanic people as "persons of Spanish origin" (U.S. Bureau of the Census, 1988). As defined by the Census, Hispanic is essentially an ethnic group designation, as such people "may be of any race." Despite the necessary exclusion of Hispanic people from this tabulation, however, the percentage of contacts involving children of color tends to mirror their respective numbers in the general population for each site.

Variables

The reporting forms completed by CPS workers contained data on 14 variables. These variables can be grouped into two conceptually distinct categories, the eight report variables (Table 4-4) and the six child, family, and community variables (Table 4-5). Both tables contain the number of responses in each variable category as well as the percentages of each response for a particular variable. For contacts involving more than one child, the authors analyzed the data for the child with the most severe alleged injuries. If they could make no distinction based on severity of injury, then the youngest child became the unit of analysis.

Table 4-4: Descriptive Statistics for Report Variables with Specific Allegations of Child Abuse/Neglect or Injury (N = 960)

Report Variables	Frequency	Percentage
Allegation		
Neglect	359	37.4
Physical abuse	268	27.9
Multiple maltreatment	198	20.6
Sexual abuse	101	10.5
Emotional maltreatment or fostering delinquency	34	3.5
Injury Type		
No injury	490	51.0
Minor	135	14.1
Unknown	113	11.8
Severe	70	7.3
Other injury	61	6.4
Missing	49	5.1
Suspected	35	3.6
Multiple injuries	7	0.7
Prior Reports		
None or Unknown	662	69.0
Child	242	25.2
Child and family or perpetrator	45	4.7
Family or perpetrator	11	1.1
Perpetrator		
Perpetrator in home	685	71.4
Other perpetrator	185	19.3
Perpetrator unknown	81	8.4
Missing	9	0.9
Source of Report		
Other professional	413	43.0
Friend, relative, other (not categorized)	163	17.0
Medical professional	102	10.6
Nonperpetrating parent	98	10.2
Neighbor	91	9.5
Anonymous	49	5.1
Self	36	3.8
Missing	8	0.8
Completeness of Report		
Mostly complete	342	35.6
Complete on critical variables	260	27.1
Somewhat complete	222	23.1
Incomplete	136	14.2
Number of Children Reported		
One	569	59.3
More than one	391	40.7
When Report Was Made		
Workday	595	62.0
Missing	236	24.6
Evening/weekend	129	13.4

Table 4-5: Descriptive Statistics for Child, Family, and Community Variables with Specific Allegations of Child Abuse/Neglect or Injury (N = 960)

Variable	Frequency	Percentage
Gender of Children		
All female	362	37.7
All male	344	35.8
Mixed	205	21.4
Missing	49	5.1
Ethnicity of Children		
Unknown	390	40.6
White	335	34.9
Hispanic	109	11.4
Missing	45	4.7
African American	44	4.6
Other	37	3.9
Age of Children		
Teenage	265	27.6
2–5	264	27.5
6–12	249	25.9
<2	182	19.0
Type of Household		
Child living with parent/other	755	78.6
Unknown	196	20.4
Missing	9	0.9
Parent Problems		
No additional problems recorded	404	42.1
Health	230	24.0
Drugs or alcohol	145	15.1
Child care	74	7.7
Child care	74	7.7
Marital	33	3.4
Housing/other	30	3.1
Community		
K	266	27.7
L	245	25.5
C	165	17.2
E	162	16.9
F	122	12.7

Logistic Regression Modeling

The purpose of this chapter is to contribute to the research considering which factors are pertinent in decisions to screen in reports to CPS for investigation and to determine whether, in a more focused analysis, the issue of race and ethnicity plays a role in such decisions. One aim was to discern which variables were statistically significant predictors of the decision to screen in a report for CPS investigation. The authors also intended to understand the degree to which the variables predicted screening decisions when examined in the presence of other variables. They used SPSS 10.0 to construct logistic regression models that best explained these decisions.

In developing logistic regression models with 960 cases from five sites, the authors began by creating a series of single-factor models, running each independent variable separately against the dependent variable: the screening decision (0 = case screened out, 1 = case screened in). They then entered all 14 variables individually into a model in descending order of their R^2 values. They based their decision to retain a particular variable in this model on the difference in model chi-square values. First, the authors subtracted the chi-square value of the model with the additional independent variable from the same value of the model without it. Based on this difference and the difference in degrees of freedom between the two models, they consulted a chi-square table to determine the statistical significance of the difference in models with and without the variable. They retained the new model when the inclusion of the additional variable was statistically significant. This method is also known as the *likelihood-ratio test* or the *chi-square difference test*.

After all 14 variables were introduced individually and significant variables were retained, the authors reintroduced those variables that were not exposed to the final model. They continued this process until all initially excluded variables had been reintroduced after all other retained variables had been included in the model. This ensured that the model did not exclude a variable that might gain significance in the presence of other variables.

To strengthen model efficiency and to increase the ease of interpretation, the researchers then collapsed the independent variables where appropriate. They entered all 14 uncollapsed variables simultaneously into a logistic regression model so that they could control the effects of all other variables on individual variable categories. They based their decision to collapse variable categories on conceptual as well as statistical similarities. Prior knowledge of factors influencing decisionmaking (for example, children with severe injuries are more likely to be screened in) guided the decision to collapse variables based on conceptual congruencies. The authors examined betas, standard errors, and standardized coefficients when taking into consideration statistical similarities. They only collapsed variables to the extent that conceptual and statistical similarities in each variable permitted. Tables 4-6 and 4-7 delineate the collapsed variable categories along with the number and percentage of cases screened in for each category (note that the category "children of color" includes African American and Hispanic children, as well as children from other racial and ethnic groups).

Table 4-6: Percentage of Cases with Specific Allegations Screened in by Report Variables

Variable	Number of Cases	Percentage Screened in
Total	960	50.8
Allegation		
All other child abuse and neglect	859	48.9
Sexual abuse	101	67.3
Type of Injury		
No injury	490	39.8
All other injury except severe	203	68.0
Missing, unknown, suspected	197	49.7
Severe injury	70	81.4
Prior Reports		
None or Unknown	662	47.7
Child	242	59.5
Child and family or perpetrator	21	46.7
Family or perpetrator	11	63.6
Perpetrator		
Perpetrator in home	685	51.2
Other perpetrator	185	50.8
Missing or unknown	90	47.8
Source of Report		
All others	663	56.7
Friend, relative, other (not categorized)	163	39.3
Self or nonperpetrating parent	134	35.8
Completeness of Report		
All or mostly complete on critical variables	602	57.5
Somewhat complete	222	43.7
Incomplete	136	33.1
Number of Children Reported		
One	569	49.4
More than one	391	52.9
When Report Was Made		
Workday	595	61.2
Missing	236	37.7
Evening/weekend	129	53.8

Using the collapsed versions of the independent variables, the researchers reintroduced all 14 variables using backward-stepwise logistic regression, which employed the likelihood-ratio test as the exclusionary criterion, to determine the exclusion of variables from the model. This was done to ensure that variables that were initially excluded from the final model in their uncollapsed versions did not regain significance when introduced into the model with collapsed versions of the variables. The resulting model thus contained all variables that were significant predictors of the screening decision.

Table 4-7: Percentage of Specific Allegations Screened in by Child, Family, and Community Variables

Variable	Number of Cases	Percentage Screened in
Total	960	50.8
Gender of Children		
All other	598	53.5
All female	362	46.4
Ethnicity of Children		
Missing or unknown	435	51.0
White	335	47.8
Children of color (African American, Hispanic, other)	190	55.8
Age of Children Reported		
<2	1,872	61.0
2–12	513	52.2
Teenage	265	41.1
Type of Household		
Child living with parent	696	54.5
Missing and unknown	205	37.1
Other	59	55.9
Parent Problems		
No additional problems recorded/other problems	842	50.8
Custody dispute	74	64.9
Child care	44	27.3
Site		
C	165	60.6
E	162	80.9
K	266	35.3
L	245	37.1
F	122	59.0

The authors constructed logistic regression models for individual sites using a similar approach. Two differences are noteworthy. First, they only used the collapsed versions of the independent variables. Again, they based the decision to exclude variables from the model based on the likelihood-ratio test. Second, they only used 13 variables in creating models for individual sites. This is because one variable, site, was excluded from the analysis.

Following the model creation for the model containing the 960 cases, the authors ran a series of interaction terms, each containing race/ethnicity and one other factor. By examining interaction effects between two variables, they could discern whether the two variables were associated with each other in explaining the variance in the dependent variable. They accomplished this by introducing the interaction term (for example, Race/Ethnicity X Type of Injury), along with the main effect variables (such as, race/ethnicity, type of injury). Again, the authors employed the likelihood-ratio test to determine if the introduction of the interaction term significantly contributed to the model. One interaction term and corresponding main effect variables were entered into the full model, resulting in 13 different models.

Model Fit Summary Statistics

The analysis generated several statistics to determine the goodness of fit for the main effects model ($N = 960$), individual site models, and the models including interaction terms. The researchers used Cohen's Kappa (ranging from 0–1) to assess the fit between observed and expected values of the dependent variable. A higher Kappa value shows that a greater degree of association exists between the observed and expected values of the screening decision. The percentage correct simply indicates what percentage of the dependent variable was predicted by the independent variables. Finally, the researchers used the Hosmer-Lemeshow goodness-of-fit test (Hosmer & Lemeshow, 2000). Available in SPSS 10.0, this test generates a significance value ranging from 0 to 1, which tests the hypothesis that the independent variables do not explain the dependent variable better than chance alone. Thus, insignificant values ($p > .05$) are desirable, indicating that the independent variables are significant in predicting the decision to screen; however, Hosmer and Lemeshow (2000) noted that the presence of a few deviant cases may have the effect of rendering the model unfit. They recommended performing residual analyses to examine the possibility that such cases may deem the model no better in predicting the screening decision than chance alone. The authors performed limited residual analyses, including inspection of dBeta, leverage statistics, and standardized residual values, as suggested by Menard (1995).

Race and Ethnicity of CPS Workers in Screening Decisions

The cases on which this chapter is based contain data on the CPS workers included in the screening decisions. Not all contacts contained such data, however. There were 640 valid cases for which data on the race or ethnicity of the CPS worker were available. This study examined whether racial differences existed among CPS workers associated with screening decisions.

An additional aim was to investigate if the interaction between the race or ethnicity of the CPS worker and the race or ethnicity of the child affected the screening decision. For many of these cases, the child's race or ethnicity was either missing or unknown. Consequently, of the 640 cases for which data on the worker's race or ethnicity were available, only 342 also contained data on the child's. These 342 cases from all five sites (C, 24; E, 44; F, 71; K, 154; L, 49) represent 42 workers, as most of the workers made numerous contacts. The authors performed cross-tabulations on the race or ethnicity of the worker and child by the screening decision. Note that because systematic bias may be present with regard to the missing and unknown cases, no conclusions or inferences should be made from these analyses; that is, they are solely exploratory.

Findings

This section presents findings from logistic regression modeling for 960 valid cases and the five individual sites. It also presents the results of logistic regression models that included the addition of interaction terms. Finally, it reports the findings on the relationship between the race or ethnicity of CPS workers and children in the context of workers' screening decisions.

Logistic Regression Model for All 960 Cases

The main effects model included eight independent variables that were significant predictors of the screening decision in the five sites included in the analysis. These variables were the CPS site, allegation, type of injury, source of the report, completeness of the data recording form, gender of child, age of the youngest child, and type of parental problems. Table 4-8 presents the betas, standard errors, probabilities, and the log odds of variable categories. The child's race or ethnicity did not have an overall effect on the decision to screen in a case for investigation. When introduced in the presence of the other eight variables, it was not significant ($\chi^2 = 1.249$; $df = 2$; $p < .50$) in predicting the decision to screen in a case for investigation.

The location at which cases were reported was a strong predictor of cases being screened in for investigation. The model reveals that in the presence of the other seven independent variables, cases reported to Site E were 8.5 times more likely to be screened in than cases from Site L, the "reference category," or the category to which other sites are compared. Reports to Site K were only 60% as likely to be screened in. That is, compared to Site L, the reference category, and taking into consideration all other variables, reports to Site K had a 6 out of 10 chance of being screened in for investigation. Another strong predictor of the screening decision was the type of injury reported to the CPS worker. The model reveals that compared with when no injury was reported, reports involving severe injuries were nearly eight times more likely to be screened in for investigation. Likewise, reports to CPS alleging less-than-severe injuries were screened in 4.4 times more often than reports with no injury alleged. When people made allegations of sexual abuse to a worker, the case was 4.8 times more likely to be screened in compared with all other allegations of maltreatment. In addition, the model shows that younger children were more likely to be screened in than teenagers. Compared to teenagers, re-

Table 4-8: Logistic Regression Beta Weights, Standard Errors, *p* Values, and Log Odds of Being Screened in Compared to Selected Category and Controlling for Other Variables

Variables	Beta	*SE*	*p*	Odds
Site				
C	1.270	.244	<.001	3.6
E	2.142	.270	<.001	8.5
F	0.587	.259	<.05	1.8
K	-0.443	.215	<.05	0.6
L	—	—	—	—
Allegation		—	—	—
Sexual abuse	1.567	.265	<.001	4.8
Other	—	—	—	—
Type of Injury	—	—	<.001	—
Missing, unknown, suspected	0.818	.213	<.001	2.3
Other than severe	1.485	.206	<.001	4.4
Severe	2.064	.351	<.001	7.9
No injury reported	—	—	—	—
Source of Report	—	—	<.001	—
Friend, relative, other (not categorized)	0.716	.303	<.05	2.0
All other categories	1.012	.249	<.001	2.4
Self or nonperpetrating parent	—	—	—	—
Completeness	—	—	<.001	—
All/most	1.166	.263	<.001	3.2
Some	0.647	.272	<.05	1.9
Incomplete	—	—	—	—
Gender of Children	—	—	—	—
All female	-0.465	.166	<.01	0.6
All other (male, mixed, or missing)	—	—	—	—
Age of Youngest Child	—	—	<.01	—
<2	0.756	.241	<.01	2.1
2–12	0.303	.190	.111	1.4
Teenage	—	—	—	—
Parent Problems	—	—	<.05	—
Child care	0.571	.307	.063	1.8
Custody	-0.720	.433	.097	0.5
No problems/other problems	—	—	—	—
Constant	-3.115	.396	<.001	0.04
Number of Cases	**960.000**			
Cohen's Kappa	**0.490**			
Percentage Correct	**75.000**			
Hosmer-Lemeshow Goodness of Fit	**0.005**			

Note: Model chi-square = 311.499; $df = 17$; $p < .001$.

ports involving children younger than 2 years of age and children ages 2 to 12 years were respectively 2 and 1.5 times more likely to be screened in for investigation. When a report involved all female children, the case was 60% as likely to be screened in for investigation than if the report involved all male children or a mix of male and female children. When parental problems were mentioned in the report to CPS and involved custody disputes, the case was only half as likely (log odds = .5) to be screened in for investigation compared with cases with no problems or problems other than child care. On the other hand, cases involving child care problems were 1.8 times more likely to be accepted for investigation.

This logistic regression model presents mixed results compared to earlier findings based on the same data set (Wells, Fluke, & Brown, 1995). The original analysis was based on 1,627 cases and 12 sites in five states and included locations that screened in 94% or more of reports received. An allegation of sexual abuse, the reporting of severe injuries, complete or mostly complete reporting forms, and the presence of children younger than 2 years of age were factors associated with the decision to screen in a case for investigation in both current and previous analyses. Likewise, the site of the report strongly predicted the decision to investigate.

One difference between the analyses concerns the source of the report. In the original analysis, self-reports and reports made by nonperpetrating parents, friends, relatives, or others were less likely to be investigated than anonymous reports and reports made by professionals or neighbors, and contacts for which the reporting source was not collected. The current analysis reveals that reports made by professionals or neighbors and anonymous and missing reports, as well as reports made by friends, relatives, or others, are more likely than self-reports and reports made by nonperpetrating parents to be screened in for investigation. Another difference is that the original analyses found that when the children reported were all female, the case was more likely to be screened out. In addition, the reporting of certain types of other parental problems emerged as a significant factor only in the current analysis.

The indications of the strength of association and goodness of fit and statistics for the present model were mixed. The independent variables predicted the decision to screen in 75% of the cases. Cohen's Kappa indicated a moderate level (.49) of agreement between the number of observed and expected cases screened in and out. Moreover, strong associations are shown for the sensitivity (.75), the measure of agreement between the observed and expected cases screened in, and specificity (.75), the measure of agreement between the observed and expected cases screened out, for the model.

The Hosmer-Lemeshow goodness of fit test value of .005 for the model shows that the model does not significantly predict variance in the decision to screen a report in for investigation. That is, according to this statistic, the presence of the eight independent variables do not significantly reduce the proportion of variance in the dependent variable that could be attributed to chance alone. As noted by Hosmer and Lemeshow (2000), however, this test is sensitive to cases that deviate substantially from the model.

Residual analyses identified eight cases that deviated substantially from the model. As a final inspection, the authors ran eight logistic regression models, excluding one case in each model, to examine the effect on the Hosmer-Lemeshow goodness of fit test. They found that two cases exhibited considerable influence on the test. Standardized residual values for the two cases were of 3.27 for the first case and -5.601 for the second. By excluding either of the cases, the Hosmer-Lemeshow goodness of fit test indicated that the variables in the model were significant predictors of the screening decision. Significance levels for the Hosmer-Lemeshow goodness of fit test with the two cases excluded were $p = .244$ and $p = .306$, respectively. Despite the better fit of the model to the data by excluding either of these cases, they authors retained all 960 variables for analyses because, on inspection, it was plausible that the characteristics of both cases were valid.

It appears these two cases had such an effect due to their particular characteristics. Specifically, in the first case no injury was reported, parental problems involved a custody dispute, no sexual abuse was alleged, and the report was made by either the perpetrator or a nonperpetrating parent. For the main effects model, all of these characteristics were indicative of a case being screened out, but this particular case was screened in. The second case presented relatively opposite dynamics in relation to the screening decision. This case, which was screened out, was reported in Site E, involved an infant for whom less-than-serious injuries were reported and which involved children who were either all male or mixed by gender. In this second case, the CPS worker fully or mostly completed the reporting form. Based on the specific case characteristics, this case had a greater expected chance of being screened in according to the model, but was screened out.

Individual Sites

Results of logistic regression models revealed that the child's race or ethnicity was not a statistically significant factor in the screening decision for any of the five sites. When race/ethnicity was introduced into the main effects models for each site, the difference in chi-square values ($df = 2$) ranged from .903 ($p < .70$) in Site L to 5.368 ($p < .10$) in

Site E and 5.434 in Site K ($p < .10$). Thus, the difference in chi-square test revealed that race/ethnicity emerged only as a marginally significant ($.10 > p > .05$) factor in the decision to screen for Sites E and K.

The findings from logistic models created for individual sites highlight the importance of site in screening decisions. As shown in Table 4-9, three variables (sexual abuse allegation, type of injury, and source of report) merged as predictors of the decision to screen in three or more sites, and usually log odds for the respective variable categories followed similar patterns. For example, when the type of injury was found to be a significant predictor, severe cases were always more likely to be screened in than when no injury was reported. The values of specific coefficients for variable categories differ to a fair extent between the five sites, however. In addition, although three factors were common to three or more sites, the combinations of variables in each site reveal the extent of intersite variability. Of the nine variables that were included in one or more models for individual sites, the number of variables included in site logistic regression models ranged from two in Site E to five in Site K.

Three report variables were significant predictors in the presence of other variables in three or more sites. The type of injury reported to CPS workers emerged in the models for four (C, F, K, L) of the five sites. Moreover, in three sites (C, E, K), workers were more likely to screen in contacts with severe injuries for investigation than contacts for which no injury was reported, nonsevere injuries were reported, or in cases for which the type of injury was missing, unknown, or suspected. In Site K, reports of severe injuries were 31 times as likely to be screened in. In all three sites, injuries reported as other than severe were the next most likely category to be screened in. For Site L, reports in which the type of injury was missing, unknown, or suspected were slightly more likely to be screened in than those which reported severe injuries (3.1 times vs. 2.9 times).

In three sites (C, F, K), an allegation of sexual abuse also predicted the decision of the CPS worker to screen in a case for investigation. Compared with all other allegations—physical abuse, neglect, multiple maltreatment, and emotional abuse fostering delinquency—reports in which sexual abuse allegations were made were from 10.9 to 12.2 times more likely to be screened in.

The decision to screen also depended in part on the nature of the relationship between the reporter and the child. For three sites (E, F, K), the source of the report emerged as a significant predictor. In these sites, when compared with reports made by the perpetrator or a nonperpetrating parent, reports made by professionals, neighbors, or anonymous or missing sources were more likely to be screened in. For Sites E and F, when friends, relatives, or others (excluding professionals, neighbors, anonymous, or miss-

Table 4-9: *p* Values and Odds of Being Screened in Compared to Selected Category and Controlling for Other Variables in Individual Sites

	C		E		F		K		L	
Variable	*p*	**Odds**	*p*	**Odds**	*p*	**Odds**	*p*	**Odds**	*p*	**Odds**
Allegation	—	—			—	—	—	—		
Sexual abuse	<.01	10.9			<.01	12.2	<.001	11.7		
Other	—	—			—	—	—	—		
Type of Injury	<.05	—			<.01	—	<.001	—	<.01	—
Missing, unknown, suspected	.568	1.3			.243	2.3	<.05	2.5	<.01	3.1
Other than severe	<.05	2.4			<.01	6.1	<.001	12.3	.065	2.2
Severe	<.05	7.0			.075	8.1	<.001	31.1	.086	2.9
No injury reported	—	—			—	—	—	—	—	—
Perpetrator Identification			<.05	—						
Missing and unknown			.415	0.6						
Perpetrator in home			.074	2.5						
Other			—	—						
Source of Report			<.05	—	<.05					
Friend, relative, other (not categorized)			.068	5.1	<.05	10.4	.857	0.9		
All other categories			<.05	3.4	<.01	7.9	<.05	3.6		
Self or nonperpetrating parent			—	—	—	—	—	—		
Completeness	<.05	—							<.05	—
All/most	<.01	4.0							<.05	3.5
Some	.093	2.2							.101	2.3
Incomplete	—	—								—
Gender of Children	—	—					—	—		
All female	<.05	0.4					<.05	0.5		
All other (male, mixed, or missing)	—	—					—	—		
Age of Youngest Child					<.01	—			<.05	—
<2					<.05	6.2			<.01	3.4
2–12					.848	1.1			.108	1.8
Teenage					—	—			—	—
When Report Was Made									<.05	—
Evening/weekend									<.01	3.1
Missing									.992	1.0
Workday									—	—
Prior Reports							—	—		
Child							<.05	2.4		
None or unknown							—	—		
Constant	**.149**	**0.57**	**.918**	**0.94**	**<.01**	**0.05**	**<.001**	**0.05**	**<.001**	**0.06**
Number of Cases	**165.000**		**162.000**		**122.000**		**266.000**		**245.000**	
Cohen's Kappa	**0.380**		**0.150**		**0.540**		**0.560**		**0.240**	
Percentage correct	**72.000**		**80.000**		**78.000**		**80.00**		**67.000**	
Hosmer-Lemeshow goodness of fit	**0.925**		**0.915**		**0.179**		**0.763**		**0.204**	

Note: Sites C, F, K, L: significance of model chi-square: $p < .001$; Site E: significance of model chi-square: $p < .01$.

ing) made the report, such cases were respectively 5.1 and 10.4 times more likely to be investigated. For Site L, friends, relatives, or others were 90% as likely to have their reports screened in than perpetrators or nonperpetrating parents were.

The six remaining variables remained significant predictors in the models for either one or two sites. The completeness of the report, the gender of the child, and the age of the youngest child each predicted the decision to investigate in two sites. In the sites for which the age of the youngest child was included in the model (F, L), children younger than 2 were more likely to be screened in than 2- to 12-year-olds, who in turn were more apt to be screened in than when the youngest child was a teenager. Contacts in which all children reported were female were significantly less likely to be screened in for investigation for two sites. Specifically, in Sites C and K, reports involving female children were only 40% and 50% as likely to be screened in for investigation, respectively, than reports about male children or both male and female children. Contacts for which the CPS worker mostly or fully completed the reporting form were more likely to be screened in than partially complete or incomplete forms. Finally, three variables only emerged in one site each. Cases in which the perpetrator was in the home (Site E), the report was made in the evening or on a weekend (Site L), and prior reports existed for the child (Site K) were all more likely to be screened in for investigation.

Overall, the logistic regression models for individual sites predicted the screening decision moderately well. Cohen's Kappa showed fair to moderate agreement between predicted and observed cases. Site E showed a fair level of agreement (kappa = .15), whereas Site K showed a moderate level of agreement (kappa = .56). The insignificant values of the Hosmer-Lemeshow goodness of fit test indicate that we can reject the null hypothesis that the independent variables are not significant in explaining the decision to screen for all five models.

The Effects of Interaction Terms

Out of the 13 logistic regression models created by adding interaction terms to the main effects model (Race/Ethnicity X one other variable), interaction terms in two models emerged as significant additions to the existing model ($N = 960$). Table 4-10 illustrates the model when Allegation X Race/Ethnicity was included as an interaction term. The interaction of race/ethnicity and allegation was significant at the $p < .05$ level. Reports involving sexual abuse of white children were more likely to be screened in for investigation than reports in which race or ethnicity was missing or unknown, which in turn were more likely to be screened in than reports involving children of color. Figure 4-1 presents the percentage of cases screened in for investigation by allegation and race/ethnicity. Of reports involving allegations of sexual abuse of white children, 76% were

Table 4-10: Logistic Regression Model with
Bivariate Interaction Effects of Allegation X Race/Ethnicity

Variables	Beta	*SE*	*p*	Odds
Site	—	—	<.001	—
C	1.316	.248	<.001	3.7
E	2.155	.273	<.001	8.6
F	0.580	.269	<.05	1.8
K	-0.426	.253	.092	0.7
L	—	—	—	—
Allegation	—	—	—	—
Sexual abuse	2.316	.455	<.001	10.1
Other	—	—	—	—
Type of Injury	—	—	<.001	—
Missing, unknown, suspected	0.829	.215	<.001	2.3
Other than severe	1.512	.208	<.001	4.5
Severe	2.077	.352	<.001	8.0
No injury reported	—	—	—	—
Source of Report	—	—	<.001	—
Friend, relative, other (not categorized)	0.755	.308	<.05	2.1
All other categories	1.074	.254	<.001	2.9
Self or nonperpetrating parent	—	—	—	—
Completeness	—	—	<.001	—
All/most	1.196	.280	<.001	3.3
Some	0.665	.274	<.05	1.9
Incomplete	—	—	—	—
Gender of Children	—	—	—	—
All female	-0.484	.167	<.01	0.6
All other (male, mixed, or missing)	—	—	—	—
Age of Youngest Child	—	—	<.01	—
<2	0.742	.242	<.01	2.1
2–12	0.307	.191	.107	1.4
Teenage	—	—	—	—
Parent Problems	—	—	<.05	—
Child care	0.633	.310	<.05	1.9
Custody	-0.728	.442	.099	0.5
No problems/Other problems	—	—	—	—
Race/Ethnicity [a]	—	—	.146	—
Children of color	0.453	.232	.051	1.6
Missing/Unknown	0.213	.229	.352	1.2
White children	—	—	—	—
Allegation X Race/Ethnicity	—	—	<.05	—
Sex abuse X Children of color	-1.952	.663	<.01	0.1
Sex abuse X Race missing/unknown	-0.651	.589	.270	0.5
Sex abuse X White children	—	—	—	—
Constant	-3.397	.463	<.001	0.03
Number of Cases	**960**			
Cohen's Kappa	**.50**			
Hosmer-Lemeshow goodness-of-fit	**.648**			
Percentage correct	**75**			

Note: Model chi-square = 321.539; $df = 21$; $p < .001$.
[a] $.10 < p < .20$.

Figure 4–1: Screening Decision by Allegation and Race/Ethnicity

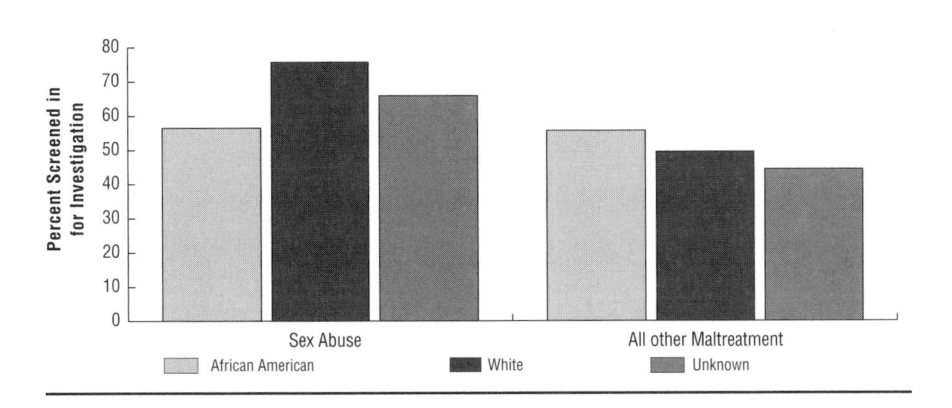

screened in compared with 57% of reports of children of color involving such allegations. This trend reverses for allegations of maltreatment other than sexual abuse: Cases involving allegations of maltreatment other than sexual abuse for children of color were more likely to be screened in compared with cases of white children (55.7% vs. 49.5%).

Table 4-11 presents the second logistic regression model that emerged when the authors examined race/ethnicity as a function of the number of children reported to CPS. The addition of the interaction term was significant at the $p < .01$ level, and the model was significant at the $p < .001$ level.

As shown in Figure 4-2, reports to CPS involving one child of color were less likely to be screened in for investigation compared with reports involving one white child (48.3% vs. 51.5%). In comparison, reports involving white children were considerably less likely to be screened in compared with children of color when the report involved more than one child (42.2% vs. 62.1%).

Both models fit the data fairly well. For the model that includes the term Allegation X Race/Ethnicity, Cohen's Kappa was .50. The Kappa value for the model with Number of Children X Race/Ethnicity was slightly less (kappa = .48). Hosmer-Lemeshow goodness of fit tests illustrate that both models are significant in fitting the data.

Worker's and Child's Race or Ethnicity Associations with Screening Decisions

This section presents the results of the examinations of workers' and children's race or ethnicity and their effects on the screening decision. Again, note that due to the number of cases for which data were unavailable, these findings are exploratory and should be interpreted with caution.

Table 4-11: Logistic Regression Model with
Bivariate Interaction Effects of Race X Number of Children Reported

Variables	Beta	*SE*	*p*	Odds
Site	—	—	<.001	—
C	1.291	.247	<.001	3.6
E	2.166	.272	<.001	8.7
F	0.615	.270	<.05	1.9
K	-3.99	.252	.113	0.7
L	—	—	—	—
Allegation	—	—	—	—
Sexual abuse	1.639	.269	<.001	5.2
Other	—	—	—	—
Type of Injury	—	<.001	<.001	—
Missing, unknown, suspected	0.821	.217	<.001	2.3
Other than severe	1.572	.213	<.001	4.8
Severe	2.055	.352	<.001	7.8
No injury reported	—	—	—	—
Source of Report	—	—	<.001	—
Friend, relative, other (not categorized)	.712	.307	<.05	2.0
All other categories	.993	.252	<.001	2.7
Self or nonperpetrating parent	—	—	—	—
Completeness	—	—	<.001	—
All/Most	1.189	.282	<.001	3.3
Some	0.636	.275	<.05	1.9
Incomplete	—	—	—	—
Gender of Children	—	—	—	—
All female	-0.432	.172	<.05	0.6
All other (male, mixed, or missing)	—	—	—	—
Age of Youngest Child	—	—	<.05	—
<2	0.708	.249	<.01	2.0
2–12	0.270	.195	.167	1.3
Teenage	—	—	—	—
Parent Problems	—	—	<.05	—
Child care	0.611	.309	<.05	1.8
Custody	-0.723	.439	.100	0.5
No problems/Other problems	—	—	—	—
Race	—	—	<.05	—
Children of color	0.845	.317	<.01	2.3
Missing/Unknown	0.747	.315	<.05	2.1
White children	—	—	—	—
Number of Children Reported[a]	—	—	—	—
One child	0.494	.276	.073	1.6
More than one child	—	—	—	—
Number of children reported X Race/ethnicity	—	—	<.01	—
One child X Children of color	-1.213	.446	<.01	0.3
One child X Race missing/unknown	-0.948	.360	<.01	0.4
One child X White children	—	—	—	—
Constant	-3.565	.495	<.001	0.03
Number of Cases	**960**			
Cohen's Kappa	**.470**			
Hosmer-Lemeshow goodness-of-fit	**.392**			
Percentage correct	**73**			

Note: Model chi-square = 323.706; $df = 22$; $p < .001$.
[a] $.10 < p < .20$.

Figure 4–2: Screening Decision by Number of Children Reported and Race/Ethnicity

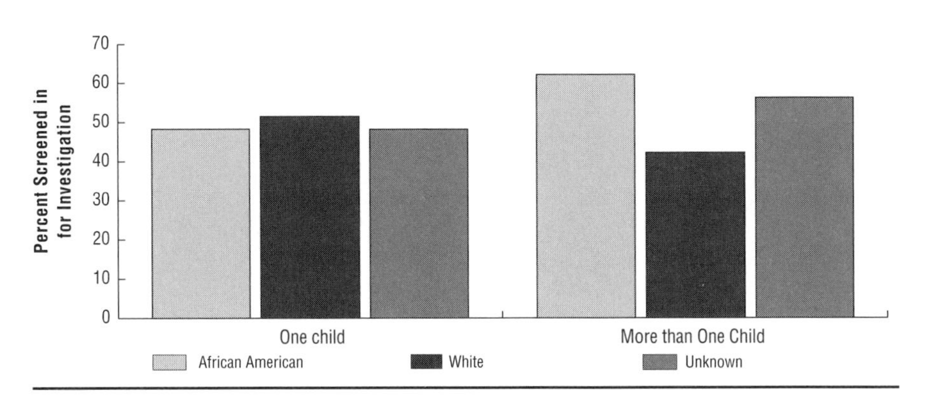

First, the researchers examined the relationship between worker race and the decision to screen. Due to the small number of cases handled by CPS workers of color, the authors collapsed the race of the worker into two categories—workers of color and white workers. Table 4-12 presents the breakdown of worker race by the screening decision. As a single worker usually had numerous contacts, this table reflects the screening decisions of 45 workers (7 of color, 38 white). As shown by the table, overall, workers of color screened in 65% of their cases for investigation, whereas white workers screened in slightly less than 50% of their cases.

To examine whether the site of the contact influenced screening decisions between workers of color and white workers, the authors inspected individual site characteristics. They found that the aggregation of cases masks considerable intrasite variation regarding the relationship between worker race and screening decision. Sites C, E, F and L contained 10 or fewer valid cases handled by workers of color, precluding comparisons of screening decisions to white workers. In Site K (59 cases screened by workers of color, 112 cases screened by white workers), workers of color screened in 27% of cases, compared with 41% for white workers.

Although in the aggregate nearly half of all cases were screened in for investigation, differences emerged based on the child's race or ethnicity. As Table 4-13 shows, 52% of white children were screened in for investigation, compared with only 44% of cases involving children of color. Nearly half of cases in which the child's race or ethnicity was missing or unknown were screened in.

Finally, the authors examined screening decisions in terms of the association between the worker's and child's race or ethnicity. There were 342 cases for which data on both the race or ethnicity of the worker and child were available. Table 4-14 illustrates the findings. Nearly half of all cases in which the worker and child were of color (46.2%)

Table 4-12: Child Protective Services Worker Race by Screening Decision (N = 640)

Race of Worker	Percentage Cases Screened in (n)	Percentage Cases Screened out (n)	N
Workers of color	65.1 (54)	34.9 (29)	83
White workers	49.2 (274)	50.8 (283)	557
Total	51.3 (328)	48.7 (312)	640

Note: Pearson chi-square: $p < .01$.

or the worker and the child were white (49.1%) were screened in for CPS investigation. When workers of color made decisions on cases in which the child was white, however, 76.6% of such cases were screened in for investigation. On the other hand, white workers screened in 40.4% of cases involving a child of color. Again, other factors such as within-site trends or severity of reports may contribute to the explanation of such findings.

Discussion

As noted in other chapters in this book, African American children, and children of color generally, are obviously overrepresented in the foster care system. The question is when, where, and why this occurs. Only by examining the decisionmaking process in its entirety can we begin to understand the issue and address it. In CPS, the first decision about acceptance into or exclusion from the system is the determination of whether an investigation should be conducted; that is, the screening of reports.

A number of studies have examined screening, but few have followed similar methods or even used the same definitions. For example, the statutory definitions of child abuse and neglect differ from state to state. Interpretations of these definitions may vary according the cultures of local CPS offices, as well. These differences would have an obvious effect on identifying factors related to the screening decision. In addition, the major issues examined in these studies vary considerably. For example, some studies focus on African American children specifically, whereas others may use the category "children of color," incorporating all nonwhites and sometimes Hispanic children. In the latter case, the researcher is really investigating whether white, non-Hispanic children are treated differently than all other children.

An examination of the literature reveals that in some studies, reports concerning children of color or African American children specifically (depending on the study) were *more likely* to be investigated than those concerning white children. This finding occurred in the following circumstances.

Table 4-13: Race of Child by Screening Decision (N = 960)

Race of Child	Percentage Cases Screened in (n)	Percentage Cases Screened out (n)	N
Children of color	44.2 (84)	55.8 (106)	190
White children	52.2 (175)	47.8 (160)	335
Missing/unknown	49.0 (213)	51.0 (222)	435
Total	49.2 (472)	50.8 (488)	960

Note: Pearson chi-square: p = .21.

- All reports (Siegel & Loman, 1997)
- Physical neglect (English & Aubin, 1991; Sedlak & Schultz, Chapter 5, this volume)
- Emotional maltreatment (Sedlak & Schultz, Chapter 5, this volume)
- Perpetrator involved with alcohol or other drugs (Sedlak & Schultz, Chapter 5, this volume)

Some studies suggest that children of color may sometimes be *less likely* to be the subject of investigation. In Washington State, families of children of color who were assigned low-risk status were more likely to be referred to voluntary services than to be the subject of CPS investigation. In NIS-3, when parents of African American children were unemployed, the allegations about their maltreatment were less likely to be investigated than reports about white children in the same circumstance.

The findings in the analyses conducted for this chapter were also somewhat contradictory and dependent on interaction effects. There was no finding of race effect in the sample as a whole. Reports regarding children of color were, however, *more likely* to be investigated than reports concerning white children when they involved the following:

- More than one child reported
- Reports other than sexual abuse (physical abuse, physical neglect, emotional maltreatment)

Allegations were *less likely* to be investigated than reports concerning white children when they involved the following:

- Sexual abuse
- One child reported

Table 4-14: Worker and Child Race by Screening Decision ($N = 342$)

Race of Pair	Percentage Cases Screened in (n)	Percentage Cases Screened out (n)	N
Both worker and child of color	46.2 (12)	53.8 (14)	26
Both worker and child white	49.1 (81)	50.9 (84)	165
Worker of color/child white	76.6 (36)	23.4 (11)	47
Worker white/child of color	40.4 (42)	59.6 (62)	104
Total	50.0 (171)	50.0 (171)	342

Note: Pearson chi-square: $p < .01$.

The findings regarding the possible relationship between worker and child race/ethnicity indicate, however, that this is an important area for further exploration. Tentatively, the authors found that when a white child was reported to a nonwhite worker, cases were much more likely to be screened in than in any other combination (about 30% more likely than if the subject of the report was a child of color). The second strongest relationship was that when the worker was white and the child nonwhite, cases were more likely to be screened out (almost 10% more likely than white children).

In thinking about the meaning of these findings, it could be argued that willingness to investigate a report signals a willingness to protect the child who is the subject of that report. On the other hand, CPS investigation might be regarded as unwarranted intrusion into family life. When race and ethnicity are included in the mix, the issue is even less clear. For example, if some degree of physical punishment is valued more among African Americans, after controlling for income and region (Flynn, 1994), does that acceptance sometimes equate to less CPS intervention on behalf of African American children? Although it is not possible to definitively answer these questions, it is possible to take a closer look at how worker decisionmaking and child race may interact to result in a possible racial imbalance in the investigation caseload.

As in a number of other studies of decisionmaking, any differences in decisionmaking based on race tend to wash out when examining main effects, however, some interesting dynamics exist when one examines race in the context of other case characteristics. These data cannot say why this might be so, nor whether being screened out or in is the most desirable alternative. Recalling that in these analyses, all cases examined met the standard of having a specific allegation of maltreatment or injury, one might wonder whether the desirable alternative would be to be screened in, that is, to at least have an investigation conducted. The negative aspect of that, of course, is that once brought to the attention of the state, underprivileged children and children of color may often be at a distinct disadvantage with respect to the treatment afforded them and their families, due to these characteristics alone. Furthermore, it may be that workers of color screening out cases involving children of color at higher rates than white children may be due in part to those workers' perceptions of the child welfare system as being more harmful than helpful to families of color.

Clearly, additional research on the decisionmaking processes of CPS workers is needed. In-depth qualitative research on the perceptions and beliefs of workers and how such constructs influence decisions should be conducted. Moreover, researchers could examine more fully how workers' assessments of specific factors of a report (for example, severity and type of alleged maltreatment, and age of child) and characteristics of the workers themselves (for example, race/ethnicity and years of experience) interact to guide decisionmaking. As the screening literature has consistently identified location as a key variable in decisionmaking, exploration of how the organizational culture of CPS sites may influence screening assessments would help identify potentially biased decisions. Finally, a more concerted effort should be undertaken to employ similar methods and operational definitions across studies so that cross-study comparisons can be made.

References

Costin, L. B., Karger, H. J., & Stoesz, D. (1996). *The politics of child abuse in America.* New York: Oxford University Press.

English, D., & Aubin, S. (1991). *Impact of investigations outcomes for child protective services cases receiving differential levels of service.* Olympia, WA: Washington State Department of Social and Health Services, Children's Administration.

Flynn, C. P. (1994). Regional differences in attitudes toward corporal punishment. *Journal of Marriage and the Family, 56,* 314–324.

Garland, A. F., Ellis-MacLeod, E., Landsverk, J. A., Ganger, W., & Johnson, I. (1998). Minority populations in the child welfare system: The visibility hypothesis reexamined. *American Journal of Orthopsychiatry, 68*(1), 142–146.

Gelles, R. J. (1982). Child abuse and family violence: Implications for medical professionals. In E. H. Newberger (Ed.), *Child abuse* (pp. 25–41). Boston: Little, Brown.

Gilbert, N., Karski, R. L., & Frame, L. (1997). *The emergency response system: Screening and assessment of child abuse reports. Final Report.* Berkeley, CA: University of California, Berkeley, Center for Social Services Research.

Hampton, R. L., & Newberger, E. H. (1985). Child abuse incidence and reporting by hospitals: Significance of severity, class, and race. *American Journal of Public Health, 75*(1), 56–60.

Hosmer, D. W., & Lemeshow, S. (2000). *Applied logistic regression* (2nd ed.). New York: John Wiley and Sons.

Johnson, M. A., & Wells, S. J. (2000). *Screening in child protective services: A literature review.* Urbana-Champaign, IL: University of Illinois at Urbana-Champaign, School of Social Work.

Menard, S. (1995). *Applied logistic regression analysis.* Thousand Oaks, CA: Sage.

Morton, T. D. (1999, December). The increasing colorization of America's child welfare system: The overrepresentation of African-American children. *Policy and Practice, 57*(4), 23–30.

Peddle, N., & Wang, C. T. (2001). *Current trends in child abuse prevention, reporting, and fatalities: The 1999 Fifty State Survey* (Working paper Number 808). Available from http://www.preventchildabuse.org/research_ctr/1999_50_survey.pdf.

Schorr, L. B. (1997). *Common purpose: Strengthening families and neighborhoods to rebuild America.* New York: Doubleday.

Sedlak, A. J., & Broadhurst, D. D. (1996). *Executive summary of the Third National Incidence Study of Child Abuse and Neglect.* Available from http://www.calib.com/nccanch/pubs/statinfo/nis3.htm.

Siegel, G. L., & Loman, A. (1997, November). *Child protection services family assessment and response demonstration. Impact evaluation: Final report.* St. Louis, MO: Institute of Applied Research.

Tumlin, K. C., & Geen, R. (2000). *The decision to investigate: Understanding state child welfare screening policies and practices. Assessing the new federalism, issues and options for states, No. A-38.* Washington, DC: Urban Institute.

U.S. Bureau of the Census. (1988). *County and city data book, 1988.* Washington, DC: U.S. Government Printing Office.

U.S. Department of Health and Human Services, Children's Bureau. (1997). *National study of protective, preventive and reunification services delivered to children and their families.* Available from http://www.acf.dhhs.gov/programs/cb/publications/97natstudy/natstudy.htm.

U.S. House of Representatives. (1987). *Abused children in America: Victims of official neglect. A Report of the Select Committee on Children, Youth, and Families.* Washington, DC: U.S. Government Printing Office.

Wells, S. J. (1985). Decisionmaking in child protective services intake and investigation. *Protecting Children, 2,* 3–8.

Wells, S. J., Fluke, J. D., & Brown, C. H. (1995). The decision to investigate: Child protection practice in 12 local agencies. *Children and Youth Services Review, 17,* 523–546.

Wells, S. J., Fluke, J. D., Downing, J. D., & Brown, C. H. (1989). *Final report: Screening in child protective services* (Grant 90-CA-1265, Administration for Children, Youth, and Families). Washington, DC: American Bar Association.

CHAPTER 5

Racial Differences in Child Protective Services Investigation of Abused and Neglected Children

Andrea J. Sedlak and Dana Schultz

Background and Purpose

The National Incidence Study of Child Abuse and Neglect (NIS) is a periodic federal effort that provides estimates of the number of children who are abused and neglected in the United States. NIS gathers data through two principal sources: (1) child protective services (CPS) agencies submit information about the cases they investigate, and (2) community professionals in a variety of agencies (e.g., police, schools, hospitals, etc.) serve as sentinels for the study and provide information about all abused and neglected children they encounter. NIS integrates the cases obtained from these two sources, generating estimates of the numbers of abused and neglected children that include both those who receive the attention of CPS agencies and those who do not (Sedlack & Boardhurst, 1996). Figure 5–1 provides a schematic summary of the NIS methodology.

The government has implemented NIS three times to date: NIS-1 provided annual estimates for children abused or neglected in 1980 (National Center on Child Abuse and Neglect, 1981), NIS-2 gave estimates for 1986 (Sedlak, 1991), and NIS-3 estimates reflected the number of children maltreated in 1993 (Sedlack & Boardhurst, 1996). NIS has consistently found no significant racial differences in the overall incidence of abuse and neglect. In fact, the authors' recent analyses to unravel racial differences in risk from the confounding effects of other risk factors (such as family income, parental employment, etc.) have found that when one takes into account the joint influences of a number of

Figure 5–1: Nationally Representative Sample of Counties

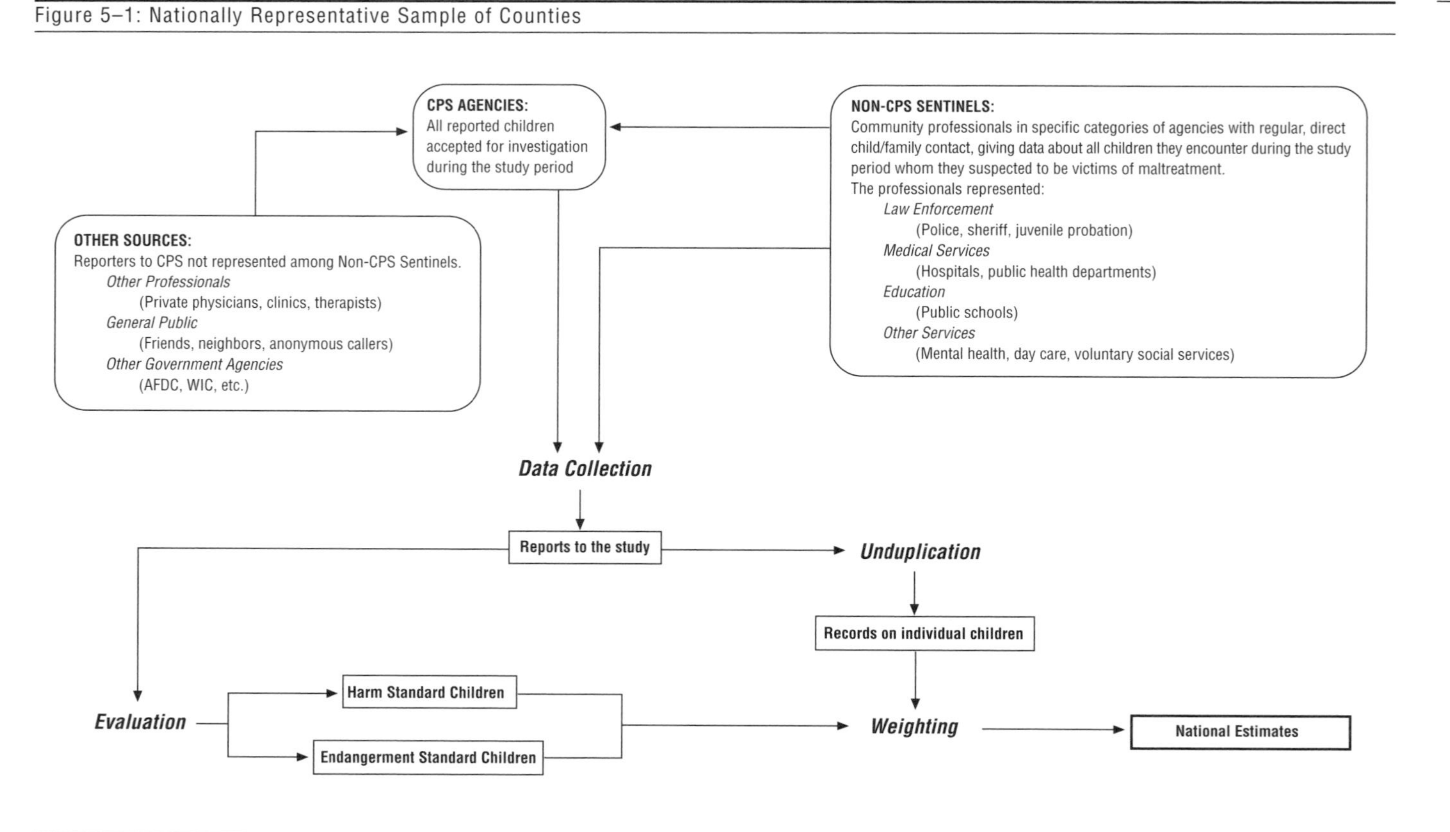

Note: CPS = child protective services; AFDC = Aid to Families with Dependent children; WIC = Women, Infants, and Children.

demographic risk factors, African American children actually have a significantly lower risk of being abused and neglected than white children do in a number of circumstances (Sedlak & Schultz, Chapter 3, this volume). Specifically, African American children have a significantly lower risk of being sexually abused and physically neglected and a marginally lower risk of being physically abused. The racial difference in the risk of physical abuse is especially pronounced among children whose parents are not in the labor force (disabled, retired, or on welfare). Also, among children whose families have annual incomes of less than $15,000 a year, African American children have a significantly lower risk of suffering physical neglect and marginally lower risks of emotional maltreatment and of any maltreatment overall. Racial differences in risk of any maltreatment emerged from the study, and risk of physical neglect was exacerbated among children who came from larger families (with four or more children in the household), with white children at higher risk (Sedlak & Schultz, Chapter 3, this volume).

At the same time, children of color are overrepresented in the child welfare system, well above their representation in the general child population (Morton, 1999). If, as the NIS findings on maltreatment risk indicate, this situation does not stem from higher rates of abuse and neglect of children of color, then it suggests that they may enter the CPS system at higher rates than white children. CPS is the primary portal for bringing children into the child welfare system. This chapter reports on analyses that examined the factors that predicted CPS investigation among the nationally representative sample of abused and neglected children in NIS-3, with specific focus on uncovering any latent racial differences.

As mentioned previously, NIS obtained information about a representative sample of maltreated children from two sources: CPS agencies and sentinels. The authors identified and removed duplicate data forms and unified the two data sources, thereby permitting NIS to provide unduplicated estimates of the number of maltreated children in the United States. Note that this process also revealed children who had not received CPS investigation but whom sentinels recognized as maltreated. The analyses reported here capitalized on this information to explore the issue at hand: patterns of differential entry into the CPS system by African American and white maltreated children. At the same time, it must be recognized at the start that the policy implications of CPS investigation patterns in NIS are not straightforward. This is because children CPS did not investigate represent an enigma—one cannot tell whether no one reported them to CPS or CPS screened out their cases without an investigation.[1]

[1] For this reason, this chapter does not use the term *reporting rate* but instead refers only to "child protective services (CPS) investigation" of the children. Earlier reports have sometimes referred to "CPS awareness" of the children or to children who were "officially known to CPS."

Method

To identify factors related to the likelihood of a maltreated child receiving CPS investigation, it was first necessary to limit the analyses to the most appropriate sectors of the NIS database. The study used three constraints to delimit the subset of NIS cases extracted for analysis here: (1) the maltreatment definitions and classifications, (2) the source recognizing the maltreatment, and (3) children's race or ethnicity.

Maltreatment Definitions and Classifications

The authors evaluated all children submitted to NIS as maltreated according to standard study definitions of abuse and neglect. They only considered as maltreated those children who fit the standards and used them to generate the national estimates. Although the analyses initially focused on children classified as maltreated under the NIS-3 definition of the Harm Standard abuse and neglect, the authors performed further analyses to examine the patterns for children who were counted as maltreated under the Endangerment Standard. Harm Standard maltreatment has been preferred in most analyses because it relies on more objective criteria, generally requiring evidence of demonstrable harm from abuse or neglect before classifying a child as maltreated.[2] For the Harm Standard analyses, the authors reduced the NIS-3 database to the 3,109 children whose maltreatment met the Harm Standard, which represented 1,553,800 children nationwide. For the Endangerment Standard analyses, the authors used the full database of 5,427 children, representing an estimated 2,815,600 children nationwide.

In preparation for the analyses reported here, the authors categorized maltreatment into six mutually exclusive classes. This was necessary to systematically compare the likelihood of CPS investigation as a function of the type of maltreatment involved. Note that the nonoverlapping character of the categories used here distinguishes them from the maltreatment categories that have been used in other reports.

Table 5-1 presents the number of unweighted sample cases in these six nonoverlapping maltreatment categories, together with their weighted totals for both the Harm and Endangerment Standards. As the table indicates, the first four mutually exclusive categories listed (physical abuse, sexual abuse, emotional maltreatment, and physical neglect) included children who experienced these forms of maltreatment either alone or only in conjunction with educational neglect. This strategy reflected the assumption that educational neglect is irrelevant to CPS investigation.[3]

[2] In contrast, the alternative *Endangerment Standard* includes children as maltreated on the basis of subjective judgments about whether they were endangered by the acts or omissions of their caregivers. Judgments about endangerment can vary in indeterminate ways from respondent to respondent, confounding findings regarding the predictors of child protective services investigation.

[3] The majority of states define educational neglect as partially or entirely outside of child protective services jurisdiction.

Table 5–1: Cases in the Third National Incidence Study over Six Nonoverlapping Maltreatment Categories

		Harm Standard		Endangerment Standard	
Category	**Maltreatment Included**	**Unweighted *n***	**Weighted *N***	**Unweighted *n***	**Weighted *N***
Physical abuse	Alone or with educational neglect	951	312,781	1,020	315,659
Sexual abuse	Alone or with educational neglect	600	189,665	713	204,654
Emotional maltreatment	Emotional abuse, emotional neglect, or both, with or without educational neglect	402	309,346	691	467,909
Physical neglect	Alone or with educational neglect	570	289,461	1,665	924,246
Multiple maltreatment	Combinations of physical abuse, sexual abuse, emotional maltreatment, and physical neglect (ignoring educational neglect)	356	110,660	269	260,316
Educational neglect	Alone with no other type of maltreatment	230	341,873	1,069	642,820
Total		**3,109**	**1,553,786**	**5,427**	**2,815,603**

Recognition Source

By design, NIS includes only children whose maltreatment is investigated by CPS agencies and, beyond those, children whose maltreatment is recognized by sentinels in specified categories of community agencies. A broad spectrum of potential reporters of maltreatment are not represented among the NIS sentinels, including physicians, therapists, social workers in private practice, and the family, friends, and neighbors of maltreated children. Children whose maltreatment is recognized by these sources can enter NIS only through CPS data. This means that 100% of children whose maltreatment is recognized by these sources are investigated by CPS, by definition.[4]

Table 5-2 schematically illustrates the NIS design in relation to a four-quadrant categorization of the full population of children who are recognized as maltreated.

[4] Note that a further implication of this is that the National Incidence Study (NIS) estimates of the total number of abused and neglected children in the United States and of the subtotal of countable children not investigated by child protective services (CPS) are underestimates. There is yet another part of the "iceberg" of children not investigated by CPS who are not addressed in NIS, and who are therefore not represented in any of the figures here (i.e., children countable under the Harm Standard recognized by professionals in private practice and by the general public but not investigated by CPS).

Table 5-2: Conceptual Framework Showing
National Incidence Study (NIS) Coverage of Recognized Maltreated Children

	CPS Investigation Status	
Recognition Source	**Investigated by CPS**	**Not Investigated by CPS**
Recognized by NIS sentinels (in hospitals, schools, law enforcement agencies, day care centers, etc.)	*Quadrant 1* Included in NIS	*Quadrant 2* Included in NIS
Recognized by others (family, friends, neighbors, private physicians, etc.)	*Quadrant 3* Included in NIS	*Quadrant 4* Not included in NIS

Note: CPS = child protective services.

It seems reasonable to expect that children who only come to the attention of nonsentinel sources would have different characteristics from those who come to the attention of the NIS sentinel sources. Because children recognized by nonsentinel sources are not fully represented in the NIS children (that is, there are none from Quadrant 4), conclusions about the features associated with CPS investigation can be seriously distorted if one uses the NIS data uncritically. To avoid such distortions, analyses that purport to examine factors that affect CPS investigation in the NIS should *exclude* Quadrant 3 children and focus solely on the union of Quadrants 1 and 2 (Sedlak, 1995).

Thus, the authors reduced the NIS-3 Harm Standard cases by eliminating the 407 cases from Quadrant 3 (338 of which had been recognized by the general public, including self, family member, and anonymous). This left 2,702 Quadrant 1 and 2 children, representing a weighted total of 1,415,415. For the Endangerment Standard analyses, the authors eliminated 906 cases (771 of which had been recognized by the general public), leaving 4,521 Quadrant 1 and 2 children, representing a weighted total of 2,474,834.

Data Extract of White and African American Children

Preliminary analyses revealed that race effects were diverse and difficult to interpret when all children, including those of Hispanic and "other" racial origins, were included. To simplify and focus the analyses reported here, the researchers focused solely on uncovering the dynamics of CPS investigation among white and African American children.

Analyses used a reduced Harm Standard database, one restricted to this subset of children. To minimize the reduction of cases at this final stage, the authors retained 43 children whose race had been imputed as African American or white in a companion analysis (Sedlak & Schultz, Chapter 3, this volume). This extract database comprised 2,001 child-level records (including 1,326 white children and 675 African American children), which represented a weighted total of 1,143,783 children nationwide (853,491 white children and 290,292 African American children). For the Endangerment Standard analyses, the database contained 3,344 child-level records (including 2,172 white children and 1,172 African American children), which represented a weighted total of 1,987,370 children nationwide (1,478,396 white children and 508,976 African American children).

Logistic Models

The researchers examined a number of logistic regression models to determine whether racial differences in the likelihood of CPS investigation would emerge when other potential predictors of CPS investigation were taken into account. They examined models for both Harm Standard and Endangerment Standard children, in both cases assessing a series of two-factor logistic models, each of which attempted to predict CPS investigation as a function of race and one other factor. The two-factor models included both simple main effect models and models with interaction terms. Following this approach, the analyses explored racial differences in CPS investigation in the context of the factors listed in Table 5-3. Note that NIS obtains only basic demographic information about children and their families and only enough information about the maltreatment situation to permit the case to be evaluatively coded for its fit or nonfit with the study definitions. Thus, the list in Table 5-3 was partly limited by the available data items gathered in NIS.

The following section provides findings for children maltreated under the Harm Standard. When the results differed for Endangerment Standard children, the text notes the differences. When a given model revealed that particular levels of a factor affected CPS investigation in similar ways, the authors combined the levels and assessed the simpler form of the model. This improved the efficiency of the model and reassessed the role of racial differences in a more streamlined context.

As indicated in Figure 5-1, NIS-3 used a multistage sample design that involved the clustering of sentinels in agencies and agencies in counties. Special measures are required in this context to compute unbiased variance estimates (Brogan, 1998; Lee, Forthofer, & Lorimor, 1989). Otherwise, findings will be distorted by the misspecification effect. Because this effect varies with the specific analysis in the NIS data, no simple "fix" for it exists in the context of standard statistical packages. Standard packages almost always assume that data derive from simple random samples. NIS provides for computing variances and significance tests using a replication approach, the jackknife (Sedlak et al., 1997; Sedlak, Hantman, & Schultz, 1997).[5] The models reported here were developed using WesVar, a program that computes estimates, variances, and measures of fit for linear and logistical regression models using replication methods (Westat, 2000).

[5] Replication methods of analyzing data from complex surveys have been shown to have several advantages even when other methods can be applied (Brick & Morganstein, 1996, 1997).

Table 5–3: Factors Tested with Race in Logistic Models Predicting Child Protective Services Investigation

Factors	Categories
Child Characteristics	
Child's age	Age at last birthday in years: Birth–2; 3–5; 6–8; 9–11; 12–14; 15–17
Child's gender	Male; Female
Family Characteristics	
Number of children in the household	1 child; 2–3 children; 4 children
Family structure	Two parents or parent substitutes; Single parent or parent substitute
Parental employment	Employed (full- or part time)[a]; Unemployed (looking for work and no parent employed; Not in the labor force (retired, disabled, or on Aid toFamilies with Dependent Children)
Annual household income	<$15,000; $15,000–$29,999; $30,000
Maltreatment Characteristics	
Category of maltreatment[b]	Physical abuse; sexual abuse; emotional maltreatment; physical neglect; multiple maltreatment; educational neglect
Severity of most serious harm	Fatal or serious; Moderate injury/harm; Inferred injury/harm[c]
Recognition source	Law—police, sheriff, juvenile probation; Medical—hospital, public health department; School—school, day care center; Mental/social—mental health clinic or other social services
Perpetrator Characteristics	
Perpetrator's relationship to child[d]	Birthparent; other parent/substitute; other, nonparental perpetrator
Perpetrator's alcohol or drug involvement[e]	Involved; not involved

[a] The employed category was more finely differentiated and consisted of two distinct levels during imputation and synthetic database construction. These were combined in all subsequent analyses.

[b] Defined as mutually exclusive categories, as described earlier.

[c] Harm Standard guidelines permit inferring injury or harm in cases of blatant abandonment, for the more extreme types of sexual abuse, and when close confinement included tying or binding.

[d] The most closely related perpetrator of harm standard maltreatment.

[e] See text footnote 8.

Findings

Child Characteristics

The analyses revealed that child's race had no overall influence on CPS investigation. Nearly equal percentages of white (23%) and African American (20%) children had their Harm Standard maltreatment investigated by CPS. This pattern was also true for children maltreated under the Endangerment Standard.

The authors examined two additional child characteristics (age and gender) in combination with race to determine whether race affected the likelihood of CPS investigation when these were taken into account. The models revealed that, although the child's gender predicted CPS investigation, the child's race continued to have no bearing on investigation when taking gender into account, and race did not emerge selectively in connection with either males or females (that is, the Race X Gender interaction was nonsignificant). Similarly, although child's age predicted CPS investigation, race did not play a role in the context of these age effects, and no age interactions emerged with race. The same findings emerged for both the Harm Standard and Endangerment Standard models.

Family Characteristics

A series of logistic models examined several family characteristics in conjunction with race to determine whether their influences might be masking racial differences in the likelihood of CPS investigation. For both Harm Standard and Endangerment Standard maltreatment, the models showed no racial differences in the likelihood of investigation in the context of family income, family structure, or number of children in the household.

Parental employment, however, modified the effect of race on the likelihood of CPS investigation for children maltreated under the Harm Standard, as Table 5-4 shows. The overall model is significant at the .01 level with an *F* value of 5.354. Parental employment did not modify the effect of race in predicting CPS investigation for children maltreated under the Endangerment Standard.

The relationship between child's race and parental employment in predicting CPS investigation is graphed in Figure 5-2. Among children with an employed parent, white and African American children were investigated at similar rates. Among those with an unemployed parent, the figure reveals a nonsignificant trend toward more investigations of white children. Much larger differences appear among children whose parents are not in the labor force. Among this group, significantly higher proportions of white children were investigated than African American children (37% versus 28%).

Maltreatment Characteristics

As outlined in Table 5-3, the study incorporated three characteristics of the maltreatment in logistic models with race: the category of maltreatment, the severity of injury or harm from maltreatment, and the source that recognized the child's maltreatment.

Maltreatment Category

As explained previously, the authors classified children into mutually exclusive categories on the basis of the types of maltreatment they had experienced. The physical abuse

Table 5-4: Logistic Regression Model Predicting Child Protective Services Investigation of Children Maltreated Under the Harm Standard as a Function of Child's Race and Parental Employment

Parameter	Parameter Estimate	Standard Error	*t* Value	*t* Value Probability
Intercept	-1.57	0.277	-5.671	<.001
African American (AA)	0.31	0.331	0.927	.364
Unemployed	0.29	0.433	0.662	.515
Not in the labor force	1.05	0.221	4.755	<.001
AA X Unemployed	-0.69	0.426	-1.625	.119
AA X Not in labor force	-0.72	0.273	-2.625	.016

Overall Model Fit	
F value	5.354
Probability of *F*	0.004
Estrella likelihood ratio	0.023

category included children whose only countable maltreatment was physical abuse, or physical abuse and educational neglect. The sexual abuse, physical neglect, and emotional maltreatment categories were similarly defined to include children with only the maltreatment of focus, ignoring educational neglect. The educational neglect category represented those children whose only countable maltreatment was educational neglect. The multiple maltreatment category included children with more than one form of maltreatment (excluding educational neglect; see Table 5-1). The authors made this classification separately for Harm Standard and Endangerment Standard children.

Table 5-5 shows the logistic regression model with child's race, the full set of maltreatment categories, and their interactions. Overall, the model significantly predicted CPS investigation among children who were maltreated under the Harm Standard at the .01 level with an *F* value of 7.99. Attempts to simplify this model did not affect the significance of the race parameters, so the model is presented in its detailed form here, despite the fact that some of the parameters are not significant.

As Table 5-5 indicates, the likelihood of CPS investigation was significantly affected by the interaction between race and two categories of maltreatment, physical neglect and emotional maltreatment. Figure 5-3 shows the percentages of white and African American children in each of these maltreatment categories who received CPS investigation. The figure illustrates that among emotionally maltreated children, African American children were

Figure 5–2: Race and Parental Employment as Predictors of Child Protective Services Investigation

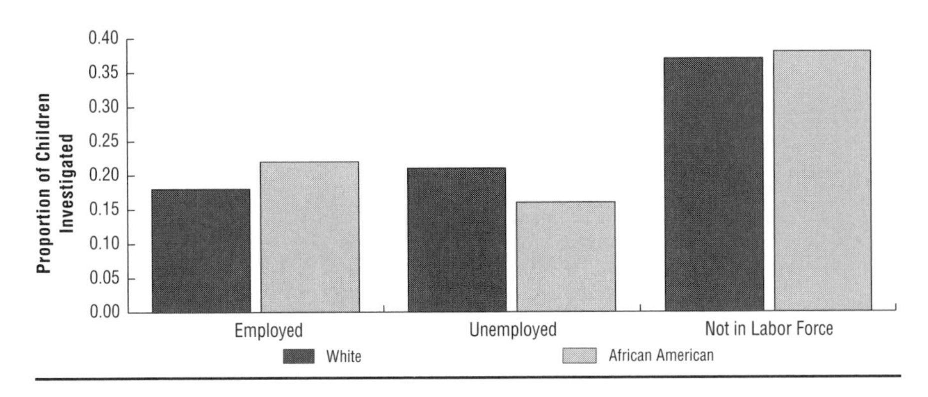

Figure 5–3: Race and Form of Maltreatment as Predictors of Child Protective Services investigation

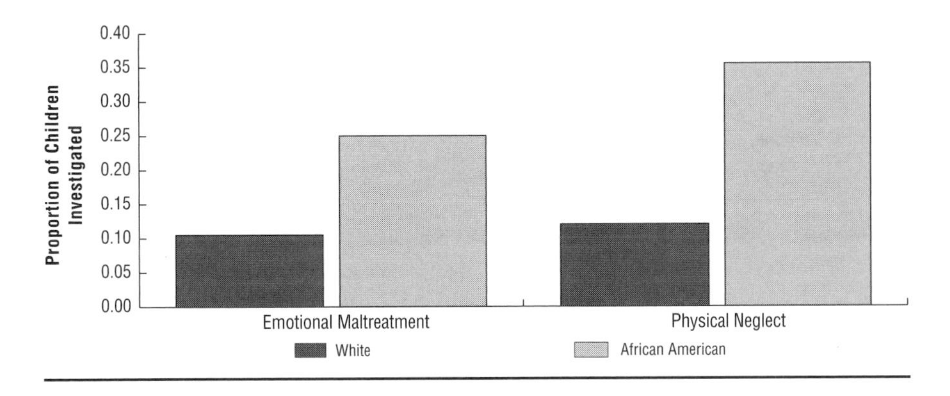

much more likely than white children to be investigated by CPS. Of African American children who were emotionally maltreated, 25% were investigated by CPS, compared with 11% of white children. The figure shows a similar pattern among the physically neglected children. African American children who were physically neglected were more likely to be investigated than physically neglected white children (35% versus 11%).

The type of maltreatment also modified the effect of race on the likelihood of CPS investigation for children maltreated under the Endangerment Standard, but in different ways, as shown in Table 5-6. The overall model is significant at the .01 level with an *F* value of 7.536.

Table 5-5: Logistic Regression Model Predicting Child Protective Services Investigation of Children Maltreated Under the Harm Standard as a Function of Child's Race and Maltreatment Category

Parameter	Parameter Estimate	Standard Error	*t* Value	*t* Value Probability
Intercept	-0.69	0.382	-1.816	0.084
African American (AA)	-0.87	0.662	-1.314	0.203
Physical abuse	0.34	0.446	0.763	0.454
Sexual abuse	0.08	0.245	0.333	0.743
Emotional maltreatment	-1.43	0.229	-6.261	<0.001
Physical neglect	-1.38	0.533	-2.590	0.017
Educational neglect	-2.22	1.304	-1.703	0.103
AA X Physical abuse	0.86	0.858	1.006	0.326
AA X Sexual abuse	0.29	1.192	0.240	0.813
AA X Emotional maltreatment	1.91	0.830	2.297	0.032
AA X Physical neglect	2.34	0.692	3.376	0.003
AA X Educational neglect	0.64	1.482	0.431	0.671
Overall model fit				
F value			7.993	
Probability of *F*			0.001	
Estrella likelihood ratio			0.130	

Table 5-6: Logistic Regression Model Predicting Child Protective Services Investigation as a Function of Child's Race and Maltreatment Category Among Children Maltreated Under the Endangerment Standard

Parameter	Parameter Estimate	Standard Error	*t* Value	*t* Value Probability
Intercept	-1.45	0.232	-6.234	<0.001
African American (AA)	0.82	0.421	1.935	0.067
Physical abuse	1.24	0.244	5.094	<0.001
Sexual abuse	1.18	0.353	3.344	0.003
Emotional maltreatment	-0.54	0.330	-1.643	0.115
Physical neglect	-0.04	0.151	-0.233	0.818
Educational neglect	-0.76	0.506	-1.505	0.147
AA X Physical abuse	-0.91	0.391	-2.336	0.029
AA X Sexual abuse	-1.76	1.074	-1.642	0.116
AA X Emotional maltreatment	-0.64	0.535	-1.192	0.246
AA X Physical neglect	-0.40	0.281	-1.440	0.165
AA X Educational neglect	-0.46	1.113	-0.417	0.681
Overall model fit				
F value			7.536	
Probability of *F*			0.001	
Estrella likelihood ratio			0.065	

Table 5-6 shows a marginal main effect for the race variable, with African American children somewhat more likely to be investigated than white children when type of maltreatment is taken into account. Across all of these analyses, this model proved to be the only one that showed a main effect for race. This Endangerment Standard model also revealed different patterns of noteworthy interaction terms. Race and only one type of maltreatment, physical abuse, affected the likelihood of CPS investigation for children maltreated under the Endangerment Standard. Workers investigated white children who were physically abused much more often than African American children (56% versus 40%).

Severity of Injury or Harm

The authors assessed the severity of the injury or harm resulting from Harm Standard maltreatment in combination with race to examine their joint and interactive effects on the likelihood of CPS investigation. As indicated in Table 5-3, codes for the severity of injury or harm reflected three levels: fatal or serious, moderate, and inferred.[6] For children who had multiple types of injury or harm, or who suffered injury or harm from multiple types of Harm Standard maltreatment, the authors used the severity of their most serious outcome.

Table 5-7 shows that the overall Harm Standard model approaches significance at the .05 level and that a marginal main effect for fatal or serious injury and a marginal interaction effect for race and fatal or serious injury exist. The same pattern emerged when the model was run for children maltreated under the Endangerment Standard.

Figure 5-4 shows how the probability of CPS investigation depends on both child's race and the severity of the injury or harm from maltreatment. Race was not related to the likelihood of CPS investigation among children with moderate or inferred (or probable) injuries. African American children who suffered fatal or serious injury, however, were much more likely to receive CPS investigation than white children with comparably severe injuries. Of African American children with fatal or serious injuries, 30% were investigated, compared with just 17% of fatally or seriously injured white children.

Source Recognizing the Maltreatment

The authors also examined race effects in the context of the source that recognized the child's maltreatment to unravel the joint influences of these factors and determine whether race interacts with recognition source in affecting the probability of CPS investigation. Table 5-8 reveals that the overall Harm Standard model with these two factors and their interaction terms was statistically significant. No relationship existed between race and recognition source in predicting CPS investigation for children maltreated under the Endangerment Standard.

[6] This classification combined the National Incidence Study codes for inferred injury and for injury judged as "probable" on the basis of the maltreatment itself.

Table 5-7: Logistic Regression Model Predicting Child Protective Services Investigation of Children Maltreated Under the Harm Standard as a Function of Child's Race and Severity of Injury or Harm

Parameter	Parameter Estimate	Standard Error	*t* Value	*t* Value Probability
Intercept	-1.34	0.282	-4.754	<0.001
African American (AA)	-0.17	0.376	-0.447	0.659
Fatal/serious injury	-0.25	0.257	-0.973	0.342
Inferred/probable injury	0.77	0.459	1.680	0.108
AA X Fatal/serious injury	0.93	0.457	2.032	0.055
AA X Inferred/probable injury	-0.15	1.076	-0.143	0.888

Overall model fit	
F value	2.798
Probability of *F*	0.051
Estrella likelihood ratio	0.015

Figure 5–4: Race and Severity of Injury as Predictors of Child Protective Services investigation

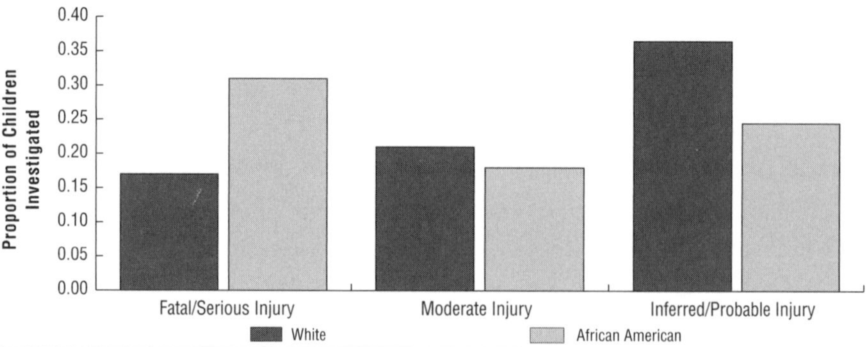

Figure 5-5 graphs the interaction between child's race and recognition source as predictors of CPS investigation of the Harm Standard children. Among children whose maltreatment was recognized by mental health or social-service professionals, African American children were more likely to receive CPS investigation than white children. Among children whose maltreatment was recognized by all other sources, no statistically reliable differences existed in the proportions of white and African American children who received CPS investigation.

Perpetrator Characteristics

In this study, analyses also examined the effects of race on CPS investigation in the context of two perpetrator characteristics: the perpetrator's relationship to the child and the perpetrator's involvement with alcohol or drugs.

Table 5-8: Logistic Regression Model Predicting Child Protective Services Investigation of Children Maltreated Under the Harm Standard as a Function of Child's Race and Source Recognizing Abuse or Neglect

Parameter	Parameter Estimate	Standard Error	*t* Value	*t* Value Probability
Intercept	-1.670	0.277	-6.034	<0.001
African American (AA)	-0.130	0.392	-0.338	0.739
LE/JP	1.180	0.485	2.437	0.024
Mental health/social services	0.430	0.911	0.470	0.643
Medical	1.030	0.353	2.928	0.008
AA X LE/JP	0.650	0.626	1.046	0.308
AA X Mental health/social services	1.530	0.823	1.858	0.077
AA X Medical	0.140	0.643	0.217	0.830
Overall model fit				
F value	5.198			
Probability of *F*	0.004			
Estrella likelihood ratio	0.054			

Note: LE = law enforcement; JP = juvenile probation.

Figure 5–5: Race and Reporting Source as Predictors of Child Protective Services investigation

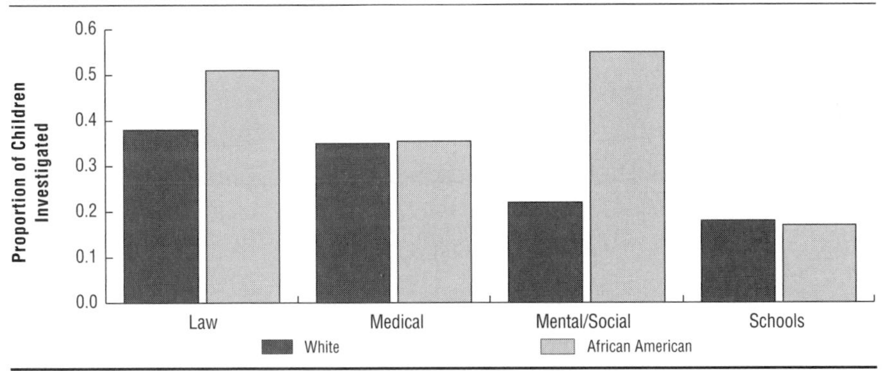

Perpetrator's Relationship to Child

The study classified children into three categories on the basis of their relationship to the perpetrator of their Harm Standard abuse or neglect: their birthparent, including in-home and out-of-home birthparents; other parents or parent substitutes, including in-home stepparents, other in-home parents such as foster and adoptive parents, and parent substitutes, such as parents' boyfriends or girlfriends[7]; and other people, includ-

[7] It should be noted that parents' boyfriends and girlfriends do not constitute parent substitutes for purposes of deciding on allowable perpetrators of Harm Standard maltreatment (Sedlak, 2001). They are classified with parent substitutes here to parallel the perpetrator categorization that was used in the report on the third National Incidence Study findings (Sedlak & Broadhurst, 1996).

ing other family members and other unrelated adults. Because the NIS-3 codes allowed for up to four perpetrators of each of three forms of maltreatment, the classification used here is a summary variable. The relationship used was that of the perpetrator of the most harmful or injurious abuse or neglect, and if multiple perpetrators were involved in this maltreatment, the relationship between the child and the most closely related perpetrator is indicated.

Table 5-9 provides the logistic regression model that combined the child's race and the perpetrator's relationship to child as predictors of CPS investigation for Harm Standard maltreatment. Overall, the model is significant at the .01 level with an F value of 4.74. The authors found the same pattern when the model was run for children maltreated under the Endangerment Standard.

Figure 5-6 graphs the proportions of children who received CPS investigation as a function of their race and their relationship to the perpetrator of their Harm Standard maltreatment. Among children who were abused or neglected by their birthparents, white and African American children evidence no differences in their probability of receiving CPS investigation. Among children maltreated by other parents or parent substitutes, there appears to be a tendency for African American children to be investigated more often. This pattern dramatically reverses when the perpetrator is some other person, such as a family member or an unrelated adult. Among children in this group, white children were investigated significantly more often than African American children (51% versus 20%).

Perpetrator's Alcohol or Substance Abuse Involvement

Race effects on the likelihood of CPS investigation were also examined in the context of whether there was any mention of alcohol or drug involvement on the part of a perpetrator.[8] Table 5-10 provides the resulting logistic regression model for the Harm Standard. Race and the perpetrator's alcohol or substance abuse involvement were not related to CPS investigation for children maltreated under the Endangerment Standard.

Figure 5-7 depicts the overall effect of the perpetrator's alcohol or drug involvement as well as the interaction between this factor and child's race in predicting the likelihood that a maltreated child will receive CPS investigation. Among children whose data forms mentioned a perpetrator's alcohol or drug involvement, African American children were much more likely to receive CPS investigation than white children. Workers investigated more than three-quarters (78%) of African American children with mention of a perpetrator's alcohol or drug involvement, compared with just 41% of white

[8] At the time of these analyses, supplementary codes for the perpetrator's alcohol or substance abuse involvement were not available in the same database as the imputed values for child's race. As a result, the models involving this factor were tested on an extract database that excluded 5 of the 2,001 children who were used in the other analyses.

Table 5-9: Logistic Regression Model Predicting
Child Protective Services Investigation of Children Maltreated
Under the Harm Standard as a Function of Child's Race and Perpetrator's Relationship

Parameter	Parameter Estimate	Standard Error	*t* Value	*t* Value Probability
Intercept	0.030	0.318	0.085	0.933
African American (AA)	-1.400	0.843	-1.656	0.113
Birthparent	-1.620	0.325	-4.986	<0.001
Other Parent	-0.960	0.326	-2.939	0.008
AA X Birthparent	1.650	0.807	2.049	0.053
AA X Other Parent	1.880	1.071	1.753	0.094

Overall model fit	
F value	4.742
Probability of *F*	0.007
Estrella likelihood ratio	0.034

Figure 5–6: Race and Perpetrator's Relationship to Child as Predictors of Child Protective Services Investigation

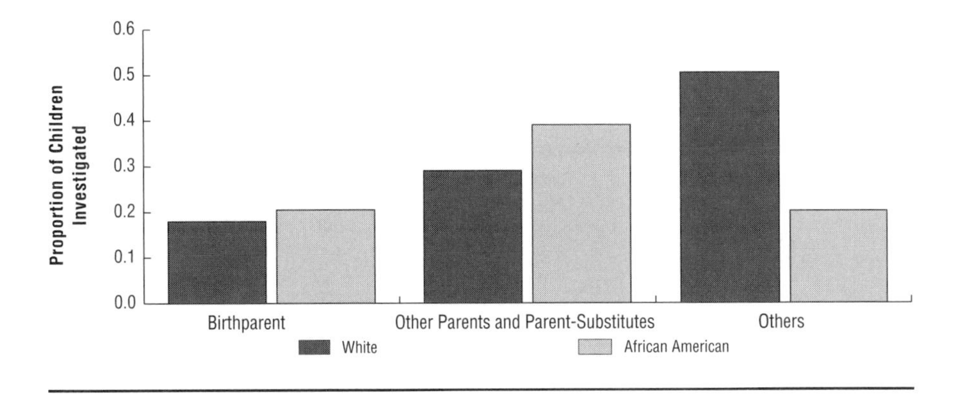

children with similar mentions. CPS investigation rates did not differ by race for children with no mention of a perpetrator's alcohol or drug involvement in narrative descriptions of their circumstances.

Conclusion and Next Steps

The NIS-3 data revealed that, among children who experienced Harm Standard maltreatment, similar percentages of African American and white children had their mal-

Table 5-10: Logistic Regression Model Predicting Child Protective Services Investigation of Children Maltreated Under the Harm Standard as a Function of Child's Race and Perpetrator's Alcohol/Drug Involvement

Parameter	Parameter Estimate	Standard Error	*t* Value	*t* Value Probability
Intercept	-1.450	0.255	-5.683	<0.001
African American (AA)	0.020	0.306	0.059	0.954
Alcohol/Drug Involvement	0.650	0.369	1.772	0.091
AA X Alcohol/Drug Involvement	1.540	0.662	2.321	0.030
Overall model fit				
F value	5.095			
Probability of *F*	0.009			
Estrella likelihood ratio	0.025			

Figure 5–7: Race and Perpetrator Alcohol/Drug Involvement as Predictors of Child Protective Services investigation

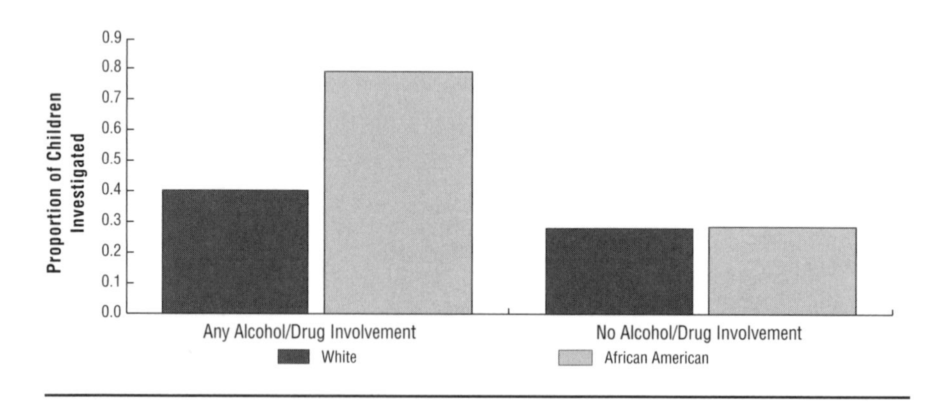

treatment investigated by CPS. The analyses presented here reveal racial differences in patterns of CPS investigation in relation to other factors. Several racial differences did emerge when other potential predictors of CPS investigation were taken into account. The key findings include:

- African American children who were emotionally maltreated or physically neglected were much more likely to be investigated than white children similarly maltreated.

- African American children who suffered fatal or serious injury were much more likely to receive CPS investigation than white children with comparably severe injuries.
- African American children whose maltreatment was recognized by mental health or social service professionals were more likely to be investigated than comparable white children.
- African American children whose perpetrator was involved with alcohol or drugs were much more likely to receive CPS investigation.

Prior analyses of the risk of maltreatment in the general population showed no overall differences in the rate of maltreatment for African American and white children. Table 5-11 shows the rate of maltreatment for white and African American children under both the Harm Standard and the Endangerment Standard. Although it appears that African American children are maltreated more often than white children, these differences are not statistically significant. Moreover, the pattern reflects the influences of a variety of disadvantaging characteristics (that is, low income, large family size, etc.), because African American children are actually maltreated at lower rates when these factors are taken into account (Sedlak & Schultz, Chapter 3, this volume).

Table 5-11 also shows the rate of CPS investigation for white and African American children. The table shows CPS investigation rates in terms of the numbers of children in the general population, thereby using the same unit of measurement as was used for calculating the overall risk of maltreatment. Here, the differences between white and African American children are statistically significant. African American children are significantly more likely than white children to be investigated by CPS for Harm Standard maltreatment. The Harm Standard CPS investigation rate was 9.3 per 1,000 for African American children and 5.6 per 1,000 for white children. The same pattern emerges in connection with CPS investigation of Endangerment Standard maltreatment, in which 18.6 African American children per 1,000 were investigated compared with 11.7 white children per 1,000.

Further work is needed to clarify the implications of these findings. The authors are planning analyses on two fronts to do this. First, they will investigate the effect that the various patterns of selection into CPS investigation have on the overall race distribution of children coming into the system. In this regard, their effect can only be understood against the backdrop of the race distribution of all Harm Standard–maltreated children on the characteristics listed at the outset of this conclusion. That is, what do these racial differences in selection into CPS investigation mean in terms of the resulting differen-

Table 5-11: Risk of Maltreatment and
Child Protective Services (CPS) Investigation by Child's Race

Parameter	Rate of Maltreatment	Rate of CPS Investigation
Harm Standard		
White children	20.35	5.61
African American children	29.98	9.32
Endangerment Standard		
White children	36.86	11.71
African American children	53.57	18.58

Note: All rates are per 1,000 children.

tial distributions of African American and white children in the investigated population? If these selection differences lead to concentrations of African American children in certain sectors of the investigated population (e.g., children whose perpetrators were involved with alcohol or drugs), then they could be contributing to the disproportionate representation of African American children in the child welfare population. To inform this issue, the authors will examine the differences in distribution between African American and white children in the population of those who receive CPS investigation.

Second, NIS-3 produced a CPS-only database, which provides information about the disposition of a nationally representative sample of children who had their maltreatment investigated by CPS. This affords further opportunity to follow the implications of the present findings, and of any distributional differences we observe, to the next stage. That is, if racial distribution differences exist in factors that play a role in substantiation decisions, or if racial differences exist in the degree to which different factors affect substantiation, then those differences might also explain why African American children are disproportionately represented in the child welfare population.

References

Brick, J. M., & Morganstein, D. (1996). WesVarPC: Software for computing variance estimates from complex designs. *Proceedings of the 1996 Annual Research Conference* (pp. 861–866). Washington, DC: U.S. Bureau of the Census.

Brick, J. M., & Morganstein, D. (1997). Computing sampling errors from clustered unequally weighted data using replication: WesVarPC. In *Bulletin of the International Statistical Institute, Proceedings* (Book 1, pp. 479–482). The Netherlands: International Statistical Institute.

Brogan, D. J. (1998). Software for sample survey data: Misuse of standard packages. In P. Armitage & T. Colton (Eds.), *Encyclopedia of biostatistics* (Vol. 5, pp. 4167–4174). New York: John Wiley & Sons.

Lee, E. S., Forthofer, R. N., & Lorimor, R. J. (1989). *Analyzing complex survey data*. Newbury Park, CA: Sage.

Morton, T. D. (1999). The increasing colorization of America's child welfare system: The overrepresentation of African American children. *Policy & Practice*, 23–30.

National Center on Child Abuse and Neglect, Children's Bureau. (1981). *Study findings: National study of the incidence and severity of child abuse and neglect* (DHHS Publication No. [OHDS] 81-30325). Washington, DC: U.S. Department of Health and Human Services.

Sedlak, A. J. (1991). *National incidence and prevalence of child abuse and neglect: 1988 (Revised report)*. Rockville, MD: Westat.

Sedlak, A. J. (1995). *Study of high risk child abuse and neglect groups: NIS-2 reanalysis report.* Washington, DC: U.S. Department of Health and Human Services.

Sedlak, A. J. (2001). *A history of the National Incidence Study of Child Abuse and Neglect*. Rockville, MD: Westat.

Sedlak, A. J., & Broadhurst, D. D. (1996). *Third National Incidence Study of Child Abuse and Neglect: Final report.* Washington, DC: U.S. Department of Health and Human Services.

Sedlak, A. J., Broadhurst, D., Shapiro, G., Kalton, G., Goksel, H., Burke, J., et al. (1997). *Third National Incidence Study of Child Abuse and Neglect: Analysis report.* Rockville, MD: Westat.

Sedlak, A. J., Hantman, I., & Schultz, D. (1997). *Third National Incidence Study of Child Abuse and Neglect (NIS-3): Public use files manual.* Washington, DC: U.S. Department of Health and Human Services.

Skinner, C. J. (1989). Domain means, regression and multivariate analysis. In C. J. Skinner, D. Holt, & T. M. F. Smith (Eds.), *Analysis of complex surveys* (pp. 59–87). New York: John Wiley & Sons.

Westat. (2000). *WesVar™ 4.0 user's guide*. Rockville, MD: Westat.

CHAPTER 6

Indicated Child Abuse and Neglect Reports

Is the Investigation Process Racially Biased?

Nancy Rolock and Mark F. Testa

The overrepresentation of African American children in the child welfare system is as true for Illinois as for the nation as a whole (Hampton, 1987; Morton, 1999; Saunders, Nelson, & Landsman, 1993). African American children constitute 19% of the child population in Illinois, but they represent 46% of indicated reports of abuse and neglect and 76% of open child cases at the Illinois Department of Children and Family Services (IDCFS).

The reasons for the overrepresentation of African American children reflect a variety of historical conditions that transcend location and a host of specific factors that are unique to Illinois. The chief complaint lodged against the Illinois child welfare system in the past was that private child welfare agencies systematically excluded African Americans ("the left-out child") from their services (Stehno, 1990). As Illinois has taken deliberate steps to facilitate the inclusion of African American children, particularly through its generous kinship care policies, the scales of concern have tipped in the opposite direction.

In an effort to understand the overrepresentation of African American children in the Illinois child welfare system, this chapter examines the critical decision point of child protection investigations. The investigation of allegations of child abuse and neglect to establish credible evidence of child maltreatment is the second stage of involvement for children and families in the child protection system. The first stage is the decision of the system to accept a report for investigation. Evidence exists that a powerful racial disparity arises at the initial reporting stage. African American children are reported to child protective services in Illinois at three times the rate of white children.

Subsequent decisions made in behalf of these children by child protection staff can either amplify or diminish the size of this initial disparity. This chapter looks at the next stage, the child protection investigation, to assess whether any evidence of racial bias on the part of the IDCFS investigators in deciding whether to substantiate an allegation of maltreatment exists.

Data and Method

This analysis focuses on administrative data from the IDCFS for a 10-year period, 1989 through 1999. For inclusion in this analysis, allegations of maltreatment had to meet the following criteria:

- The report of maltreatment associated with the child was the child's first report (sequence A).
- The report included a finding of an allegation of maltreatment as either indicated (substantiated) or unfounded (unsubstantiated). This excludes all pending cases or cases in which the finding was missing or miscoded. (The authors excluded approximately 0.2% of the data from analysis for these reasons.)
- The investigation involved an African American or white family and an African American or white investigator. Excluded cases include incidents in which one of the two parties involved—the investigator or the family—was not African American or white.
- The report included the most serious allegation of multiple allegations. The researchers ranked seriousness of allegations in the following order: death due to abuse, sexual abuse, physical abuse, blatant disregard, substance misuse, emotional abuse, environmental neglect, lack of health care, lack of supervision, risk of harm, and all other allegations.

The authors formulated logit models that predict the log odds of substantiation as a function of the race of the family and the race of the investigator. A general logit model for the three-way contingency table under consideration is:

$$\Phi_{jk} = \beta + \beta^{F}_{j} + \beta^{I}_{k} + \beta^{FI}_{jk} \quad (1)$$

where,

Φ_{jk} = logarithm of the odds that an allegation of maltreatment is substantiated

β = constant: logarithm of the general mean

β^{F}_{j} = main effect of race of family: logarithm of the average change in the odds of substantiation associated with the investigation of an African American versus a white family

β^{I}_{k} = main effect of race of investigator: logarithm of the average change in the odds of substantiation associated with an investigation by a white versus an African American investigator

β^{FI}_{jk} = interaction effect: logarithm of the average of the cross-product odds ratio (i.e., the dependence of the effect of the race of the investigator on the race of the family)

The following restricted logit models are of special interest:

- H_0: *Equal probability*—No main or interaction effects ($\beta^{F}_{j} = \beta^{I}_{k} = \beta^{FI}_{jk} = 0$) is the null hypothesis that the odds of substantiation are equal regardless of the race of the family or investigator (see Figure 6-1a).
- H_1: *Racial bias*—Equal positive main and interaction effects ($\beta^{F}_{j} = \beta^{I}_{k} = \beta^{FI}_{jk} > 0$) is the alternative hypothesis that bias occurs in the finding of an allegation of maltreatment when an African American family is investigated by a white investigator (see Figure 6-1b).

Model H_0 is of obvious relevance because it tests whether a "bias problem" exists. That is, if H_0 is true, the odds of substantiation are constant across all racial combinations of family and investigator and no disproportionality is introduced at the investigation stage. The leading alternative to the null hypothesis is Model H_1, which tests whether white investigators are more likely to substantiate an allegation of maltreatment when an African American family is the subject of the report. If H_1 is true, this would be strongly suggestive of discrimination against African American families by white child protection investigators.

Figure 6–1a: H_0—Equal Probability Model

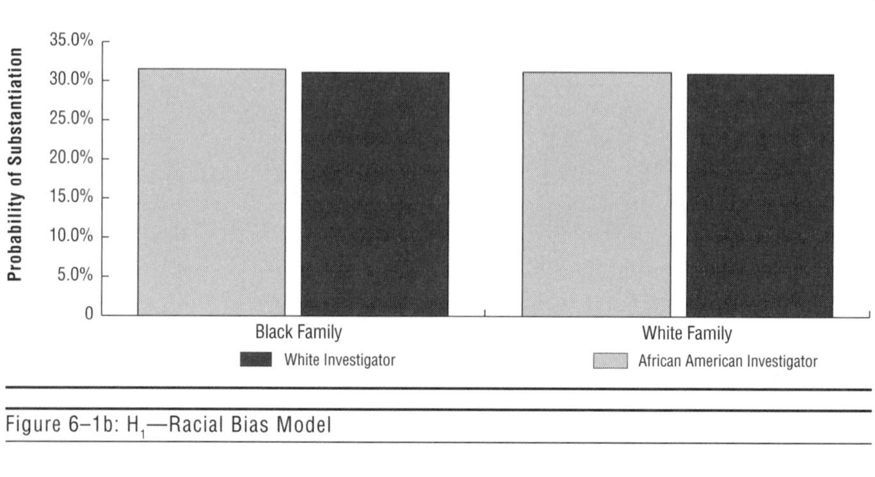

Figure 6–1b: H_1—Racial Bias Model

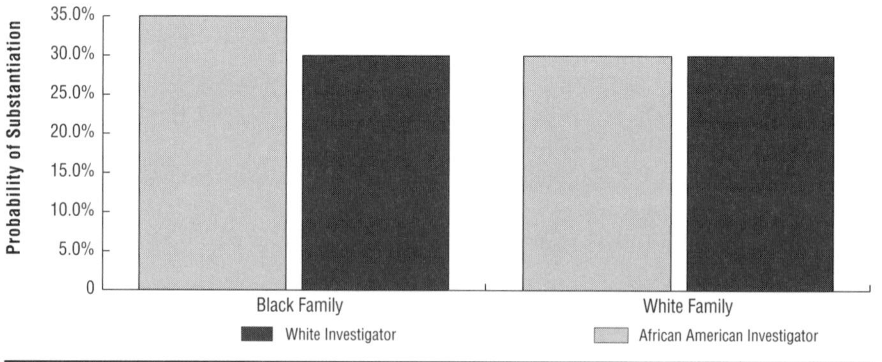

Model H_1 represents the conventional way that racial bias is believed to increase disproportionality, however, other alternatives to the null hypothesis exist, and they are also consistent with racial bias. They include:

- H_2: *Cross-racial bias*—No main effects and positive interaction effect ($\beta^F_j = \beta^I_k = 0$, $\beta^{FI}_{jk} > 0$) is the alternative hypothesis that families are more likely to be indicated if they are investigated by workers of the opposite race (see Figure 6-1c).

- H_3: *Institutional bias*—Main effect of the race of the family but no interaction and main effect of the race of the investigator ($\beta^I_k = \beta^{FI}_{jk} = 0$) is the alternative hypothesis that bias against African American families occurs at the institutional level irrespective of the race of the investigator (see Figure 6-1d).

Figure 6–1c: H_2—Cross-Racial Bias Model

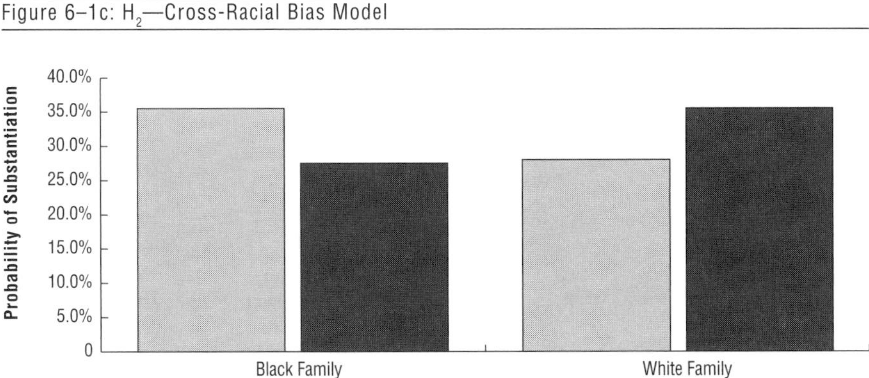

Figure 6–1d: H_3—Institutional Bias Model

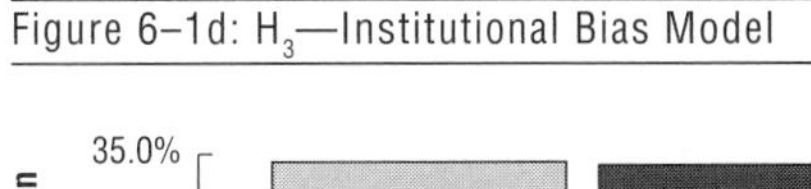

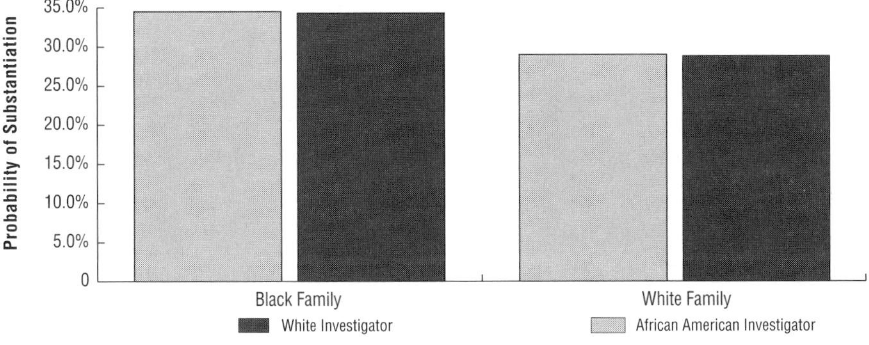

Many other logit models, of course, might fit the data better, and the authors will discuss these alternatives in the course of presenting the findings. This analysis begins with the models H_1 to H_3 because they represent the standard alternatives to the null hypotheses of equal treatment.

Any test of the racial bias hypothesis must assume that the families of different races are statistically equivalent with respect to relevant background characteristics. Although this assumption is clearly unrealistic for all families, it is more tenable for families under investigation because they represent a selective subsample of families reported for child abuse and neglect. They are more homogeneous with respect to income, family structure, social isolation, and discipline practices than are families of different races in the general population. But despite the greater similarities, other nonrandom differences may exist, such as type of allegation and county of investigation, which make the groups noncomparable. Therefore, the analyses attempt to take into consideration these remaining differences by controlling statistically for the following factors: type of allegation, year of the investigation, the age of the child being investigated, the type of initial reporter, the educational status of the investigator, the tenure of the investigator at IDCFS, and the local area networks (LANs, or service area) where the investigation occurred.

Findings

The authors examined Child Abuse and Neglect Tracking System data using log-linear regression to build logit models that explain the factors that predict an investigator's decision to substantiate an allegation. The first model, H_0, is the null hypothesis that the odds of substantiation are constant across all combinations of family race and investigator race. If true, the odds of substantiation for all families would equal the exponentiation of the general mean ($e^{-.786} = .456$), or 31.3% in probability terms. As shown in Table 6-1, the null hypothesis can be rejected because of its poor fit to the observed data, that is, the log-likelihood chi-square (χ^2) is large and statistically significant.

The first alternative tested is the racial bias model H_1. This is the hypothesis that white investigators indicate African American families at a much higher rate than either African American investigators indicate African American and white families or white investigators indicate white families. Although many parameter estimates could satisfy this restriction, the log-likelihood chi-square is smallest when the main and interaction effects are set to .060. The expected probabilities associated with this model are graphed in Figure 6-1b. But as shown in Table 6-1, this model also fits the observed data poorly and can be rejected.

The cross-racial bias model (H_2) displays an even worse fit. The parameters set the indication rates higher if the family's race is different from the investigator's race and lower if the races of the families and investigators match. In fact, the poorer fit reflects the fact that investigators are less likely, rather than more likely, to indicate a family of the opposite race than families of the same race.

Of the alternatives considered so far, the institutional bias model (H_3) yields predictions that are closest to the observed data, and Figure 6-1d graphs it. If true, the system would indicate African American families at a higher rate than white families, regardless of the race of the investigator. Although the predicted odds from H_3 are closer to the observed data, the fit is still poor enough that other alternatives should be considered.

When the model is allowed to take the shape of the actual data, we obtain a saturated model (H_4) that reproduces the observed frequency counts exactly. Thus, the fit is perfect ($G_2 = 0$). The saturated model shows that, like the institutional bias model, African American children are indicated at a significantly higher rate than white children. The need table title

Table 6–1: Logit Models Predicting an Investigator's Decision to Substantiate Allegation

Model	β^{Fam}_{1} = Black	β^{Inves}_{1} = White	β^{F1}_{11}	G^2	Probability
H_0: Equal Probability	0	0	0	4569.2	.000
H_1: Racial Bias	0.060	0.060	0.060	3012.3	.000
H_2: Cross-Racial Bias	0	0	0.180	11478.0	.000
H_3: Institutional Bias	0.120	0	0	1685.9	.000
H_4: Saturated Model	0.178	0.105	-0.038	0	—
H_5: Main Effects Model	0.170	0.100	0	208.6	.000

Note: Constant = general mean = -.786.

odds that an African American child will be indicated are 1.19 times greater ($e^{.178}$) than the average rate of substantiation, regardless of investigator race. Evaluated at the general mean, the substantiation rate is 3.9 percentage points higher if the family is African American rather than white. The saturated model also shows that the odds that a white investigator will substantiate an allegation of maltreatment are 1.11 times greater ($e^{.105}$) than the average rate of substantiation, regardless of the family's race. Evaluated at the general mean, the substantiation rate is 2.3 percentage points higher if the investigation is conducted by a white worker instead of a black worker.

Here we have powerful evidence of two sources of disparity. It is interesting to note that cross-race investigations, however, appear to diminish rather than amplify the disparities associated with the main effects of family and investigator race. The interaction effect of the race of the investigator and the race of the family shows that both white and African American investigators indicate opposite-race families at slightly less than the average (0.8 percentage points less than the general mean). Given that interaction effect is substantively negligible, it is more parsimonious to drop the interaction term and re-estimate the model with only the main effects. The best-fitting restricted model (H_5) suggests that African American children are at higher risk of substantiation, regardless of investigator race, and white investigators indicate families at a higher rate, regardless of family race.

Before pursuing whether these two sources of racial disparity reflect institutional biases that prejudice the attitudes of white and African American investigators alike or cultural biases that cause white and African American investigators to assess maltreatment differently, it is important to revisit the question of whether these differences have anything to do with race at all. As mentioned previously, the analysis thus far assumes that African American and white families under investigation are alike in all relevant background characteristics. But it could be otherwise. African American families may be reported more often than white families for certain allegations, such as substance-exposed infants (SEIs), who are more likely to be indicated because of positive toxicology tests than other reports of maltreatment. Thus the higher rate of substantiation may be spuriously related to family race and instead reflect the higher incidence of SEI reports among African American families. Of course, this higher incidence might reflect, in turn, biases in hospital testing procedures, however, biases are a potential source of racial disparity at the first stage of reporting rather than investigation. Similarly, the higher rate of substantiation by white investigators may reflect differences in education, job tenure, and county of investigation rather than investigator race. Once these differences in worker characteristics are controlled for statistically, the main effect of investigator race might wash out.

In an effort to explore these alternative sources of racial disparity, the researchers estimated several additional log-linear models for more complex contingency tables. They used the following variables to form eight separate four-way contingency tables, using indicated report by family race by investigator race by:

1. year of the investigation,
2. age of the child being investigated,
3. type of allegation,
4. type of initial reporter,
5. educational status of the investigator,
6. tenure of the investigator at IDCFS,
7. type of allegation of maltreatment, and
8. LANs or community where the investigation occurred.

When the researchers statistically controlled each of these variables, the main effect of family race persisted. In other words, these variables did not illuminate why African American children are indicated at a higher rate. Of these factors, two diminished the main effect of the investigator's race: type of allegation and the community in which the investigation took place. Before considering these two factors in greater detail, we review briefly the results for the remaining models. None of these remaining models, it should be noted, changed the significance of the race effects.

- *The year of the investigation.* This model confirms that fewer cases are indicated today in Illinois than 10 years ago and that African American families have been indicated at a higher rate for the entire 10-year history.

- *The age of the child at the time of the report.* The age of the child did not substantially change the likelihood of indication.
- *The source of the initial report.* Prior research shows that if a mandated reporter was the source of the report, it was more likely to be substantiated than if the reporter was nonmandated (Hutchison, 1989). The authors found no significant difference on indication rates based on the type of reporter.
- *The highest educational degree the investigator has received.* No significant difference existed in indication rates based on the educational background of the reporter.
- *The investigator's tenure at IDCFS.* This refers to the length of time that the investigator has been working with the IDCFS at the time of the investigation. This variable was not significantly related to indication rates.

Type of Allegation

For purposes of this analysis, the authors categorized allegations into one of the following types: physical abuse, sexual abuse, other types of maltreatment, and SEI. *SEI* is defined as an allegation of the presence of a controlled substance in a newborn's system or other forms of substance exposure or misuse during the child's first year of life. As Illinois law requires that all positive hospital tests for alcohol and other drugs in an infant's blood result in a substantiated allegation, the authors chose SEI as the comparison group for the allegation model.

As displayed in Model H_6 in Table 6-2, this is a well-fitting model. The log-likelihood chi-square is 100.84. The main effect of family race is still highly significant, but the main effect of the race of the investigator becomes insignificant at the .06 level when controlling for the type of allegation. At first glance, this suggests that investigators of different races act similarly. Although it is true that both African American and white investigators are indicating African American families at a much higher rate than white families, the interaction of investigator race and type of allegation deserves a closer look.

White investigators are much more likely to indicate allegations of physical abuse than African American investigators, but they are less likely to be involved with an indicated SEI report. They are also only slightly more likely to indicate allegations of sexual abuse and other forms of maltreatment, such as neglect, lack of supervision, or risk of harm. We can only speculate about the reasons that white investigators are more likely to indicate families for physical abuse than African American investigators. Some research suggests that white

Table 6–2: Model H_6—Allegation

Parameters	Estimate	Significance
β (Constant)	0.1036	*
β^{Family}_{1} = Black	0.2244	*
$\beta^{Investigator}_{1}$ = White	0.0243	ns
β^{FI}_{11} (Family x Investigator Interaction)	0.0119	ns
$\beta^{Allegation}_{1 = Physical\ Abuse}$	-0.8839	*
$\beta^{Allegation}_{2 = Sexual\ Abuse}$	-0.0885	*
$\beta^{Allegation}_{3 = Other}$	-1.2090	*
$\beta^{Allegation}_{4 = SEI}$	2.1813	*
β^{FA}_{11} (Family x Physical Abuse Interaction)	-0.0464	*
β^{FA}_{12} (Family x Sexual Abuse Interaction)	-0.1577	*
β^{FA}_{13} (Family x Other Maltreatment Interaction)	0.0134	ns
β^{FA}_{14} (Family x SEI Interaction)	0.1907	*
β^{IA}_{11} (Investigator x Physical Abuse Interaction)	0.1704	*
β^{IA}_{12} (Investigator x Sexual Abuse Interaction)	0.0851	*
β^{IA}_{13} (Investigator x Other Maltreatment Interaction)	0.0682	*
β^{IA}_{14} (Investigator x SEI Interaction)	-0.3536	*
β^{FIA}_{111} (Family x Investigator x Physical Abuse Interaction)	0.00328	ns
β^{FIA}_{112} (Family x Investigator x Sexual Abuse Interaction)	-0.0667	*
β^{FIA}_{113} (Family x Investigator x Other Maltreatment Interaction)	-0.0403	*
β^{FIA}_{114} (Family x Investigator x SEI Interaction)	0.1038	*

Note: SEI = substance-exposed infant.
* Indicates that the estimate is statistically significant, whereas ns = not significant.

families look less approvingly on the use of corporal punishment than African American families, which may explain the higher indication rates by white investigators.

When it comes to SEI reports, the pattern is reversed. White investigators are less likely to be involved with an indicated SEI report than African American investigators. The estimated probability of a family being indicated by a white investigator is substantially lower than that of a family being indicated by an African American investigator. Because the testing of newborns for substance exposure is largely out of the hands of IDCFS investigators, the only plausible explanation is that regional differences in the hospital practices may exist, which put families investigated by African Americans at significantly greater risk of SEI findings than whites. Because African American investigators are concentrated in Cook County, differential testing practices in Cook County hospitals may put families at a higher risk of SEI substantiation. This might help to explain why African American families, who are also more heavily concentrated in Cook County, are indicated for SEI at a greater rate than their white counterparts.

In reports in which sexual abuse is the allegation, although white investigators continue to indicate slightly more often than their African American counterparts do, less disparity in substantiation rates by the race of the worker exists. The same holds true for the race of the family. Consequently, the racial pattern for sexual abuse investigations more closely approximates the equal probability model than any other allegation. Unlike physical abuse, there may be greater societal consensus on what constitutes sexual abuse.

In the analysis for the category of "other" allegations, the researchers found the same patterns: African American families are most likely to be indicated, and white investigators are more likely to indicate, but the white racial and cross-racial bias models are not adequate explanations for the pattern.

Area of the State Where Investigation Occurred

The researchers looked at the community where the allegation was investigated. The effects of both the race of the family and the race of the caseworker change significantly in this model. The main effect of investigator race appears to be related to specific practices in certain communities. Those communities that indicate at a higher rate are also those communities with a higher proportion of investigators who are white. When the researchers plotted the main effect of the race of the family, they found a lack of clustering, suggesting that no strong geographic component exists for the main effect of the race of the family.

Small areas exist where white workers indicate African American families at higher rates than white families, but little suggests that this is a statewide bias. There are, perhaps, some clusters of bias, particularly in the suburban Cook County area and in the southeastern part of the state. To help understand what these communities might have in common, the authors mapped poverty rates and examined the race of the children living in the communities; however, adding community-level poverty rates for children to the analysis did not change in an appreciable way the main effects of the race of the family and of the investigator, which still remained significant.

Discussion and Conclusion

African American children constitute 19% of the child population in Illinois, but they represent 46% of indicated reports of abuse and neglect and 76% of open child welfare cases. In an effort to understand the overrepresentation of African American children in the Illinois child welfare system, this chapter looked for evidence of racial bias in the investigation of child abuse and neglect. The authors found evidence of strong main effects of family race and investigator race on the odds of substantiation. That is, children in African American families are more likely to be indicated, regardless of the race of the investigator, and white investigators are more likely to indicate a report, regardless of family race. Apart from these main effects, the authors found no evidence that investigators are racially biased against families of the opposite race. No interaction effect boosts the substantiation rate for African American families investigated by white investigators beyond the main effects of family and investigator race.

Although the authors found that allegations of maltreatment against African American children run a higher risk of being substantiated than allegations involving white children, nothing in the analysis helped us understand why this disparity exists. On the other hand, two factors stood out in illustrating why allegations of maltreatment are more likely to be indicated by white investigators, regardless of the race of the family: the type of abuse investigated and the region of the state where the abuse occurred. White workers have a greater propensity for indicating physical abuse allegations than black investigators, but a lower propensity for indicating SEI allegations. The authors surmise that these differences may reflect variation in community norms regarding the acceptance of corporal punishment as a disciplinary method and community variations in hospital testing practices for intrauterine substance exposure.

References

Hampton, R. L. (1987). Race, class and child maltreatment. *Journal of Comparative Family Studies, 18*, 113–126.

Hutchison, E. D. (1989). Child protective screening decisions: An analysis of predictive factors. *Social Work Research & Abstracts, 25*(3), 9–16.

Morton, T. D. (1999). The increasing colorization of America's child welfare system: The overrepresentation of African American children. *Policy & Practice, 57*(4), 23–30.

Saunders, E. J., Nelson, K., & Landsman, M. J. (1993). Racial inequality and child neglect: Findings in a metropolitan area. *Child Welfare, 72*, 341–354.

Stehno, S. M. (1990). Public responsibility for dependent black children: The advocacy of Edith Abbott and Sophonisba Breckinridge. *Social Service Review, 62*, 485–503.

CHAPTER 7

The Effect of Risk Assessments and Their Relationship to Maltreatment Recurrence Across Races

Christopher Baird

Over the past two decades, America's child protective service (CPS) systems have seen the number of African American families on caseloads increase. In most jurisdictions, African Americans are more likely than whites, Hispanics, or Asians to have allegations of maltreatment substantiated and to have children placed in out-of-home care. In many states, the placement rates for white children are substantially different than for African American children.

This trend is particularly disturbing when viewed in the context of the National Incidence Studies (NISs), which concluded that no differences exist in maltreatment rates for African Americans and whites.[1] If this is accurate, NISs raise serious questions about the disproportionate number of African American families in America's child protection system. Ample evidence exists, however, that rates of maltreatment do vary by economic status and other family characteristics, which, in turn, could well be reflected in what appear to be different rates of maltreatment by race.

Some have worried (or even concluded) that as more and more CPS agencies implement actuarial risk assessment systems, racial bias will be exacerbated. They reason that because actuarial systems use simple objective factors such as income levels, fam-

[1] The National Incidence Studies develop estimates of abuse and neglect prevalence rates for the general population. These studies combine data from several sources, including child protective services (CPS) and professionals from non-CPS agencies likely to come in contact with maltreated children. Participants included law enforcement, schools, day care centers, hospitals, voluntary social service agencies, mental health agencies, juvenile probation, and public health departments.

ily size, and number of caregivers in the home, they will rate more African Americans than whites as being at high risk for child maltreatment. Because more African American families than white families live in poverty, have more single-parent households, and have three or more children residing in the household, these fears seem, at least on the surface, to have some foundation. If bias exists, it could result in additional overrepresentation of African Americans in both the CPS and foster care systems.

Rather than speculate about the potential effect of actuarial risk assessment models on the overrepresentation of African Americans, however, the National Council on Crime and Delinquency's Children's Research Center (CRC) has reviewed data from agencies using actuarial risk assessments to determine if these systems have actually resulted in a greater level of disparity between African Americans and whites. The number of agencies that have implemented actuarial systems has increased considerably in recent years. Consequently, risk ratings on many thousands of families, both African American and white, are available for analysis. This chapter presents data from the three largest states using CRC actuarial risk assessment systems: California, Georgia, and Michigan. It also includes the presentation of data from a national study of risk assessments in which the Michigan risk assessment model was applied to cases from four geographically dispersed jurisdictions. These presentations are followed by an in-depth discussion of results and a presentation of the issues raised regarding risk assessment and the disproportionate representation of African Americans in child welfare systems throughout the country.

This chapter will answer questions about the relationships among risk, race, and the recurrence of abuse and neglect. It presents the actual experiences of states using actuarial risk assessment and clarifies precisely how equity issues should be evaluated.

Defining Equity

To judge the level of equity attained by actuarial risk assessment models, the authors invoked the criterion used by the educational testing industry. Racial and ethnic bias have long been a concern in educational testing because of their ramifications on admissions to schools and school programs. The American Educational Research Association on Measurement in Educations stated that "examinees of equal standing with respect to the construct the test is intended to measure, should, on average, earn the same test score, irrespective of group membership" (*Standards for Educational and Psychological Testing*, p. 153).

To guard against this bias in child welfare, African American and white families rated as high, moderate, and low risk must exhibit similar rates of subsequent maltreatment. If, for example, a system rated 25% of both races as high risk, but 50% of high-risk white families had a subsequent report of abuse or neglect, whereas only 30% of high-risk African American families abused or neglected their children again, then the term *high risk* would mean something very different for the two groups.

Although minor differences in rates of subsequent abuse and neglect reports and substantiation are unavoidable, the instruments should (a) demonstrate a significant level of discrimination among high-, moderate-, and low-risk cases in each racial group, and (b) never create a situation in which high-risk cases of one race do not exhibit significantly higher rates of subsequent abuse or neglect than moderate-risk cases of any racial group. Moderate-risk cases must, in turn, exhibit significantly higher rates of subsequent abuse or neglect than rates found for low-risk cases of any racial group. When CRC joins with a state to develop a CPS risk-assessment system, it is careful to ensure that differences among races in maltreatment rates recorded at each risk level are minimized. As a result, each group exhibits similar rates of subsequent maltreatment within risk levels. Table 7-1 presents related data from the California and Michigan scale construction samples. Baird (in press) found similar results in revalidation studies using cohorts of 6,000 to 9,000.

Race and Risk Information from States Using Actuarial Assessments

Alaska was the first state to use actuarial risk assessment in CPS, and it has now done so for more than a decade. Soon after Alaska implemented its system, Michigan followed suit, and it has since accumulated a massive amount of data on family risk levels, needs, services, and outcomes. From the beginning, CRC and Michigan officials were highly cognizant of potential racial bias and made equity an essential principle of the development effort. They tested risk instruments independently on families of each race to ensure that equity was maintained. Because overall recurrence rates are similar for African Americans and whites, agencies should expect similar proportions of each population to be classified as high, moderate, and low risk. The results are clear: Despite using factors that some have worried are biased, essentially equal proportions of African Americans and whites can be classified into each risk level in Michigan. Table 7-2 presents risk assessments from assessments of nearly 12,000 Michigan cases. Obviously, the degree of equity attained in classifying Michigan families into risk levels is quite remarkable.

Another simple method for exploring the equity issue is to compute an average risk level for each group.[2] Using this approach to compare risk ratings of different groups again demonstrates that the Michigan risk assessment tools do not discriminate against

[2] This is done by assigning a value to each risk level, multiplying the value by the number of cases at each level, summing the totals, and dividing by the total population of each group. The following values were assigned to Michigan risk levels: low risk = 1; moderate risk = 2; high risk = 3; very high risk = 4.

Table 7-1: Subsequent Substantiation Rates by Race and Risk Level (in percentages)

	Michigan[a]		California[a]	
Risk Level	**African Americans**	**Whites**	**African Americans**	**Whites**
Low/moderate[b]	6.0	5.0	9.0	15.0
High	15.0	12.0	29.0	33.0
Very high	28.0	30.0	42.0	50.0

[a] Michigan rates reflect a 12-month follow-up. California rates reflect a 24-month follow-up.
[b] Because of the small number of cases rated low risk when the sample is subdivided by race, the researchers have combined the low and moderate categories.

Table 7-2: Michigan: Percentage of Families at Each Risk Level

Risk Level	**White (*N* = 6,651)**	**African American (*N* = 5,296)**
Low	10.5	11.3
Moderate	30.7	30.0
High	45.1	46.0
Very High	13.7	12.7

African Americans. African Americans had an average risk rating of 2.601, whereas whites averaged 2.620. In sum, whites—not African Americans—had a marginally higher risk rating when the actuarial assessment was applied.

The Michigan experience is not an anomaly. In fact, findings from all states using actuarial risk assessments are notably consistent. Georgia adopted the Michigan system, modified it to a small degree, and then implemented it statewide. Data are now available on nearly 8,000 assessments conducted in a sample of Georgia counties. Table 7-3 outlines the results of these assessments by race. Again, more whites than African Americans score at the higher risk levels. Using average risk ratings for comparison purposes, whites in Georgia have an average risk rating of 1.859, whereas the average rating for African Americans is 1.772.

California began implementing a structured decisionmaking system in 1996 in several pilot counties. Actuarial risk assessment is an important component of this system. California, with assistance from CRC, developed its own risk assessment instrument. The designers based development on a random sample of more than 2,500 families from seven pilot counties.[3] The research resulted in risk assessment tools similar in both content and format to the Michigan system. Classification results by race using data from the scale construction effort again illustrate that actuarial risk assessment models do not systematically rate African Americans as being as higher risk levels (see Table 7-4). Using the average risk rating of each race to compare results indicates that

[3] The counties included as pilots were Alameda, Humboldt, Los Angeles, Orange, Sacramento, San Bernardino, and Santa Clara.

Table 7-3: Georgia: Percentage of Families at Each Risk Level

Risk Level	White (*N* = 3,441)	African American (*N* = 3,985)
Low	26.7	31.7
Moderate	60.7	59.1
High	12.6	9.1

Table 7-4: California: Percentage of Families at Each Risk Level

Risk Level	African American (*N* = 413)	Hispanic (*N* = 682)	White (*N* = 1,103)
Low	17.4	13.8	11.5
Moderate	39.0	47.2	39.2
High	32.7	29.9	37.3
Very High	10.9	9.1	12.1

whites, not African Americans, have a slightly higher risk profile. Whites in California had an average risk rating of 2.582, whereas African Americans averaged 2.337. The California database also provides one of the best observations available to date on how risk levels of Hispanic families correspond to those of whites and African Americans. As Table 7-4 illustrates, risk ratings of Hispanic families do not exceed those of whites. The average risk rating for Hispanic families in the California study was 2.343.

In a national study funded by the Office on Child Abuse and Neglect (OCAN) comparing different risk assessment systems, researchers applied the Michigan system to cases from Florida, Missouri, California, and Michigan. The data from these four states serve as the final example. As Table 7-5 illustrates, no significant differences existed in the number of whites and African Americans scoring in each risk level, and again, the average risk rating computed for each group indicates that whites have a slightly higher overall risk profile (2.147 for whites vs. 2.105 for African Americans).

Finally, in CPS, actuarial risk assessment is not used to guide placement decisions. It is used only to help determine which cases are facing the greatest risk. Most cases need in-home services to protect children and to designate the level of intervention required.

Figure 7-1 demonstrates how using valid risk assessment systems can help offset possible bias found at other decision points in the CPS process. Although workers judged 6% more African American families than white families to require an "immediate response" from investigators, and they substantiated 4.4% of allegations involving African American families, only 0.9% more African American cases were opened for services. Case opening is the point at which risk assessment begins to play a role in decisionmaking. Differences between races found at earlier decision points decrease significantly when actuarial risk is introduced.

Table 7-5: Michigan Risk Assessment Applied to Cases from Four Jurisdictions: Percentage of Families at Each Risk Level

Risk Level	White ($N = 684$)	African American ($N = 581$)
Low	13.5	15.2
Moderate	58.3	58.8
High	28.2	25.9

Figure 7-1: Comparisons at Various Decision Points for African American and Whites in Georgia

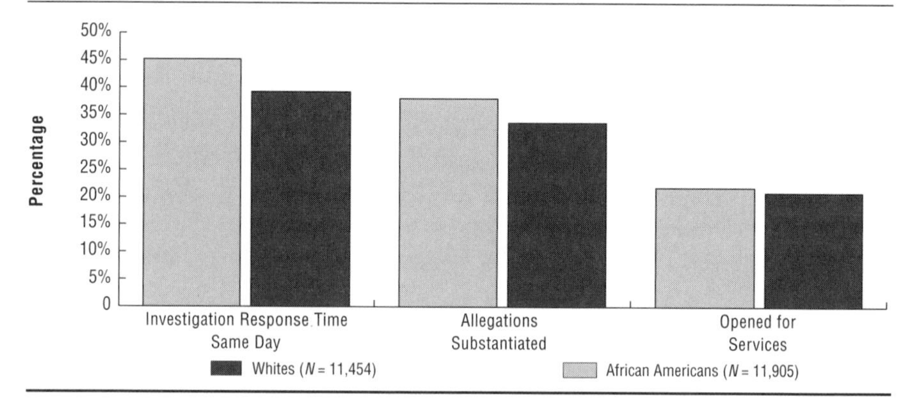

The Purpose of Risk Classification Systems

Before discussing why actuarial risk instruments increase equity in decisionmaking, it is important that the CPS field has a full understanding of the purpose of these systems. The field should move beyond traditional notions of what risk assessment is all about. Validity of decision systems has until lately been measured by the degree to which predictions about case outcomes are realized. For example, Ruscio (1998) defined validity in the following manner:

> The efficacy of your decision policy can be examined through the use of a simple fourfold classification table crossing the optimal outcome for each child (kept at home vs. placed into care) with the decision that is reached. There are two types of correct decisions, or "hits," that are possible: True positives are decisions that place children into care when appropriate, and true negatives are decisions that keep children at home when appropriate. There are also two types of incorrect decisions, or "misses," that are possible: False positives are decisions that unnecessarily place children into care, and false negatives are decisions that fail to place children into care when placement is necessary. Based on this classifica-

> tion table, the effectiveness of a decision policy may be evaluated in several ways. For instance, one could determine how many of the decisions to place a child into foster care were correct (true positives divided by the sum of true and false positives); how many children who optimally should have been kept in the home actually were (true negatives divided by the sum of true negatives and false positives); or how many placement decisions, overall, were correct (the sum of true positives and true negatives divided by the total number of cases). (p. 145)

Although calculations of false positives, false negatives, and the overall percentage of correct predictions are useful in many settings, they may not be the best method for gauging the efficacy of a risk assessment system when the probability of success or failure is substantially different than 50/50. When events are relatively rare, it is inherently difficult to predict them. In such instances, simply assuming an event will not occur may produce more predictive accuracy than any attempt to determine where or when occurrence is likely. For example, if subsequent maltreatment (failure) is reported in only 15% of cases opened to protective services, then simply predicting no case opened to services will have subsequent maltreatment reported produces an 85% "hit rate." Obviously, such a prediction, although highly accurate, is of little value to a CPS agency. (The sensitivity of the prediction is .85, but the specificity—the correct identification of those who do fail—is zero.) A valid and reliable risk assessment system may improve the hit rate marginally, but it is possible such a system could result in a higher percentage of false positives and false negatives and still provide the agency with quality information about the relative probability of subsequent maltreatment. Consider the scenario in which a CPS population ($N = 100$) has a subsequent maltreatment rate of 15%. A risk assessment identifies 25% of the population as high risk, which, for this example, is equated with a prediction of subsequent maltreatment. Table 7-6 presents actual versus predicted outcomes.

In Table 7-6, an overall hit rate of 82% is attained (3% lower than that attained when all cases are predicted to succeed) with a rate of false positives (subsequent maltreatment) of 56% and false negatives of 5.3%. Despite the high proportion of false positives, cases that the system rated as high risk experienced maltreatment at a 44% rate, whereas only 5.3% of those rated at lower risk levels had subsequent maltreatment. The ratio of failures in the high-risk group to failures in the low-risk group is more than 8:1. Such results help agencies identify which families are more likely to abuse or neglect their children. In addition, 11 of the 15 cases (73.3%) in which subsequent maltreatment occurred were correctly identified, a relatively high rate of specificity.

Other fields, such as medicine, juvenile justice, and adult corrections, have largely abandoned the idea that risk assessment is an exercise in prediction. Instead, terms like

Table 7-6: Example: Actual Versus Predicted Outcomes

	Predicted Outcome	
Actual Outcome	**No Subsequent Maltreatment**	**Subsequent Maltreatment**
No subsequent maltreatment	71	14
Subsequent maltreatment	4	11

base expectancy rates have replaced discussions of false positives and false negatives. In corrections, for example, high risk does not equal a prediction of failure. In fact, in most correctional systems, more high-risk cases succeed than fail. Instead, *high risk* simply denotes inclusion in a group of offenders with significantly higher historical rates of recidivism than other groups.

The field of medicine offers similar examples. In cancer research, it is common practice to identify characteristics of malignancies and surrounding tissue and to classify patients as high, moderate, or low risk based on the observed rates of recurrence in a specified time period (see, for example, the Van Nuys Prognostic Index cited in Silverstein & Lagios, 1997). A designation of high risk of recurrence does not equate with a prediction that the cancer will recur. In fact, most medical professionals carefully avoid making such predictions. As treatment options expand and improve, recurrence-free survival rates have increased to the point at which, if false positives and negatives were minimized, the best prediction for high-risk cases would be "no recurrence." Still, knowing that cases with similar characteristics have experienced a recurrence rate of 10%, 25%, or 45% helps the doctor and patient select the most appropriate treatment plan. In medical literature, the use of stark terms such as "false positives" and "false negatives" to evaluate the efficacy of cancer-classification techniques is relatively rare.[4]

Conceptually, the use of false positives and false negatives to evaluate risk assessment systems creates another dilemma. Although outcomes are often dichotomous (an event will either occur or not occur), most risk assessment systems incorporate three or more risk levels. If system efficacy is based on predicting an outcome, one must ask what prediction is being made for cases at intermediate risk levels: Is a designation of "moderate risk" a prediction that subsequent maltreatment will or will not occur? We submit that it is neither, but simply the recognition that these cases maltreat children at higher rates than some and lower rates than others. Knowing this allows workers to establish appropriate service plans, just as similar information permits doctors and patients to decide on a particular course of action.

[4] For example, two recent research studies that produced or evaluated scales to rate the risk of recurrence of breast cancer (Silverstein & Lagios, 1997; Silverstein, Lagios, & Craig, 1996) do not use the terms *false positives* and *false negatives*. What is most interesting about these articles is that the scaling methods employed mirror those used to create many child welfare risk scales.

Therefore, in evaluating the relative efficacy of risk assessment instruments, it is imperative to be very clear about expectations. Researchers often use the terms *prediction* and *classification* interchangeably, yet they really connote different expectations. Prediction is more precise than classification. According to *Webster's II* (1995), *prediction* "declares in advance on the basis of observation, experience, or scientific reason" (p. 831). To predict accurately in any field is difficult; to accurately predict human behavior is especially complex, as so many factors contribute to determining how individuals will act. *Webster's* simply defines *classification,* on the other hand, as "a systematic arrangement in groups or categories according to established criteria" (p. 209). Although accurate prediction would greatly benefit CPS and society, it has not proven feasible. We submit that the goal of risk assessment is much more modest: It is simply meant to assign cases to different categories based on observed rates of behavior.

What is important is the degree to which families in different risk groups perform differently. Classification recognizes that a high-risk designation is not a prediction of failure. It is, instead, a clear indication that such families may require more attention and more services, because cases in this designation tend to maltreat children at higher rates than cases in other classifications. Valid risk instruments achieve significant differences in rates of maltreatment among risk groups. The greater the differences, the better the instrument.

Recently, better methods of measuring the efficacy of risk assessment systems have emerged. Researchers are realizing that traditional definitions of validity do not adequately measure the power of risk classification systems. Silver and Banks (1998), for example, stated that

> the primary utility of a risk-classification model is in providing a continuum of risk estimates associated with a variety of conditions which can be used to guide a range of decision-making responses...it is for this reason that traditional measures of "predictive accuracy" which carry with them the assumption that dichotomous decisions will be made, have little utility for assessing the potency of a risk classification model. (pp. 8–9)

In essence, researchers should measure the validity of risk assessment systems by the degree to which each system identifies subgroups of a meaningful size and the degree to which each system reports different rates of subsequent maltreatment for cases at each risk level.

Why Actuarial Systems Produce Such a High Degree of Equity

Data from states using actuarial risk assessment systems clearly demonstrate that these instruments do not discriminate against African American families. In fact, they bring a level of equity to CPS decisionmaking that could very well serve as at least a partial remedy to the racial disproportionality that has plagued child welfare over the years.

Understanding why actuarial risk assessment systems work so well to increase equity in decisionmaking requires knowledge of how they are constructed, as well as a thorough understanding of national data on abuse and neglect as they relate to race. The following discussion links national data on abuse and neglect and methods used to construct systems that measure risk. It is important that CPS agencies understand these relationships.

As noted earlier, critics of actuarial risk assessments frequently cite NIS reports that claim no significant differences in maltreatment rates between African Americans and whites exist. These data really have little relevance to risk assessment research, however. NISs combine several data sources to estimate prevalence rates for the general population; they report abuse and neglect incidents as occurrences per 1,000 people in a given location. Risk assessment studies, however, focus on only a small subset of the general population: those families who have had an allegation of abuse or neglect reported and who CPS then investigates. Recurrence rates recorded for these families are much higher than incidence rates found in the general population (10 to 20 times the general incidence rate). The prevalence rates NIS cites bear little resemblance to patterns of recurrence found in a CPS cohort. Despite this limitation, NIS data can be helpful in explaining why actuarial risk assessment systems do so much to promote equity in CPS decisionmaking.

Even if no difference exists in the overall maltreatment rates reported for African Americans and whites, a review of NIS's database clearly indicates substantial differences may exist in the type of maltreatment reported by race. In general, the author's research has found that African Americans are more likely to be reported for neglect, whereas whites are more likely to face allegations of abuse.

Maltreatment, particularly neglect, is strongly correlated with poverty, the stress involved in being a single parent, and other factors that are more commonly found in African American homes. For example, far more African Americans than whites have annual incomes of less than $15,000 (30.4% vs. 11.6%), a much greater percentage of African American homes have a single female caregiver present (52% vs. 18%), and a higher proportion of African American homes have three or more children present (14% vs. 9%; U.S. Bureau of the Census, 1999). NIS-3 reports higher rates of neglect for families with each of these characteristics:

- Children in families with income of less than $15,000 are 44 times more likely to be neglected than children from higher-income families.
- Children in single-caregiver families have an 87% greater risk of physical neglect than those in two-caregiver families.

- Children in the largest families are neglected at three times the rate of single-child families.

Given that families with these characteristics have a higher level of neglect reported and that more African American families have these characteristics, only one conclusion is possible: Neglect rates are higher for African Americans than whites. It is important to remember, however, that whites facing the same stresses noted here have reported incidences of neglect at a similar rate.

Conversely, the composition of white families makes the occurrence of child abuse more likely than in African American families. Several factors contribute to this, but the most prominent is gender related. As the NISs report, abuse is most often perpetrated by males (67% of all physical abuse perpetrators are male; 89% of sexual abuse is perpetrated by males). Less than half (48%) of all African American families have a male caregiver present. About 80% of white families have a male caregiver in the household (U.S. Bureau of the Census, 1999). With more families with a male caregiver present, whites have somewhat higher rates of abuse reported.[5] (This is particularly true when researchers measure recurrence in a CPS cohort.)

When researchers do CPS cohort studies, the difference in rates of reabuse and rates of reneglect reported for African Americans and whites essentially offset each other, resulting in nearly identical rates of subsequent maltreatment. The fact that these differences exist, however, helps explain why actuarial risk assessment systems used in Michigan, Georgia, California, and other states effect such a high level of equity.

Most notably, in states using CRC risk assessment models, separate instruments are used to rate the risk of neglect and the risk of abuse. This is essential to achieving equity, as different family characteristics are related to the recurrence of different types of maltreatment. As the data presented earlier would indicate, African Americans score higher on most neglect scale items and have a higher average risk-of-neglect score. Table 7-7 presents an item analysis from Michigan and from the four sites that participated in the OCAN study; similar results from other sites are also available. The differences in average neglect scores translate into higher proportions of African Americans rated high risk for neglect (see Figures 7-2 and 7-3).

Conversely, whites, as a group, score higher on most items on abuse scales and have a higher average risk of abuse score than African Americans (Table 7-8 presents Michigan and OCAN results). As Figures 7-4 and 7-5 illustrate, more whites are rated at the higher risk levels for abuse. When researchers combine ratings from the two scales by

[5] This was uniformly true in 14 risk assessments the Children's Research Center conducted from 1986 through 2003. In New York, where legislators define abuse very narrowly, this pattern was not evident.

Table 7-7: Neglect Item Scores from Michigan and the National Office on Child Abuse and Neglect (OCAN) Study

Item	Mean Score			
	Michigan		OCAN	
	White	African American	White	African American
Current complaint is for neglect	0.641	0.743	0.539	0.617
Number of prior assigned complaints	0.912	0.816	0.916	0.892
Number of children in the home	0.373	0.487	0.349	0.472
Number of adults in home at time of complaint	0.359	0.538	0.356	0.536
Age of primary caregiver	0.317	0.406	0.340	0.348
Characteristics of primary caregiver	1.210	1.230	0.907	0.812
Primary caregiver involved in harmful relationship	0.546	0.404	0.470	0.304
Primary caregiver has a current substance abuse problem	0.589	1.064	0.329	0.613
Household is experiencing severe financial difficulty	0.220	0.267	0.154	0.151
Primary caregiver's motivation to improve parenting skills	0.727	0.721	0.403	0.474
Caregiver's response to investigation	0.803	0.909	0.553	0.629
Average neglect score	6.697	7.585	5.359	5.860

Figure 7-2: Neglect Risk Levels by Race in Michigan

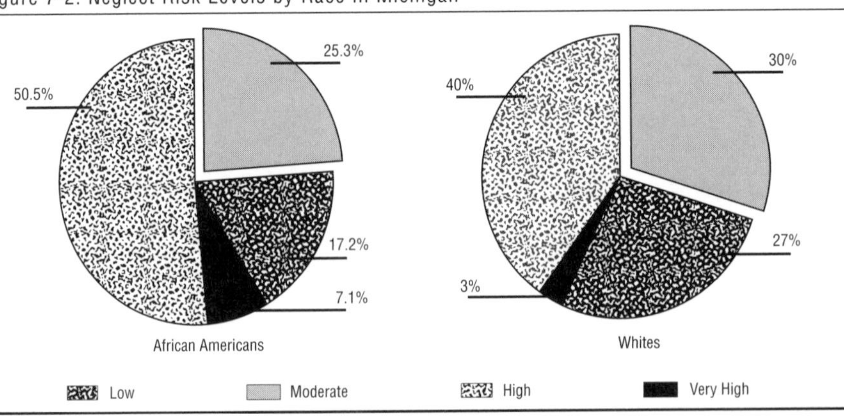

assigning the highest level of risk indicated by either scale, they essentially classify equal proportions of each race in the high, moderate, and low risk levels.

We can see that actuarial risk assessment systems produce no racial bias. The author selected the factors used to rate the risk of future abuse or neglect because they relate to

Figure 7-3: Neglect Risk Levels by Race—Office on Child Abuse and Neglect National Study

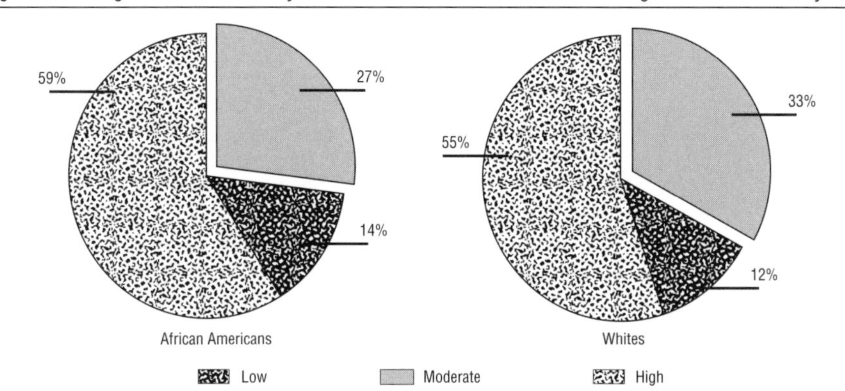

Table 7-8: Abuse Item Scores from Michigan and the National Office on Child Abuse and Neglect (OCAN) Study

	Mean Score			
	Michigan		OCAN	
Item	White	African American	White	African American
Current complaint is for abuse	0.490	0.393	0.553	0.468
Prior assigned abuse complaints	0.455	0.277	0.451	0.399
Prior child protective services history	0.465	0.454	0.420	0.444
Number of children in the home	0.686	0.720	0.716	0.737
Caregiver abused as a child	0.235	0.141	0.143	0.075
Secondary caregiver has a current substance abuse problem	0.198	0.152	0.118	0.063
Primary or secondary caregiver employs excessive/inappropriate discipline	0.684	0.533	0.626	0.526
Caregiver is a domineering parent	0.233	0.157	0.265	0.210
Child in the home has a developmental disability or history of delinquency	0.294	0.167	0.374	0.308
Secondary caregiver motivated to improve parenting skills	0.511	0.301	0.336	0.224
Primary caregiver views incident less seriously than agency	0.460	0.478	0.297	0.340
Average abuse score	5.026	3.938	4.569	3.959

subsequent reports, substantiations, injuries, and placements in families with previous investigated allegations of abuse or neglect. In instances in which the average score on an item differs between races, this reflects actual differences in outcomes. For example, as a group, African Americans score higher on "number of caregivers in the home" be-

Figure 7-4: Abuse Risk Levels by Race in Michigan

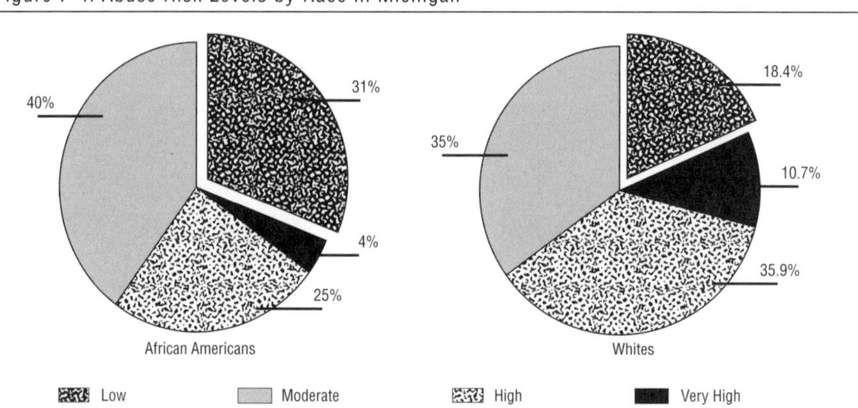

Figure 7-5: Abuse Risk Levels by Race—Office on Child Abuse and Neglect National Study

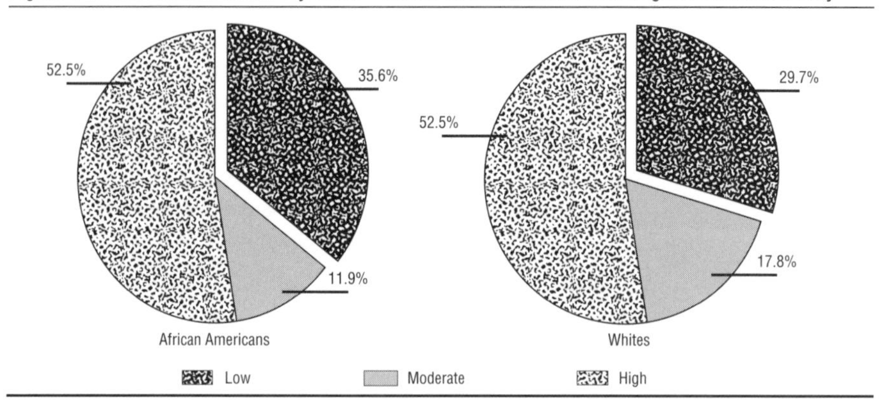

cause a greater proportion of African American households have a single caregiver, and single caregivers have higher rates of neglect reported. The level of equity attained by actuarial risk assessment systems is rarely experienced in the human service field.

Is Substantiation a Biased Outcome Measure?

Some researchers have criticized substantiation as an outcome measure because it is an administrative process subject to investigators' biases (English, 1999). Although the proclivity to substantiate more reports on African Americans is a serious issue, it has little effect on risk research. As noted earlier, risk instruments are based on recurrence rates. Cases included in risk studies are only those reported to and investigated by CPS agencies. The outcomes are subsequent reports and substantiations (and in most jurisdictions, child injuries and out-of-home placements). The question then is, are the disproportionate rates of substantiation for African American cases (for all reports received) also found in recurrence rates? Based on 15 studies conducted in nearly a dozen jurisdictions, subsequent substantiation rates of the two races appear to be very similar. In all but one CRC study, no statistically significant differences existed in the subsequent substantiation rates of African Americans and whites (Baird, Chapter 7, this volume).

In a few studies, African American subsequent substantiation rates were marginally higher than whites' rates, but these differences were not statistically significant. The OCAN study, for example, reported a subsequent substantiation rate of 15.9% for whites and 19.5% for African Americans ($p > .05$). More often, however, whites had marginally higher rates of subsequent substantiation. In California, the only site where researchers found statistically significant differences in rates of subsequent substantiation, whites had the higher rate (26.1%). Workers resubstantiated African Americans at a 19.1% rate, whereas they substantiated 19.7% of cases involving Hispanics during the two-year follow-up period. In sum, African Americans do not appear to have a higher rate of subsequent substantiation than whites. Criticism of substantiation as an outcome measure also fails to note that designers do not construct actuarial risk assessment instruments based solely on how items relate to subsequent substantiations. They use additional outcome measures, including subsequent referrals, subsequent placements, and subsequent child injuries. As Figure 7-6 from California demonstrates, families at each risk level have substantially different rates reported on each outcome measure. For example, only 1.4% of all low-risk cases in the California sample used to develop the scale had a subsequent out-of-home placement recorded. The placement rate increased at every risk level, to nearly 28% for cases rated as very high risk.

Conclusions and Implications

Clearly, African Americans are overrepresented in this nation's child welfare systems, but attempts to use this fact to discourage use of actuarial risk assessment systems are misguided. Overrepresentation of African Americans is likely due, at least in part, to unfettered discretion, not to attempts to add structure to decisionmaking. Parent (1995) noted in a *Time Magazine* article, "If you get a caseworker who goes to somebody's home and says it's fine, then it's fine. That's how important their voice is" (p. 62). And, as a Chapin Hall Center for Children report indicates, workers (and researchers) frequently disagree on what each case requires (Rossi, Schuerman, & Budde, 1996). Whenever difficult decisions affecting families are left principally to individuals, disparity is almost a certainty. The counterclaim that actuarial risk assessment systems are racially biased is primarily based on a fundamentally flawed review of a national database. Data pre-

Figure 7-6: California Risk Assessment Outcomes by Risk Level (*N* = 2,511)

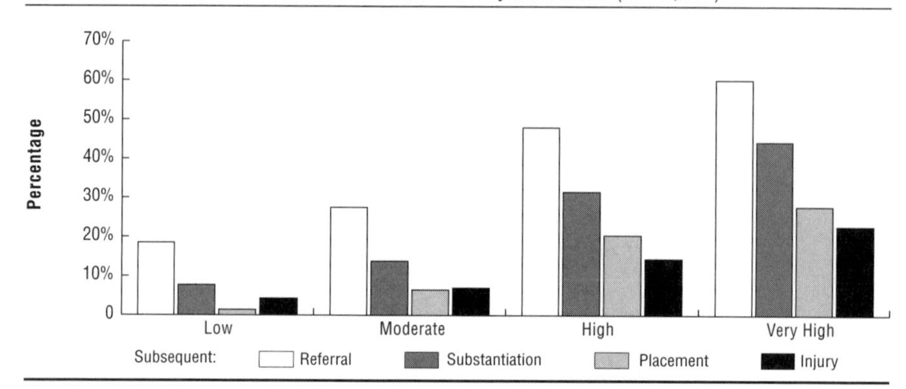

sented here demonstrate that proper use of actuarial risk assessment could well reduce overrepresentation of families of color in the child welfare system.

Overrepresentation of people of color in child welfare is a serious issue that deserves serious study. Anything less constitutes a disservice to the field. Results from states using actuarial risk assessment systems are compelling: These tools can help ensure that child welfare decisions are appropriate, consistent, and equitable for all families entering the child protection system.

References

English, D. (1999). Evaluation and risk assessment of child neglect in public child protection services. In H. Dubowitz (Ed.), *Neglected children: Research, practice, and policy* (pp. 191–210). Thousand Oaks, CA: Sage.

Parent, M. (1995, December 11). Turning stones: My days and nights with children at risk. *Time Magazine*, 62.

Rossi, P., Schuerman, J., & Budde, S. (1996). *Understanding child maltreatment decisions and those who make them*. Chicago: Chapin Hall Center for Children, University of Chicago.

Ruscio, J. (1998). Information integration in child welfare cases: An introduction to statistical decision making. *Child Maltreatment, 3*, 143–156.

Silver, E., & Banks, S. (1998, November). *Calibrating the potency of violence risk classification models: The dispersion index for risk (DIFR)*. Paper presented at the American Society of Criminology conference, Washington, DC.

Silverstein, M. J., & Lagios, M. D. (1997). Use of predictors of recurrence to plan therapy for DCIS of the breast. *Oncology, 2*, 393–410.

Silverstein, M. J., Lagios, M. D., & Craig, P. H. (1996). The Van Nuys Prognostic Index for ductal carcinoma in situ. *Breast Journal, 2*, 38–40.

U.S. Bureau of the Census. (1999). *Statistical abstract of the United States*. Washington, DC: U.S. Government Printing Office.

Webster's II New College Dictionary. (1995). Boston: Houghton Mifflin.

CHAPTER 8

Effects of a Research-Based Risk Assessment on Racial/Ethnic Disproportionality in Service Provision Decisions

Will Johnson

Beginning in early 1999, a number of California counties started to use a research-based child welfare risk assessment instrument called the California Family Risk Assessment (CFRA), developed under the auspices of the California Legislature and the California Department of Social Services by the Children's Research Center, a unit of the National Council on Crime and Delinquency. CFRA is an instrument for estimating the likelihood that children investigated for child maltreatment will experience subsequent maltreatment by their caregivers. Armed with this knowledge, child welfare workers have the information they need to allocate scarce service resources among families so that children at greater risk receive more help and families requiring little assistance will receive only those services essential to ensure child safety.

Historically, some children of color, particularly African Americans, have been disproportionately represented in foster care and in-home child maltreatment prevention programs administered by U.S. government agencies (Brissett-Chapman, 1997; Morton, 1999). Because of these racial and ethnic disparities, some writers have questioned the racial and ethnic equity of decisionmaking in child welfare. Specifically, Morton (1999) raised the concern that the overrepresentation of nonwhite group members in the child welfare population could result, in part, from the use of biased risk assessment variables contained in research-based risk assessment instruments. He noted that overrepresentation of African Americans could also come from the use of biased outcome variables (e.g., substantiated maltreatment allegations) to validate these instruments. He concluded that "if risk assessment or other assessment scales and indexes are based on characteristics that predict allegation founding, and allegation founding contains racial bias, then case-opening and service decisions resulting from such an approach have the potential to compound a race-bias effect" already present in biased risk assessment items. (p. 29)

Shortly after its creation, the California Department of Social Services undertook an analysis of CFRA to ensure that using this tool to assess child maltreatment risk and in decisions to provide child protection services would not result in a disproportionate focus on African Americans and members of other nonwhite groups.

The analysis presented in this chapter demonstrates that members of nonwhite groups are not disproportionately made the subjects of child protection intervention because of the use of CFRA in California. The analysis also specifically addresses the concerns raised by Morton (1999) regarding research-based risk assessment instruments developed using substantiated maltreatment allegations as a validation criterion.

To provide context, the following describes the California Child Welfare Structured Decision-Making (SDM) Project, of which CFRA is a part. It is followed by a detailed description of CFRA and its use, then a description of the analytic framework used in examining the possibility that the use of the CFRA might result in disproportionate focus on African Americans and members of other minority groups. Succeeding sections describe analytic methods and the results of the analysis. The analysis results suggest that the use of CFRA will not result in disproportionate focus on African Americans or other nonwhite groups.

Background

California's Child Welfare SDM Project

CFRA is one of several instruments developed as part of California's Child Welfare SDM Project. The SDM project is a partnership between the California Department of Social Services, California counties, and the Children's Research Center. The first purpose of the SDM project is to add structure to child welfare case assessment to improve the consistency (reliability) and accuracy (validity) of the assessments and the decisions that flow from them. The intent of improved decisionmaking is to better identify those children at greatest risk of future maltreatment so that planners can allocate a large proportion of scarce treatment resources to them. Provision of more treatment resources to the highest risk children is intended to accomplish the second purpose of the SDM project: reduction of rates of maltreatment recurrence, child injury, placement in foster care, and rereferral or reinvestigation of families. The SDM project currently operates in 13 California counties or portions of counties, for a total of about 39% of the state population.

Description of CFRA

CFRA is a 20-item instrument completed by child welfare workers for each maltreatment report that receives an in-person investigation leading to the conclusion that maltreatment occurred or might have occurred. Completed at the conclusion of the investigation (usually within 30 days of the receipt of the report), CFRA provides an estimate of the likelihood that caregivers who are the subjects of maltreatment allegations will maltreat their children in the future. CFRA scores are used with two sets of guidelines. One set assists child welfare workers in deciding whether to open a case to provide services at the conclusion of an investigation. Workers use the second set to decide how frequently to visit the family and children if application of the first set of guidelines has resulted in an opened case. The case-opening guidelines encourage the opening of higher risk cases, where possible, and the contact-frequency guidelines suggest that once opened, higher risk cases should receive more contacts per month than lower risk cases, up to four contacts per month for very high-risk cases.

To develop CFRA, researchers collected data in 1998 on a random sample of 2,500 California child maltreatment reports investigated between January and June of 1995 in seven counties (San Bernardino, Orange, Los Angeles, Santa Clara, Alameda, Sacramento, and Humboldt) that were the original participants in the SDM project. The researchers obtained case records for each maltreatment report. Records included information available at the time of investigation and for a period of two years afterward. The researchers analyzed more than 100 items of information available at the investigation in relation to case-outcome information on substantiated maltreatment recurrences, child injuries, foster care placements, and reinvestigations occurring within two years of investigation. They identified 20 information items having statistically significant relations with maltreatment recurrence or the other outcomes mentioned above for inclusion in the assessment tool. One criterion for the inclusion of items in the tool was that they have low or insignificant correlations with racial or ethnic group membership.

CFRA consists of two 10-item subscales, one for measuring the likelihood of future neglect and the other for measuring the likelihood of physical or sexual abuse. To score CFRA, researchers use summed item scores on each scale to place cases into risk categories (low, moderate, high, and very high) using cut points. The scoring procedure takes the highest categorized score for either scale as the scored risk estimate.

With supervisory concurrence, the child welfare worker can override the risk score, increasing it by one risk category (e.g., from moderate to high risk). This is done when the child welfare worker finds that unusual family characteristics or circumstances not captured by the 20 items of the risk instrument suggest that the risk is actually greater than indicated using the scoring procedure alone. This is called a *discretionary override.*

The discretionary override was created in recognition of the need for skilled clinical assessment of families. It is clear that no brief, easy-to-use instrument like CFRA can possibly include among its items the multiplicity of infrequently occurring case circumstances that could powerfully affect risk to children. Skilled child welfare workers are therefore needed to assess conditions in the home to identify important factors that can influence risk that are not included in CFRA.

The CFRA scoring procedure also includes *policy overrides*. Child welfare program administrators from participating SDM counties identified a small number of infrequently occurring case characteristics thought to indicate heightened risk that were not included among the 20 CFRA items. When any of these items is found in a case, a policy override is exercised by increasing the risk level to very high risk, regardless of the original scored risk category. Discretionary and policy overrides are very infrequent in practice, occurring in only about 4% of cases. Thus, CFRA is flexible in its application, but the need to exercise this flexibility is rare. Child welfare workers deem CFRA risk estimates sufficiently accurate that they use them without overrides in a very high percentage of cases.

Recent analysis of CFRA ratings made at case opening by child welfare workers in two large and two small California counties, with cases followed prospectively for 16 months, shows predictive validity for CFRA (Johnson, 2001). Instrument scores correlated positively and significantly with maltreatment recurrence in large urban and suburban counties ($r = 0.22, p = .001, N = 224$ for Los Angeles, and $r = 0.19, p < .0005, N = 793$ for Orange County). Similar results were found in small rural counties ($r = 0.26, p = 0.024, N = 74$ for Humboldt County, and $r = 0.18, p = 0.065, N = 68$ for Sutter County). In Los Angeles and Orange Counties over the 16-month follow-up period, 3% to 4% of low-risk cases, 9% to 10% of moderate-risk cases, and 21% to 23% of high- and very high-risk cases had substantiated maltreatment recurrences. In Humboldt County, the recurrence rates were 0.0% for low-risk cases, 10.7% for moderate-risk cases, and 31.0% for high- and very high-risk cases. In Sutter County, the recurrence rates were 11.1% for low-risk cases, 16.7% for moderate-risk cases, 22.7% for high-risk cases, and 42.9% for very high-risk cases. Thus, in these California jurisdictions, cases assessed as being at high or very high risk for maltreatment recurrence were several times more likely to have substantiated maltreatment recurrences within a 16-month follow-up period than were low-risk cases. These findings demonstrate the utility of CFRA for classifying investigated children as to the likelihood of future maltreatment.

Analytic Framework

To be of use, any measuring instrument must possess two major properties—convergent validity and discriminant validity. *Convergent validity* is present when associations exist between instrument scores and measures of other constructs to which theory suggests the instrument scores should be related. The previously-described correlations between CFRA scale scores and subsequent substantiated maltreatment recurrence provide evidence of convergent validity for CFRA. As noted earlier, however, Morton (1999) argued that race plays a role in determining risk assessment scale scores and in determining whether maltreatment allegations will be substantiated by child welfare workers. Morton's view implies that the previously mentioned correlations supporting the convergent validity of CFRA may be spurious. This possibility was analyzed as part of the study.

Discriminant validity, the second property of measuring instruments, is evidenced by an absence of associations between instrument scores and measures of other constructs that theory or other considerations suggest should not be related (Campbell & Stanley, 1966; Crocker & Algina, 1986; Judd, Smith, & Kidder, 1991). Morton (1999) argued that the values of individual risk variables included in risk assessments are associated with race. He also argued that total risk instrument scores based on values of individual risk variables are associated with race. Substantiation of maltreatment allegations is a third variable that Morton argued is associated with race. Using substantiation of maltreatment allegations as a criterion in risk instrument validation studies, according to Morton, could cause members of nonwhite groups to score higher on risk instruments than they would if this validation criterion was unassociated with race. Examining the associations between risk variables, allegation substantiation, and race or ethnicity was, therefore, an important focus of the study.

Method

To examine these issues, the author conducted three analyses. The first tested the possibility that group members of color would score higher on CFRA than whites, indicating an association between CFRA scores and minority-group membership that might inappropriately subject people of color to disproportionately more frequent, intrusive state action. The researcher tested this possibility by comparing item scores, subscale scores, and overall CFRA scores across racial and ethnic groups using chi-square statistics or *t* tests, depending on the measurement level of items or scores. In this analysis, the author treated subscale and overall instrument scores as interval-level measurements and used *t* tests. The analysis helped determine whether evidence exists that CFRA disproportionately assesses group members of color as being at higher risk, perhaps not because they actually are at greater risk, but because it produces biased estimates of risk.

The second analysis examined the possibility that racially and ethnically biased CFRA items would, with disproportionate frequency, produce higher scores for group members of color, and these higher scores might combine with a biased tendency of child welfare workers to find maltreatment allegations substantiated more frequently in families of color. In this scenario, higher CFRA scores would tend to pair with substantiated maltreatment allegations and lower CFRA scores would tend to pair with a lack of substantiated maltreatment allegations. If this occurred during studies done to develop CFRA, it would appear that CFRA items were validly correlated with subsequent substantiation of maltreatment allegations, as intended. If race or ethnicity were operating as described previously, however, these correlations would actually be spurious. They would result from true correlations between race and ethnicity and CFRA scores on one hand, and correlations between race and ethnicity and substantiation of maltreatment allegations on the other. Computation of partial correlations between CFRA item or scale scores and substantiated maltreatment recurrence, controlling for racial or ethnic group membership, would reveal whether the apparent correlations between the CFRA item and scale scores and substantiated maltreatment were valid or spurious. To execute this test, the author computed first-order partial correlations between CFRA items and substantiated maltreatment recurrence during a two-year follow-up period, controlling for racial and ethnic group membership.

The third and final possible problem of disproportionate focus on racial/ethnic minorities examined in this analysis was with child welfare worker's decision whether to find maltreatment allegations substantiated when investigating maltreatment reports. A tendency on the part of child welfare workers to find maltreatment allegations substantiated with disproportionately high frequency among families of color might indicate bias in this variable. Use of allegation substantiation as a criterion variable, that is, as a means of judging the accuracy of a risk assessment item or instrument, would be rendered problematic under these circumstances. To test for possible bias in findings of substantiated maltreatment allegations, the author compared racial and ethnic groups to see whether child welfare workers were more likely to find substantiated allegations of maltreatment when investigating families of color than when investigating white families.

In all of these analyses, child welfare workers' characterizations of racial and ethnic group membership taken from case records were used to define race and ethnicity. Sizeable numbers of white, African American, and Latino cases were available for analysis.

Results

The Possibility of Higher Scores on CFRA for People of Color

The first set of results allows examination of the possibility that group members of color might score higher on CFRA than whites, indicating an association between scores and minority-group membership that could inappropriately subject people of color to disproportionately more frequent state action. Tables 8-1 and 8-2 present comparisons of racial and ethnic group scores on items for CFRA's Neglect and Abuse subscales. Table 8-3 summarizes the results across all the items in both CFRA scales. The first row of Table 8-3 indicates that whites had the highest percentage or mean score among the three groups (whites, African Americans, or Latinos) on 13 of the 20 items on the two CFRA scales. African Americans scored higher than the other groups on four items, and Latinos had the highest score on three items. The second row of Table 8-3 indicates that whites scored statistically significantly higher than at least one of the other groups on 11 of the 20 items on the two CFRA scales. African Americans scored significantly higher on three items and Latinos on two items. The clear indication is that whites score higher more often than African Americans or Latinos across the individual items of the CFRA.

Table 8-4 shows the average scores of the three groups on each of the CFRA scales (Neglect and Abuse) using raw scores (point totals from the items of the scales) and categorized scores, with raw score values placed in scoring categories (i.e., low, moderate, high, and very high) according to scale cut points. The table shows that overall, whites score slightly but statistically significantly higher, on average, than African Americans or Latinos on CFRA. These results provide no evidence that nonwhite-group CFRA scores are biased upward. Using CFRA, therefore, appears unlikely to subject members of nonwhite groups to disproportionately higher rates of case opening and service provision postinvestigation.

The Possibility of Spurious Correlations Between CFRA Items and Substantiated Maltreatment Recurrence

The second possibility examined in the analysis was that racially biased CFRA items would produce higher scores for group members of color on CFRA and that these higher scores might combine with a biased tendency of child welfare workers to find maltreatment allegations substantiated more frequently in families of color. This would produce apparently valid, but actually spurious, correlations between CFRA items and CFRA scales on one hand, and substantiation of maltreatment allegations on the other. The researcher tested this possibility using partial correlations between CFRA item, scale, or overall final scores and substantiated maltreatment recurrence. Tables 8-5, 8-6, and 8-7 show bivariate and partial correlations of individual CFRA items, CFRA scales, and CFRA overall final scores with substantiated maltreatment recurrence within two years of case opening. To identify spurious correlations, it is necessary to compare the magnitude, direction (that is, the sign, + or -), and statistical significance of a bivariate correlation of a CFRA item, scale, or final score and substantiated maltreatment recurrence (second column from left in Tables 8-5 through 8-7) with the magnitude, direction, and statistical significance of the corresponding partial correlation of that item, scale, or

Table 8-1: Analysis of Item Scores for African Americans, Latinos, and Whites—California Family Risk Assessment Neglect Scale

Neglect Scale Items	Highest-Scoring Group (Score); Statistical Significance of Differences with Other Groups	Next Highest-Scoring Group (Score); Statistical Significance of Differences with Other Groups	Lowest-Scoring Group (Score); Statistical Significance of Differences with Other Groups
N1. Current complaint is for neglect	AA[a] (67%); no significant differences with other groups	W[a] (64%); no significant differences with other groups	L[a] (62%); no significant differences with other groups
N2. Number of prior investigations (mean item scores)	W (1.15); significantly higher than AA and L	AA (.98); significantly lower than W, no different than L	L (.86); significantly lower than W, no different than AA
N3. Household has previously received child protective services	W (24%); significantly higher than L, no different than AA	AA (22%); no significant differences with other groups	L (17%); significantly lower than W, no different than AA
N4. Four or more children involved in incident	L (16%); significantly higher than W and AA	AA (11%); significantly lower than L, higher than W	W (7%); significantly lower than L and AA
N5. Age of youngest child in the house (percentage younger than 2 years)	AA (35%); significantly higher than W, no different than L	L (32%); significantly higher than W, no different than AA	W (27%); significantly lower than AA and L
N6. Primary caregiver provides physical care inconsistent with child's needs	W (32%); significantly higher than AA and L	AA (26%); significantly lower than W, no different than L	L (26%); significantly lower than W, no different than AA
N7. Primary caregiver has past or current mental health problem	W (8%); significantly higher than AA and L	L (4%); significantly lower than W, no different than AA	AA (4%); significantly lower than W, no different than AA
N8. Primary caregiver has past or current drug or alcohol problem (mean item scores)	W (0.61); significantly higher than AA and L	AA (0.47); significantly lower than W, no different than L	L (0.42); significantly lower than W, no different than AA
N9. Characteristics of children in the household (mean item scores)	AA (0.39); significantly higher than W and L	W (0.27); significantly lower than AA, no different than L	L (0.25); significantly lower than AA, no different than W
N10. Housing (mean item scores)	W (0.26); no significant differences with other groups	AA (0.24); no significant differences with other groups	L (0.18); no significant differences with other groups

Note: AA = African Americans; W = whites; L = Latinos. Higher scores indicate higher risk. For items at the nominal level of measurement, the author used the chi-square test with $a = 0.05$. For items measured at the ordinal level, the author used analysis of variance with post hoc multiple comparison tests and $a = 0.05$.

[a] Sample sizes: AA, $N = 413$; L, $N = 682$; W, $N = 1103$.

Table 8-2: Analysis of Item Scores for African Americans, Latinos, and Whites—California Family Risk Assessment Abuse Scale

Abuse Scale Items	Highest-Scoring Group (Score); Statistical Significance of Differences with Other Groups	Next Highest-Scoring Group (Score); Statistical Significance of Differences with Other Groups	Lowest-Scoring Group (Score); Statistical Significance of Differences with Other Groups
A1. Current complaint is for abuse	L[a] (62%); significantly higher than W and AA	W[a] (47%); significantly lower than L, no different than AA	AA[a] (47%); significantly lower than L, no different than W
A2. Number of prior abuse investigations (mean item scores)	W (0.55); significantly higher than AA and L	L (0.45); significantly lower than W, no different than AA	AA (0.36); significantly lower than W, no different than L
A3. Household has previously received child protective services	W (24%); significantly higher than L, no different than AA	AA (22%); no significant differences with other groups	L (17%); significantly lower than W, no different than AA
A4. Prior injury to a child due to child abuse or neglect	AA (26%); significantly higher than L, no different than W	W (25%); significantly higher than L, no different than AA	L (18%); significantly lower than W and AA
A5. Primary caregiver's assessment of incident (blames child and justifies maltreatment)	W (2.4%); significantly higher than AA, no different than L	L (1.8%); no significant differences with other groups	AA (1.7%); significantly lower than W, no different than L
A6. Domestic violence in the household in the past year	W (11%); significantly higher than AA, no different than L	L (10%); significantly higher than AA, no different than W	AA (5%); significantly lower than W and L
A7. Primary caregiver characteristics (mean item scores)	L (0.43); no significant differences with other groups	W (0.38); no significant differences with other groups	AA (0.33); no significant differences with other groups
A8. Primary caregiver has history of abuse or neglect as a child	W (15%); significantly higher than AA and L)	AA (9%); significantly lower than W, no different than L	L (8%); significantly lower than W, no different than AA
A9. Secondary caregiver has past or current alcohol or drug problem	W (23%); significantly higher than AA, no different than L	L (20%); significantly higher than AA, no different than W	AA (13%); significantly lower than W and L
A10. Characteristics of children in the household (mean item scores)	W (0.28); no significant differences with other groups	L (0.26); no significant differences with other groups	AA (0.24); no significant differences with other groups

Note: AA = African Americans; W = whites; L = Latinos. Higher scores indicate higher risk. For items at the nominal level of measurement, the author used the chi-square test with $a = 0.05$. For items measured at the ordinal level, the author used analysis of variance with post hoc multiple comparison tests and $a = 0.05$.

[a] Sample sizes: AA, $N = 413$; L, $N = 682$; W, $N = 1103$.

Table 8-3: Summary of Racial and Ethnic Group Item Differences on California Family Risk Assessment Items

Item	Whites	African Americans	Latinos
Number of times had the highest raw average or percentage score	13	4	3
Number of times had the highest raw average or percentage score and was statistically significantly higher than one or more other groups	11	3	2

Table 8-4: Comparison of Risk Assessment Raw Scale Scores, Scale Scores Categorized, and Final Risk Assessment for African Americans, Latinos, and Whites

Overall Scale Raw and Categorized Scores and Final Risk Level	Highest-Scoring Group (Mean Score); Statistical Significance of Differences with Other Groups	Next Highest-Scoring Group (Mean Score); Statistical Significance of Differences with Other Groups	Lowest-Scoring Group (Mean Score); Statistical Significance of Differences with Other Groups
Abuse raw score (range: 0–14)	W[a] (2.90); significantly higher than AA, no different than L	L[a] (2.75); significantly higher than AA, no different than W	AA[a] (2.31); significantly lower than W and L
Abuse raw score categorized (low, moderate, high, very high; range: 1–4)	W (1.92); significantly higher than AA, no different than L	L (1.87); significantly higher than AA, no different than W	AA (1.72); significantly lower than W and L
Neglect raw score (range: 0–13)	W (3.98); significantly higher than L, no different than AA	AA (3.78); significantly higher than L, no different than W	L (3.31); significantly lower than W and AA
Neglect raw score categorized (low, moderate, high, very high; range: 1–4)	W (2.24); significantly higher than L, no different than AA	AA (2.14); no significant differences with other groups	L (2.03); significantly lower than W, no different than AA
Final risk score (range: 1–4)	W (2.50); significantly higher than L and AA	AA (2.37); significantly lower than W, no different than L	L (2.34); significantly lower than W, no different than AA

Note: W = whites; L = Latinos; AA = African Americans. The researchers tested differences using analysis of variance with post hoc multiple comparison tests and $a = 0.05$.

[a] Sample sizes: AA, $N = 413$; L, $N = 682$; W, $N = 1103$.

final score and substantiated maltreatment recurrence controlling for racial or ethnic group membership (third, fourth, and fifth columns from the left in Tables 8-5 through 8-7). If the partial correlation of an item with substantiated maltreatment recurrence differs in direction (that is, sign) from the bivariate correlation or is statistically insignificant, evidence exists that the bivariate relation of the item to maltreatment recurrence is spurious. When this occurs, it means that racial or ethnic group membership (the control variable) is determining both CFRA scores and decisions to substantiate maltreatment recurrence.

Examination of the bivariate and partial correlations of CFRA item, scale, and final scores with substantiated maltreatment allegations reveals no evidence that race or

Table 8-5: California Family Risk Assessment Neglect Scale Item Bivariate and Partial Correlations with Maltreatment Recurrence, Controlling for Membership in Racial and Ethnic Group

Neglect Scale Items Bivariate Correlations with Maltreatment Recurrence*	**Partial Correlations with Maltreatment**	**Recurrence Controlling for Membership in Racial and Ethnic Group**		
		African American**	**Latino****	**White****
N1. Current complaint is for neglect	.10	.11	.10	.10
N2. Number of prior investigations (mean item scores)	.23	.23	.22	.22
N3. Household has previously received child protective services	.17	.17	.16	.16
N4. Four or more children involved in child abuse or neglect incident	.10	.10	.10	.11
N5. Age of youngest child in the house (percentage younger than 2 years)	.08	.08	.08	.09
N6. Primary caregiver provides physical care inconsistent with child's needs	.16	.16	.16	.15
N7. Primary caregiver has past or current mental health problem	.11	.11	.11	.11
N8. Primary caregiver has past or current drug or alcohol problem (mean item scores)	.15	.15	.15	.14
N9. Characteristics of children in the household (mean item scores)	.12	.12	.11	.12
N10. Housing (mean item scores)	.12	.12	.12	.12

* All correlations are statistically significant at $p < 0.05$.

** The sample size for all correlation coefficients is 2,208.

ethnicity is simultaneously determining CFRA scores and findings of substantiated maltreatment. Looking in any row of Tables 8-5 to 8-7, the partial correlations (within each racial or ethnic group) between the CFRA item, scale, and final scores in that row and substantiation of maltreatment have the same direction (sign) and virtually identical magnitude. Also, all the bivariate and partial correlations are statistically significant. Thus, the item, scale, and final scores are correlated with substantiation of maltreatment recurrence even when race and ethnicity is controlled statistically. In conclusion,

Table 8-6: California Family Risk Assessment Abuse Scale Item Bivariate and Partial Correlations with Maltreatment Recurrence, Controlling for Membership in Racial and Ethnic Group

Abuse Scale Items	Bivariate Correlations with Maltreatment Recurrence*	Partial Correlations with Maltreatment Recurrence Controlling for Membership in Racial and Ethnic Group		
		African American	Latino	White
A1. Current complaint is for abuse	-.11	-.11	-.10	-.10
A2. Number of prior abuse investigations (mean item scores)	.15	.15	.15	.15
A3. Household has previously received child protective services	.17	.17	.17	.16
A4. Prior injury to a child due to child abuse or neglect	.12	.12	.12	.12
A5. Primary caregiver's assessment of incident (blames child and justifies maltreatment)	.04	.04	.04	.04
A6. Domestic violence in the household In the past year	.09	.08	.09	.08
A7. Primary caregiver characteristics (mean item scores)	.09	.09	.09	.09
A8. Primary caregiver has history of abuse or neglect as a child	.08	.08	.08	.07
A9. Secondary caregiver has past or current alcohol or drug problem	.10	.10	.10	.09
A10. Characteristics of children in the house-hold (mean item scores)	.08	.08	.08	.08

Note: The sample size for all correlation coefficients is 2,208.

* All correlations are statistically significant at $p < .05$.

no evidence exists of racial or ethnic bias in the relationship between CFRA items or scale scores and decisions to find substantiated maltreatment.

The Possibility of Racial or Ethnic Bias in Decisions to Find Substantiation of Maltreatment

The third and final possible problem with regard to racial or ethnic bias that this analysis examined was whether child welfare workers are disproportionately more likely to find that maltreatment allegations are substantiated when assessing allegations against

Table 8-7: California Family Risk Assessment Scale Bivariate and Partial Correlations with Maltreatment Recurrence, Controlling for Membership in Racial and Ethnic Group

Neglect Scale Items	Bivariate Correlations with Maltreatment Recurrence*	Partial Correlations with Maltreatment Recurrence Controlling for Membership in Racial and Ethnic Group		
		African American	Latino	White
Abuse raw score (range: 0–14)	.18	.18	.18	.18
Neglect raw score (range: 0–13)	.28	.28	.28	.27
Abuse raw score categorized (low, moderate, high, very high; range: 1–4)	.18	.18	.180	.17
Neglect raw score categorized (low, moderate, high, very high; range: 1–4)	.28	.28	.28	.28
Final risk score (range: 1–4)	.28	.28	.28	.27

* All correlations are statistically significant at $p < 0.05$.

Table 8-8: Maltreatment Substantiation as a Criterion for Validating the California Family Risk Assessment Instrument: Rates of Substantiation During Two-Year Follow-Up Period by Placement Experience

Placement Experience Breakdown	Group With Highest Substantiation Rate (Rate); Statistical Significance of Differences with Other Groups	Group with Next Highest Substantiation Rate (Rate); Statistical Significance of Differences with Other Groups	Group with Lowest Substantiation Rate (Rate); Statistical Significance of Differences with Other Groups
Cases with no placement during follow-up	W (15.7%); significantly higher than AA and L	L (10.5%); significantly lower than W, no different than AA	AA (9.7%); significantly lower than W, no different than L
Cases with one or more children placed during follow-up	W (92.1%); significantly higher than AA, no different than L	L (84.5%); no significant differences with other groups	AA (81.5%); significantly lower than W, no different than L
Cases with no children placed at time of sample investigation	W (30.5%); significantly higher than L and AA	L (21.8%); significantly lower than W, no different than AA	AA (15.8%); significantly lower than W, no different than L
Cases with one or more children placed during sample investigation	AA (23.0%); no significant differences with other groups	W (20.9%); no significant differences with other groups	L (16.9%); no significant differences with other groups
Cases with no placements during sample investigation or follow-up	W (21.3%); significantly higher than L and AA	L (12.7%); significantly lower than W, no different than AA	AA (10.4%); significantly lower than W, no different than L
Cases with one or more children placed during sample investigation or follow-up	W (30.5%); no significant differences with other groups	AA (27.4%); no significant differences with other groups	L (26.5%); no significant differences with other groups

Note: W = whites; L = Latinos; AA = African Americans. The researcher used a chi-square test with $a = .05$ for all comparisons.

families of color. Table 8-8 compares rates of substantiation for different racial or ethnic groups during a two-year follow-up period, broken down by foster care placement experience. The data show that regardless of placement experience, whites are more likely than African Americans or Latinos to have substantiated maltreatment allegations made against them within two years of case opening. Bias against people of color does not appear to be a valid reason for rejecting substantiation of maltreatment allegations as a criterion for use in validating CFRA.

Summary and Conclusions

This chapter has described CFRA and examined some of its psychometric characteristics. CFRA is an instrument for classifying children investigated for child maltreatment as to the likelihood that they will experience subsequent maltreatment by their caregivers. This classification approach arms practitioners with the knowledge necessary to allocate a larger share of scarce maltreatment-prevention resources to higher risk children. The author has checked its validity for classifying investigated families in this way in a prospective analysis with positive results in both large urban or suburban and small rural communities.

The analysis conducted here examined three possible problems with racial bias in research-based risk assessment instruments (Morton, 1999) to see whether these problems were present with use of CFRA. One issue examined was whether members of nonwhite groups scored higher than whites. If true, this might disproportionately and inappropriately subject people of color to intrusive state child protection action. A second possible problem analyzed was the possible spuriousness of apparently valid correlations between CFRA item, scale, and overall final scores and subsequent maltreatment. These correlations could be spurious if child welfare workers consciously or unconsciously took into account racial or ethnic group membership while scoring CFRA items and also when deciding the accuracy of subsequent maltreatment allegations. The final possibility studied was whether nonwhites were more likely to have maltreatment allegations substantiated than whites. This could bias allegation substantiation as a criterion variable for judging the validity of research-based risk assessment instruments and disproportionately subject racial and ethnic minorities to state child-protection action.

None of the possible problems examined here was present in CFRA. Whites scored slightly higher on the CFRA than people of color. The researcher found all CFRA items to be validly correlated with maltreatment recurrence, using partial correlation analysis to control for the effects of racial and ethnic group membership. Finally, the author found that maltreatment allegations against whites are more likely to be judged accurate (substantiated) than are allegations against people of color.

In summary, detailed analysis of CFRA did not indicate that use of this risk assessment instrument would result in disproportionately frequent intrusive state child-protection action against people of color.

References

Brissett-Chapman, S. (1997). Child protection risk assessment and African American children: Cultural ramifications for families and communities. *Child Welfare, 76*, 45–63.

Campbell, D. T., & Stanley, J. C. (1966). *Experimental and quasi-experimental designs for research*. Boston: Houghton Mifflin.

Crocker, L., & Algina, J. (1986). *Introduction to classical and modern test theory.* New York: Holt, Rinehart, and Winston.

Johnson, W. (2001). [Unpublished data of the California Child Welfare Structured Decision Making Project].

Judd, C. M., Smith, E. R., & Kidder, L. H. (1991). *Research methods in social relations* (6th ed.). New York: Holt, Rinehart, and Winston.

Morton, T. (1999). The increasing colorization of America's child welfare system: The overrepresentation of African American children. *Policy & Practice, 57*(4), 22–30.

CHAPTER 9

Factors that Predict the Decision to Place a Child in Substitute Care

Gardenia Harris, Gail Tittle, and John Poertner

Substantiated reports of child abuse and neglect require investigators to determine where a child will be placed. Some children remain at home, whereas others are placed in out-of-home care. The outcome of this decision is critical to the child and the family. Placing children out of their homes may be necessary for their immediate safety, but it can also be very traumatic when they are removed from the people they know and placed with strangers, breaking important bonds. On the other hand, leaving children at home may keep them in an unsafe situation and put them at risk for additional abuse or neglect. With the complexity of the factors involved in making these decisions, it is easy for a worker or a child welfare system to err in either direction when faced with the question of which option is best to serve a child.

Literature Review

An extensive literature search on the decision to place identifies a wide range of predictive factors. Most people would agree that many of these are appropriate and important. For example, a past history of abuse or neglect seems to be a reasonable predictor of child safety. Other factors, such as the race of the child or caregiver are either inappropriate, representing a bias, or are indicators of another factor, such as poverty. This chapter will focus on the issue of race as a predictor of the decision to remove a child from the home.

Several studies have identified race as a predictive factor of the decision to place a child in foster care (Benedict, White, & Stallings, 1987; Groeneveld & Giovannoni, 1977; Lindsey, 1994; Phillips, Haring, & Shyne, 1972; Segal & Schwartz, 1985; U.S. Department of Health and Human Services [DHHS], 1997). The majority of studies that examined race and ethnicity found that race and ethnicity exerted a significant influence over the decision to place children in foster care. For example, DHHS (1997) reported that nationally, the majority of white (72%) and Hispanic (60%) children received in-home services, but most African American children (56%) were placed in foster care. Similarly, Groeneveld and Giovannoni (1977) found that workers were more likely to remove neglected children of color from their homes than neglected white children. Phillips et al. (1972) reported that although the race of the mother did not affect placement decisions, the race of the father did. Children from homes with an African American father present were far more likely to be placed in care, however, children from households with a white father present were significantly more likely to receive services in their homes.

The results of other studies further indicated that race affects placement decisions, albeit in a more complex way. Although Benedict et al. (1987) found that similar proportions of African American and white children were placed in care for abuse, neglect, or abandonment, the reason for placement varied by race. Caseworkers were more likely to place nonmaltreated African American children in foster care because of parental illness or death. In contrast, workers were more likely to place nonmaltreated white children in foster care because of housing, financial, or family problems. Furthermore, the type of placement varied by race. Workers placed a larger proportion of white children in agency foster homes. In contrast, they placed African American children more often with relatives, with friends, or in group care.

Lindsey (1994) also found that the reason for placement varied by race. He found that for dependency cases, African American and Hispanic children were twice as likely to be placed in foster care than were white children. Furthermore, African American children were at a higher risk of placement than white or Hispanic children when placement was due to environmental factors. When parental condition was a major reason for placement, however, African American (0.89) and Hispanic (0.72) children had lower odds of being placed than white (1.00) children did. In cases of neglect, workers placed African American children as often as white children. In comparison, they placed Hispanic children less often (0.60) for neglect than white children. Finally, Lindsey found that placement rates did not vary by race in cases that involved abuse, alcohol, and drugs.

Echoing the findings of Benedict et al. (1987), Lindsey (1994) discovered that although children of color were disproportionately represented in foster care, when children who received services were used as the base population, there was only a minimal association between race and placement. Workers placed white and African American children equally often. Hispanic children had a slightly lower chance of being placed than did white children.

Conversely, other studies indicated that being African American was negatively associated with the decision to place children in care. Segal and Schwartz (1985) found that although white children in a short-term emergency treatment facility tended to be discharged to a substitute care setting, African American children were more often returned to their birthfamilies. These authors speculated that this finding could reflect the shortage of substitute care alternatives available for African American children. Finally, Katz, Hampton, Newberger, Bowles, and Snyder (1986) and Runyan, Gould, Trost, and Loda (1982) concluded that race was not a significant factor in the placement decision.

Method

The Children and Family Research Center conducted two studies that examined factors that contributed to the decision to place children in foster care, seeking data on factors identified in the literature. Both studies used a retrospective cross-sectional design, with the first study using data exclusively from a state administrative database, and the follow-up study using both the state administrative database and case records. Both studies drew a random sample of cases, with the first study using cases statewide and the follow-up study choosing cases nearly evenly distributed between two middle-sized cities.

Both studies consisted of two groups of children. All of the children in the study had one indicated report of abuse and neglect in Illinois between 1995 and 1998. This report was the child's first case opening in the child welfare system. The researchers only selected those children younger than 18 years of age at the time of the case opening. One group of children remained at home. Caseworkers placed the second group of children in foster care. For children who were placed, the researchers only selected those cases that opened with a first placement in a family foster home, relative foster home, or specialized foster home. They defined children in intact family cases as those cases in which the family as a whole received services from the state child welfare agency and no children in the family were in substitute care.

The model-building process for each of the two studies focused on seeking the most parsimonious collection of variables that differentiated children who were placed in foster care from those who remained at home. Model building followed the strategy suggested by Dattalo (1994), who recommended that researchers examine the relationship between prospective independent variables and the dependent variable prior to the logistic regression analysis and that they use an alpha level of 0.15 to select variables for further analysis. The researchers then performed forward stepwise logistic regression including all of the independent variables identified as having an alpha level of 0.15 or less. They then examined the resulting model for variable interaction effects and derived a final model.

The First Study

For the first study, which used exclusively administrative data, the authors selected a random sample of cases from each group (foster care cases and intact cases) for the purpose of developing the placement decision model. They selected this sample size to meet the criteria of 95% certainty that the estimated parameter was within 3% of the true value. Consequently, they drew a random sample of 1,806 cases for the purposes of model development. This sample consisted of 842 children who were placed in foster care and 964 who received services at home.

Once the model was developed, they researchers tested it on a sample that met the criteria of 99% certainty that the estimated parameter was within 2% of the true value. This was a random sample of 4,946 cases. The test sample consisted of 2,044 children who were placed in foster care and 2,902 children who remained in their homes.

Many of the variables used in this study had highly skewed distributions, making them inadequate for further analysis. The authors coded variables with either a one or a zero to indicate the presence or absence of a condition to generate groups or categories in these variables to allow for statistical analysis.

Included as variables for this study were the race of the child and the race of the caregiver. Findings regarding the child showed that a slightly higher percentage (53.7%) of the children who were placed in foster care were African American, compared with the children who received services in their homes (45.7%). A slightly lower percentage (38%) of the children who were placed in foster care were white, compared with the children who received services in their homes (42%). Hispanic children comprised a very small proportion of the sample, with only 5.6% of the total children placed in foster care being Hispanic.

As for the caregiver's race, a larger percentage (52.6%) of the caregivers of children in placement were African American, compared with the percentage (45.3%) of caregivers of children who remained in the home. Of the caregivers of children in placement, 40% were white, compared with 43.8% of the caregivers of children who remained in their homes. A slightly larger percentage of the caregivers of children who remained at home were Hispanic (8.7%) compared with the percentage (5.6%) of caregivers of the children who were in foster care.

Using an alpha level of 0.15 as a screening criterion to ensure important variables were identified, the researchers performed a forward conditional logistic regression analysis. The child's race as white, as African American, or as Hispanic, and the caregiver's race as African American or as Hispanic met the criteria for entry into the model.

Forward conditional logistic regression analysis yielded a model that contained 12 predictor variables, as indicated in Table 9-1. This model classified 75.2% of the cases correctly. The analysis correctly classified Eighty-two percent of the intact family cases, compared with 68% of the placement cases. When the researchers tested the model with the second sample, analysis correctly classified 85% of the intact cases and 74% of the placement cases. Significant predictors of placement for both samples were:

- the number of home visits during the investigation,
- the number of previous indicated allegations,
- the child being an infant (younger than 6 months of age),
- the number of contacts made during the investigation,
- the number of allegations in the most recent reports,
- the number of previous indicated reports,
- the allegation of lack of supervision,
- the caregiver never having been married, and
- the child being a toddler (6 months to 3 years of age).

The race of the child and the race of the caregiver did not remain a factor in this final model, however. This does not mean that race was not a factor in decisionmaking, but simply indicates that for the data available for this analysis, the race variable did not meet the statistical conditions to be included in the model.

The number of investigator visits to the home and the number of other investigator contacts during the investigation are predictors of placement outcomes. One or more investigator visits to the home decreases the probability of the child being placed in foster care. Four or more other contacts during the investigation increase the probability of placement in foster care. When investigators make four or more other contacts, a child is 3.3 times more likely to be placed in foster care than when the investigator makes three or fewer other contacts.

A child's allegation history is predictive of the placement decision. Children with a previous indicated allegation are more likely to be placed in foster care. Also, the child's

Table 9-1: First Study Logistic Regression Models Test Results

Variable	*B*	*SE*	Significance	Wald	Exp(*B*)
Home visit	-0.91	0.10	.00	-.11	0.40
Number of previous indicated allegations	0.26	0.03	.00	.09	1.30
Infant	1.58	0.11	.00	.17	4.85
Number of contacts	1.19	0.09	.00	.16	3.28
Number of allegations in most recent report	-2.50	0.08	.00	-.37	0.08
Number of previous indicated reports	1.06	0.11	.00	.12	2.88
Lack of supervision	0.48	0.09	.00	.06	1.62
Risk of harm	0.19	0.10	.06	.02	1.21
Never married	0.44	0.08	.00	.07	1.55
Child age from birth to 3 years	0.68	0.10	.00	.08	1.97
Child age 9–12 years	-0.04	0.13	.75	.00	0.96
Reporter being family or friend	-0.16	0.11	.14	-.01	0.86

age is predictive of the placement decision. Infants (from birth to 6 months) or toddlers (6 months to 3 years) are more likely to be placed. An infant is 4.8 times more likely to be placed, and a toddler is twice as likely to be placed.

The number and type of allegations in the most recent report are also predictive of placement. If the report contains three or more allegations, the child is more likely to receive services in the home. Children whose most recent report contains three or more allegations have a 92% decreased probability of being placed in foster care compared with children with reports that contained one or two allegations. If the most severe allegation is "lack of supervision," however, the probability of placement increases by 2.6 times. The last variable in the model is a never-married caregiver. If the caregiver has never been married, the child is 1.5 times more likely to be placed.

The use of administrative data for this study limited the variables that could be included in the analysis as well as how the researchers could operationalize the variables identified in the literature review. Therefore, the authors conducted a follow-up study adding case record data.

The Follow-Up Study

Although using similar administrative data as the previous study, the authors added new variables to this study from case record data. Due to the constraints of using case record data, they used a smaller sample. Although the original sample consisted of 570 cases, a combination of discrepancies between administrative data and case records as well as missing data left the final sample for this study at 393 child cases. It was composed of case records of 190 children who were placed in foster care and 203 children who received services in the home.

Again, many of the variables used in the follow-up study had highly skewed distributions, making them inadequate for further analysis. The authors used dummy coding to generate groups or categories in these variables to allow for statistical analysis.

Examining the race of the caregiver, this study found that a larger percentage (37.9%) of the caregivers of the children in placement were African American compared with the percentage (30.5%) of caregivers of the children who remained in the home (Table 9-2). Slightly more than 60% of the caregivers of the children in placement were white compared with 66% of the caregivers of children who remained in their homes.

Having used an alpha level of 0.15 as a screening criterion to ensure important variables were identified, the authors performed a forward conditional logistic regression analysis. The child's race as white or as African American and the caregiver's race as African American met the criteria for entry into the model.

Forward conditional logistic regression analysis yielded a model that identified nine variables that predicted the decision to place a child into substitute care. This model accurately classified almost 78% of the intact family cases and nearly 86% of the placement cases, or 83.3% of all cases. Significant predictors of placement were:

- the child being an infant (younger than 6 months of age),
- family size,
- caregiver-to-child interaction,
- abuse and neglect history,
- the number of allegations in the most recent report,
- the reporter being anonymous,
- the reporter working for the Department of Children and Family Services,
- the number of other contacts, and
- the interaction variable of abuse and neglect history by risk of harm.

As in the previous study, however, neither race of the child nor race of the caregiver remained a factor in the final model.

Table 9-2: Follow-Up Study Logistic Regression Models Test Results

Variable	*B*	*SE*	Significance	Wald	Exp(*B*)
Infant	1.704	0.418	.00	16.590	5.498
Family size	-0.275	0.108	.02	5.675	0.773
Caregiver-to-child interaction	0.372	0.104	.00	12.678	1.450
Abuse and neglect history	-0.684	0.338	.04	4.088	0.504
Number of allegations in most recent report	-2.232	0.361	.00	38.156	0.107
Reporter being anonymous	-3.728	1.291	.00	8.336	0.024
Reporter being state child welfare agency	1.498	0.581	.01	6.661	4.475
Number of other contacts	1.714	0.364	.00	22.130	5.551
Abuse and neglect history and risk of harm	-1.990	0.973	.04	4.180	0.137

One of the strongest predicators for a child being placed in foster care was the child's age. If the child was an infant (birth to 6 months old), he or she was 5.5 times more likely to be placed into care than to remain at home following an indicated report of abuse or neglect. Family structure was also predictive of the placement decision. The child's family size was indicative of placement. Children in homes with more than four people in the family were 23% less likely to be placed in care. Children who were at risk based on caregiver-to-child interaction were 45% more likely to be placed into care.

A child's allegation history was predictive of placement outcomes. Surprisingly, a history of abuse and neglect decreased the odds of a child entering foster care. Children in families with a history of abuse and neglect were 50% less likely to come into care. Another negative predictor for entering care was the number of allegations in the most recent report. If the most recent report had three or more allegations, the child was less likely to be placed in foster care. In fact, these children were at an 89% decreased probability of being placed in foster care compared with children with reports that contained one or two allegations.

Several case processing variables were predictive of child placement. In cases in which the initial reporter of the suspected child abuse and neglect was anonymous, the child was 98% less likely to enter foster care. In contrast, if the Department of Children and Family Services made the initial report, the child was 4.5 times more likely to enter care. The number of other caseworker contacts made during the investigation was also a strong predictor of child placement. If four or more other contacts were made, the child was 5.6 times more likely to be placed into care. If abuse and neglect history and risk of harm were accounted for together, a child with an abuse and neglect history with the most severe allegation being risk of harm was 86% less likely to come into care.

Discussion

It is cause for hope that variables such as the race of the child or caregiver and the office that investigated the report did not enter the model. Some investigators find that these variables influence child welfare decisionmaking when they should not (DHHS, 1997; Groeneveld & Giovannoni, 1977). Neither of the two placement studies found variables of these types to be predictive of the placement decision. Race; economic status; family characteristics, with the exception of family size; and location of the child welfare agency were not indicators of placement decisions.

Several variables found to be predictive of the placement decision in the study using administrative data only were not predictive in the follow-up study. The authors found that several variables were predictive of child placement in both studies. These variables are the child being an infant, the number of allegations in the most recent report, the risk of harm, and the number of other contacts. In adding case record data in the second study, the authors entered new variables in the model that proved predictive of child placement. These variables are caregiver-to-child interaction and abuse and neglect history. The inclusion of a variable that accounts for the interaction of the abuse and neglect with the risk of harm allegation also helps clarify that history of abuse and neglect when accompanied by a most severe allegation of risk of harm reduces the probability of placement.

From a child welfare policy and practice point of view, the results of this study are positive. The variables found to be predictive of child placement in both studies are characteristics of the child, characteristics of the family, abuse and neglect history, and the investigative process. Rather than being factors that seemed to show a bias in the child welfare system, the majority of predictor variables were factors that appeared logical and suitable for use in decisionmaking. The age of the child for infants was related to the child being placed in foster care. Although age is not a risk factor in and of itself, the younger a child is, the more vulnerable he or she is likely to be. Therefore, as in earlier studies, this study indicated that infancy was a pivotal factor in the decision to place a child in care (DHHS, 1997; Lindsey, 1994; Phillips et al., 1972; Segal & Schwartz, 1985). A larger number of contacts with the child's school, medical personnel, or other involved parties made by the worker in the process of investigating the report was found to be related to a higher probability of placement. This may indicate the worker's uncertainty about the child's safety and the need to collect as much information as possible to clarify the situation. In addition, the number of allegations in the most recent report and the risk of harm are both logical indicators for placement.

This study had several limitations. A cross-sectional retrospective study can only demonstrate how some independent variables might predict the dependent variable. This design does not allow causal judgments. A study using a more complex design or a longitudinal design is needed to attempt to determine which case characteristics or worker behaviors more fully explain the placement decision.

These studies have many measurement problems. The researchers operationalized variables based on what was available in the administrative database or the case files. Therefore, the adequacy of the measures and their reliability are open to question. Critical variables such as the presence of mental illness or substance abuse were determined based solely on worker judgment. It is likely that workers vary greatly in their ability to assess these conditions. As is the case in most social research, additional limitations exist related to the logistic regression. These include some variables being badly skewed and the subsequent need to recategorize them, and problems of multicollinearity between the independent variables.

In spite of the normal limitations of studies such as this, the results do provide insights into the decision to place a child into substitute care. Continued research should be done to deepen our understanding of placement decisionmaking. Further research adding variables related to the cognitive processes of the decisionmaker would shed additional light on the decision of whether a child is placed in substitute care.

References

Benedict, M. I., White, R. B., and Stallings, R. (1987). Race and length of stay in foster care. *Social Work Research and Abstracts, 23,* 23–26.

Dattalo, P. (1994). A comparison of discriminant analysis and logistic regression. *Journal of Social Service Research, 19,* 121–144.

Groeneveld, L. P., & Giovannoni, J. M. (1977). Disposition of child abuse and neglect cases. *Social Work Research and Abstracts, 13*(2), 24–30.

Katz, M. H., Hampton, R. L., Newberger, E. H., Bowles, R. T., & Snyder, J. C. (1986). Returning children home: Clinical decision making in cases of child abuse and neglect. *American Journal of Orthopsychiatry, 56,* 253–262.

Lindsey, D. (1994). *The welfare of children.* New York: Oxford University Press.

Phillips, M. H., Haring, B., & Shyne, A. (1972). *A model for intake decisions in child welfare.* New York: Child Welfare League of America.

Runyan, D. K., Gould, C. L., Trost, D. C., & Loda, F. A. (1982). Determinants of foster care placement for the maltreated child. *Child Abuse and Neglect, 6,* 343–350.

Segal, U. A., & Schwartz, S. (1985). Factors affecting placement decisions of children following short-term emergency care. *Child Abuse & Neglect, 9,* 543–548.

U.S. Department of Health and Human Services, Children's Bureau. (1997). *National study of protective, preventive, and reunification services delivered to children and their families.* Washington, DC: U.S. Government Printing Office.

CHAPTER 10

The Entry of Children from the Welfare System into Foster Care

Differences by Race

Robert M. Goerge and Bong Joo Lee

Over the past decade, Illinois, as well as many other large states, has seen a larger proportion of African American children being placed in foster care than children of other ethnicities. A number of potential explanations could account for this. These range from differences in parenting and other human capital characteristics in families of different ethnicities to differences in the characteristics of neighborhoods in which families live. This chapter explores some of the possible explanations.

This chapter reports on an analysis of families who entered the Illinois welfare system from 1991 to 1998 and the placement of their children into foster care. These families began to receive either Aid to Families with Dependent Children (AFDC) or Temporary Aid to Needy Families (TANF) in these years and had not participated in the income maintenance program for at least two years before they began to receive assistance. This study followed the children in these families during from the time of entry through the end of 1998 to see whether they were placed in any type of out-of-home care supervised by the Illinois Department of Child and Family Services (DCFS).

Not all children who enter foster care come from families that have received cash assistance, but about 60% are from these families (Goerge et al., 2000). The initial reason for following these children was to evaluate the effects of welfare reform (Goerge &

Authors' Note: The data for this chapter were initially developed at the "For Better and For Worse: State Welfare Reform and the Well-being of Low-Income Families and Children" conference, Joint Center for Poverty Research, September 16–17, 1999, in Washington, DC.

Lee, 1997). Over and above the issues of welfare reform, however, the cash-assistance caseload provides an adequate risk pool from which researchers can learn a great deal about why and how certain children enter foster care and how this varies by race.

This research rests on the premise that individual-, family-, and community-level socioeconomic and demographic characteristics, along with the policies and practices, will contribute to the outcomes of reform for children. Given the availability of this kind of administrative data for research purposes in more and more states, the authors hope that this study is a key first step toward building a more nationally representative set of results.

Data and Method

This study is concerned with the foster care placement of children who receive AFDC/TANF. It focuses on the experiences of the children—at least initially the focus of welfare policies—and does not attribute the parents' AFDC/TANF receipt history to the child.

Data

The study draws its primary data from the Illinois Integrated Database on Children and Family Services (IDB). IDB is a state-level, longitudinal database constructed from administrative data gathered by public agencies that serve children and families in Illinois (Goerge, Van Voorhis, & Lee, 1994). Specifically, the researchers used individual-level longitudinal service records constructed from AFDC/TANF data from the Illinois Department of Human Services Client Database and foster care placement data from the Illinois DCFS Child and Youth Centered Information System. The authors linked the individual-level AFDC/TANF and foster care placement records by child to develop "spells" that begin with the entry to AFDC or TANF and end with either foster care placement or the latest date of observation, which was December 31, 1998.[1]

Because the original data used for this study come from two separate agency information systems that do not share a common identification, linking data records reliably and accurately across data sources (foster care and public assistance databases) is an important issue. To link individual service records, the authors used a process called *probabilistic record matching*. First developed by researchers in the fields of demography and epidemiology, probabilistic record matching is based on the assumption that no single match between variables common to the source databases will identify a client with complete reliability. Instead, the process calculates the probability that two

[1] The monthly Aid to Families with Dependent Children/Temporary Aid to Needy Families, Medicaid, and food stamp receipt information is used to construct the spell of service receipt. In constructing the welfare service spells, the study treated periods of welfare receipt that include one-month periods off welfare as continuous spells of program receipt.

records belong to the same client using multiple pieces of identifying information. These "weights" vary based on the distribution of values of the identifiers (Jaro, 1989; Newcombe, 1988; Winkler, 1988). In matching, the researchers used full name, Social Security number, birth date, gender, race and ethnicity, and origin of residence.

The Study Population

The study population was all Illinois children who entered AFDC/TANF for the first time between 1991 and 1998.[2] Although federal welfare reform was implemented July 1, 1997, Illinois had instituted many policy and program changes in both welfare and child welfare programs prior to reform. For example, Illinois instituted the Work Pays program in 1994, which implemented a generous income-disregard policy as an effort to "make work pay."

Under the Work Pays program, a client's TANF grant is reduced by $1 for every $3 of gross income earned, and clients continue to be eligible for some cash grant until their gross incomes reach the federal poverty line. In the child welfare arena, Illinois implemented the Home of Relative reform plan in 1995. Under this reform, the state abandoned the requirement of taking custody of children in informal kinship care even absent a protective need; prior to this policy change, the state took custody of children reported to a child abuse and neglect hotline whose circumstances required relatives to assume temporary guardianship. Because these changes occurred at various points during the 1990s, one must examine long-term trends to detect any gradual changes in the patterns of the transitions that might be due to policy and program changes. Thus, the authors examined the experiences of children who entered AFDC/TANF from 1991 to 1998 and followed them through the end of 1998.

The authors also selected a study population that shared similar AFDC/TANF experiences. Such shared experiences, such as entry into AFDC/TANF during the same time period, allowed the researchers to control for factors that might affect foster care placement. Choosing a point-in-time population, in contrast, would have included children with widely varying durations or histories of AFDC/TANF receipt. A population of children with different AFDC/TANF entry dates, such as that of a point-in-time population, could also fundamentally change the potential distribution of the likelihood of the events occurring. In such cases, interpreting the findings would be difficult. Another possible study population might be an exit cohort. An exit cohort, however, would exclude those children who had not formally left the programs, but who were nevertheless at risk of being placed in foster care.

[2] For the proportional hazard models, the researchers used a 10% random sample for the analyses.

In an entry cohort study such as the one used in this study, it is imperative to control for any possible effects of the study population's experiences before they entered the observation period. In studies that use similar longitudinal methods, it is well documented that experiences of the new-entry cohorts (those who enter a particular status for the first time) are often quite different from those who had previous service experiences (i.e., reentries). Thus, the authors limited their analysis to those children who entered AFDC/TANF for the first time during the study period and who had not received AFDC/TANF at least in the previous two years.[3] This definition of the new-entry cohorts allows the authors to follow experiences of children from their initial entry to AFDC/TANF as they move in and out of cash assistance.[4] This was particularly important for the analysis of foster care placement and abuse/neglect report experiences because the researchers were interested in the interaction between receiving cash assistance and experiencing child welfare events (see Study Design section for further discussion of the approach).

Table 10-1 presents selected characteristics of each AFDC/TANF entry cohort between 1991 and 1998. An almost linear decline existed in the number of new AFDC/TANF entrants during the study period. During the early 1990s, the number of new entrants stood at about 100,000. By 1998, the number had declined to about 35,000, representing an approximate 65% reduction in the number of new entrants.[5] The biggest decline in the number of new entrants occurred from 1996 to 1997. The majority of children who entered AFDC/TANF for the first time were children from birth to age 4—of the 644,570 entrants during this period, roughly 74% were children between birth and age 4. About 43% of all children were from Chicago, approximately 45% were African American, and one-third lived in communities in which 30% or more children lived in poverty.

[3] Because of the lack of the data extending back a sufficient period, the authors could not apply the same nonparticipation time for all entry cohorts. The monthly Aid to Families with Dependent Children (AFDC)/Temporary Aid to Needy Families (TANF) administrative data used for this study only date to 1989. This allowed the authors to define new entrants in 1991 as those who had not participated in AFDC/TANF for the previous two years, whereas later cohorts are defined by nonparticipation since 1989. Therefore, the 1998 entry cohorts have nine years of nonparticipation. This will present somewhat overestimated new entrant numbers for the earlier cohort years. By applying the same two-year nonparticipation rule, the analysis finds that there were about 5,000 additional new 1998 entrants added to the 35,098 entrants included in the study.

[4] An alternative way of defining the entry cohorts is to apply the same two-year nonparticipation time for all entry cohorts. This method, however, did not allow the authors to continuously follow the experiences of the entry cohorts as they moved in and out of Aid to Families with Dependent Children (AFDC)/Temporary Aid to Needy Families (TANF). Take an example of a child who enters AFDC for the first time in 1991, leaves assistance in 1992, reenters in 1996, and finally enters foster care after the 1996 entry—the method used here allowed the authors to characterize the experience of the child as entering AFDC for the first time in 1991 and being placed in foster care after leaving and returning to AFDC. The alternative definition of the entry cohorts would treat the 1996 entry to AFDC as the second "first" entry to AFDC for the same child because the child did not receive AFDC for more than two years after his or her exit from AFDC in 1992. One obvious concern for the entry cohort definition used was whether having cohorts with different lengths of nonparticipation periods would affect the results in the transition rates. The authors examined the transition patterns for the cohorts with the same two-year definition and found the results were very consistent with the results presented here.

[5] Again, the decline is somewhat overestimated due to our data limitation discussed in Footnote 3. When applying the same two-year nonparticipation rule, the decline from 1991 to 1998 is about 60%.

Table 10-1: Selected Demographic Characteristics of Illinois Children Who Entered Aid to Families with Dependent Children (AFDC) and Temporary Assistance to Needy Families (TANF) Between 1991 and 1998

		Age (%)					Race or Ethnicity (%)				Community Child Poverty Rate[b] (%)			
Entry Year[a]	Total	Birth–4	5–9	10–14	15–17	Chicago (%)	White	African American	Hispanic	Other	<10%	10%–20%	21%–30%	>30%
1991	115,853	66.9	14.9	11.6	6.6	42.1	40.2	44.4	14.1	1.3	18.5	25.0	23.3	33.2
1992	98,674	73.1	11.8	9.3	5.7	43.2	38.7	45.6	14.3	1.4	18.1	24.4	23.4	34.2
1993	101,816	74.0	11.1	9.2	5.7	45.0	37.6	45.1	15.4	1.8	18.0	24.5	23.3	34.2
1994	97,886	75.5	10.4	8.6	5.5	46.0	36.7	44.4	16.7	2.2	18.0	24.1	23.9	34.1
1995	80,024	78.5	9.5	7.3	4.7	44.5	37.2	45.2	15.7	1.9	18.1	24.4	23.7	33.8
1996	71,566	79.3	9.4	7.0	4.3	44.6	36.4	47.3	14.4	1.9	18.1	23.6	24.3	34.1
1997	43,653	73.5	12.6	8.7	5.2	39.1	42.3	42.3	13.4	2.0	—	25.7	25.4	29.0
1998	35,098	78.0	10.5	7.1	4.4	42.4	38.3	46.2	13.8	1.7	19.2	24.1	25.7	30.9
Total	644,570	74.1	11.5	8.9	5.5	43.7	38.3	45.1	14.9	1.8	18.3	24.4	23.8	33.4

[a] Number of new entries represents those entering AFDC or TANF without AFDC/TANF receipt in at least the previous two years.

[b] Communities are defined by ZIP code areas.

Study Design

It is important to note that the reliability of the estimated effect of policy reforms depends on whether a researcher has access to data on the characteristics and outcomes of the recipients both prior to and during the new programs. IDB is an ideal database for such a study design because it stores longitudinal data covering a sufficiently long period both prior to the beginning of new programs and during program operation. Longitudinal data date back eight years prior to the implementation of federal welfare reform in Illinois.

The overall effect of policies and programs on the key outcome measures depended on several distinct factors: the characteristics of AFDC/TANF recipients, area and community characteristics, and the relative effectiveness of the new policies and programs. The major challenge of the study was to develop an analytic model that researchers could use to isolate the effect of new policies and programs on the outcome measures while controlling for the characteristics of recipients and communities.

The authors employed proportional hazards modeling to examine the effects of child, parent, and neighborhood characteristics, as well as service events, on the child's entry into the foster care system.[6] For this report, they will focus on the effect of the race or ethnicity of the

[6] In separate analyses, the authors also examined the "period" effects of the year the participants were in during the study period to discern any differences between the cohort effect and the calendar year effect in terms of the transition patterns. They defined calendar variables as time-varying covariates representing the year the participants were in. They found very similar results between the two methods, which indicates that the transition patterns across different entry cohorts are not substantially different from the patterns of the "cross-sectional" population across years.

child. Race and ethnicity were coded as non-Hispanic white, African American, Hispanic, and other. In the discussion of the models, this study will focus primarily on changes in the values of the coefficients as other covariates were added to the model. Because the researchers were also interested in controlling for the change in the likelihood of entering foster care over time due to child welfare reform as well as welfare reform, they added covariates for the year of entry. These covariates represent the year of first entrance into AFDC/TANF and are defined as a set of seven dummy variables, using 1991 as the contrast year.

Transitions from AFDC/TANF to child welfare services obviously depend on family demographic and socioeconomic characteristics, such as neighborhood residence and race. Controlling for such influences when determining the effect of policies is critical. Therefore, in addition to using entry dates as proxies for policy effects, this study also examines the effect of the characteristics of children, families, and communities on the likelihood of making a transition. The covariates describing the individual child's characteristics include age at the time of AFDC/TANF entry and gender. Characteristics of families are largely measured by sociodemographic characteristics of mothers recorded in the AFDC/TANF agency administrative data. They include education, age at the birth of first child, and work experience. The researchers also examine the effects of neighborhood poverty and living in a major city (Chicago) on the likelihood of making a transition.

The researchers divided child's age at time of AFDC/TANF entry into four categories: age 4 and younger, ages 5 to 9, ages 10 to 14, and ages 15 to 17. They calculated the child poverty rate at the ZIP code level using 1990 census data. The results were divided into four levels of community poverty: fewer than 10% of the child population living below the poverty line, 10% to 20%, 20% to 30%, and 30% or more living below the poverty line. Once communities were characterized, the authors assigned a poverty status to all AFDC/TANF entrants in a particular community.[7] They classified region and gender variables as Chicago or "rest of state" and as male or female. With the division between Chicago and "rest of state," the authors captured urban and rural differences generally. They divided the mothers' characteristic variables—education, work experience, and age at first birth—into two categories each: high school graduate or non-high-school graduate, some work experience or no work experience, and age 20 or older and younger than age 20.

Findings

Descriptive Analysis

Entry into temporary foster care occurs when the court, in consultation with the public child welfare agency, determines that because of risk of additional abuse or neglect, a

[7] The authors used address information at the time of the first Aid to Families with Dependent Children/Temporary Aid to Needy Families entry to identify the child's ZIP code.

child should not live with his or her parents. A placement typically happens after an abuse or neglect report. In the late 1980s and early 1990s in Illinois, the foster care caseload increased, and it has only begun to decrease in recent years.[8]

In general, a sharp decrease has occurred in children entering foster care after their entry into AFDC or TANF since 1994. The rate of children entering foster care within six months of entry into AFDC or TANF was just below 8 per 1,000 between 1991 and 1993, increasing to a high of 10.25 per 1,000 in 1994, before decreasing to 7.95 per 1,000 in 1997 (see Table 10-2). This pattern was driven predominantly by the youngest group of children (from birth to 4 years old), who made up nearly three-quarters of child entrants to AFDC/TANF between 1991 and 1998. For this group, the highest six-month entry rate was also seen in 1994 (12 per 1,000); it decreased to 9.3 by 1997. The other 25% of entries show no notable patterns over this time period.

The 1994 cohort and those children who were at risk during 1994 seemed to have an increased risk of entering foster care. 1994 was the first year of full implementation of the Work Pays program in Illinois, and it was also the year before the manner in which children were placed with relatives in the state's foster care system was significantly reformed (as described previously). The patterns for the cumulative rates of entry into foster care from one year to five or more years after entering AFDC/TANF are similar to those for the first six months, but at a quite lower magnitude. Although the first-year rate remains above 12 per 1,000, in subsequent years, the incremental percentage of children who enter foster care is lower than 12 per 1,000, with a few exceptions. These exceptions appear to be for those children who were at risk of entry into foster care during 1994.

Multivariate Analysis

Table 10-3 presents the results of the multivariate analysis starting with a simple model that contains year of entry, race, gender and age at entry. Subsequent models contain additional covariates, which in some way were expected to change the race variable coefficients. Model 1 shows that African American children were more likely to enter foster care and Latino children were less likely to enter foster care than white children. It also shows that children younger than 5 were much more likely to enter foster care placement than older children. The researchers found no gender effect. They also found that the likelihood of placement decreased over time in a statistically significant manner beginning in 1994.

Model 2 added the region effect of living in Chicago. Given the greater numbers and of African American children in Chicago, the researchers expected a significant effect of

[8] Various changes in types of entry into foster care are only one possible outcome of welfare reform. To get a complete picture, one must look at exits from foster care. One might hypothesize that once families are cut off from cash assistance, they may have a reduced chance of being reunified with their child because they have fewer resources to care for him or her.

Table 10-2: Patterns of Foster Care Placement Among Children Who Entered Aid to Families with Dependent Children (AFDC) and Temporary Assistance to Needy Families (TANF) Between 1991 and 1998

Year of Entry to AFDC/TANF	Number of New Entries to AFDC/TANF	Rates of Being Placed in Foster Care (per 1,000) Within:						
		6 Months	1 Year	2 Years	3 Years	4 Years	5 Years	>5 Years
Birth–4 Years								
1991	77,503	9.32	15.43	25.72	36.11	47.59	54.58	65.00
1992	72,160	8.51	15.58	29.46	40.95	49.20	55.63	61.70
1993	75,376	9.67	18.18	32.25	41.15	49.02	52.87	**54.81**
1994	73,907	12.12	19.85	31.15	38.03	43.35	**45.48**	
1995	62,823	10.86	17.80	27.68	33.40	**36.74**		
1996	56,741	10.84	16.00	24.57	**28.04**			
1997	32,076	9.32	15.00	**19.33**				
1998	27,381	**8.66**	**10.52**					
5–9 Years								
1991	17,309	4.22	6.47	10.98	14.96	19.64	24.15	30.85
1992	11,643	4.55	7.30	12.80	16.49	20.36	23.19	26.20
1993	11,281	2.04	4.52	9.48	11.97	15.51	17.46	**18.17**
1994	10,213	4.41	6.95	9.50	11.36	14.88	**15.76**	
1995	7,581	5.14	7.39	10.82	12.80	**13.85**		
1996	6,761	2.37	5.03	8.13	**9.02**			
1997	5,501	4.54	7.82	**10.73**				
1998	3,675	**2.45**	**3.27**					
10–14 Years								
1991	13,441	5.58	9.52	16.44	21.87	25.97	28.79	30.06
1992	9,209	6.08	11.62	20.41	27.04	30.84	33.12	34.21
1993	9,317	3.01	6.87	13.09	16.31	18.57	20.39	**21.14**
1994	8,398	4.76	9.05	13.34	15.48	17.39	**17.86**	
1995	5,834	2.91	5.31	8.91	12.00	**12.68**		
1996	4,981	5.62	9.44	14.86	**15.46**			
1997	3,811	3.94	9.71	**12.60**				
1998	2,498	**3.60**	**4.80**					
15–17 Years								
1991	7,600	3.95	5.13	7.37	7.76	N/A	N/A	N/A
1992	5,662	4.95	7.06	9.89	10.07	N/A	N/A	N/A
1993	5,842	4.11	6.68	8.22	8.73	N/A	N/A	N/A
1994	5,368	4.10	4.66	5.03	5.03	N/A	N/A	
1995	3,786	3.17	4.23	4.23	4.49	N/A		
1996	3,083	4.22	5.51	6.16	**6.16**			
1997	2,265	3.53	6.62	**7.51**				
1998	1,544	**1.94**	**1.94**					
All Ages								
1991	115,853	7.77	12.73	21.23	29.44	38.29	43.97	52.09
1992	98,674	7.61	13.74	25.53	34.99	41.83	47.08	51.98
1993	101,816	7.90	14.97	26.60	33.79	40.21	43.44	**45.02**
1994	97,886	10.25	16.74	25.93	31.51	36.05	**37.79**	
1995	80,024	9.37	15.26	23.61	28.52	**31.29**		
1996	71,566	9.39	14.06	21.55	**24.43**			
1997	43,653	7.95	13.19	**17.04**				
1998	35,098	**7.35**	**8.97**					

Note: Bold-printed entries represent partially censored observations.

Table 10-3: Estimated Conditional Risk Ratios: Movement from Aid to Families with Dependent Children (AFDC)/Temporary Assistance to Needy Families (TANF) to All Foster Care Placements 1991–1998 of AFDC/TANF Entry Cohorts in Illinois

Variable	Model 1	Model 2	Model 3	Model 4	Model 5[a]
Entry to AFDC/TANF Year					
1991	1.00	1.00	1.00	1.00	1.00
1992	1.04	1.04	1.04	1.04	1.00
1993	0.95	0.95	0.95	0.95	0.93
1994	0.82*	0.82*	0.83*	0.83*	0.84*
1995	0.85*	0.84*	0.87	0.87	0.92
1996	0.77 *	0.77*	0.82 *	0.81*	0.87
1997	0.78 *	0.78*	0.85	0.85	0.87
1998	0.66 *	0.66*	0.71	0.72	0.92
Race/Ethnicity					
White	1.00	1.00	1.00	1.00	1.00
African American	1.95 *	1.94*	1.74*	1.68*	1.55*
Hispanic	0.55 *	0.54*	0.54*	0.53*	0.47*
Other	1.13	1.12	1.05	1.07	1.26
Gender					
Male	1.00	1.00	1.00	1.00	1.00
Female	0.98	0.98	0.97	0.97	1.00
Age of Child					
Birth–4	1.00	1.00	1.00	1.00	1.00
5–9	0.38 *	0.38*	0.41*	0.41*	0.48*
10–14	0.58 *	0.58*	0.64*	0.64*	0.73*
15–17	0.40 *	0.40*	0.43*	0.43*	0.48*
Region					
Rest of State		1.00	1.00	1.00	1.00
Chicago		1.01	0.95	0.90*	0.83*
Being on AFDC/TANF[b]					
No				1.00	1.00
Yes			2.04*	2.02*	1.93*
Community Poverty					
<10%				1.00	1.00
10% to less than 20%				1.17*	1.21*
20% to less than 30%				1.10	1.11
≥30%				1.27*	1.21*
Mother's Education					
No High School					1.00
High School Graduate					0.50*
Mother's Work Experience					
No					1.00
Yes					0.92
Mother's Age at First Birth					
≥20 and older					1.00
<20					0.99
-2 Log Likelihood	53,765.20	53,765.10	53,544.90	53,531.10	35,847.78
df	14	15	16	19	22

Note: Baseline levels are indicated as risk ratio of 1.

[a] Model 5 is estimated only for children who had mothers identified in AFDC/TANF cases.

[b] The variable *Being on AFDC/TANF* is specified as time-varying covariate.

*Estimates are statistically significant at the 0.05 level.

regions and perhaps a decrease in the coefficient for African American children. This effect was not present, however. Furthermore, the addition of this covariate changed none of the other risk ratios for the other covariates.

In Model 3, the authors added the effect of whether a child was still receiving AFDC or TANF. Because they continued to track children after they exited AFDC/TANF, this was an important indicator of whether the possible additional surveillance of AFDC/TANF cases by welfare or related agencies affected entry into foster care or whether lower income and assets associated with AFDC/TANF affected entry into foster care. The researchers did see a significant effect among children who were in an active AFDC or TANF case; they were twice as likely to enter foster care as those children who were not in an active case. This covariate did decrease the magnitude of race effects slightly (by about 10%), but not enough to make it statistically insignificant.

As to which of the two hypotheses—heightened surveillance or fewer resources—would explain this effect, it is difficult to determine. Because very few reports of child maltreatment come from TANF workers, the authors and other experts in the field generally do not favor the surveillance hypothesis. During the study period, however, if families left AFDC or TANF, it is likely that this indicated an increase in their economic status. Even during TANF implementation (because time limits have not yet been reached), it is still likely that leaving TANF is a signal of improved economic status of families, even if the improvements are small. Therefore, while families are on cash assistance, it is likely that they are poorer and they are less likely to be employed—thereby affecting their ability to keep the child safe and perhaps also to parent.

Model 4 added community poverty level. A child who resides in a community with more than 30% of children living in poverty has a 27% greater likelihood of entering foster care than a child who lives in a community where fewer than 10% of children live in poverty. Communities where between 10% and 30% of children live in poverty also have a greater likelihood of placement. Adding these covariates reduces the race effect slightly (about 3%) and makes the effect of region significant, but in the opposite direction one would typically expect. The authors found that children in Chicago were less likely to enter foster care than in the balance of the state. It is clear, however, that community-level poverty and race account for much of the effect of living in Chicago because of the high concentration of child poverty in Chicago as well as the high concentration of African American children.

In the last model (Model 5), the authors added the child's mother's characteristics to the model. Mother's education is a significant factor determining the likelihood of a child being placed in foster care. Children of mothers who finished high school were about 50% less likely to be placed in foster care than those of mothers who did not finish high school in this study. Again, including mother's characteristics decreased the African American race coefficient by about 4%. Surprisingly, the mother's work experience and the mother's age at first birth did not affect either the likelihood of entry into foster care or the magnitude of the race effect.

The race effect is always difficult to interpret. Especially when looking at entry into foster care, child welfare researchers are constantly challenged to explain why African American children are more likely to enter foster care. As the results in Table 10-3 demonstrate, controlling for factors other than individual child's characteristics, such as region, receiving AFDC/TANF, community poverty, and mother's characteristics reduce the race effect from the odds ratio of 1.95 (in Model 1) to 1.55 (in Model 5). As the results in Model 5 indicate, however, even after controlling for the effect of the other covariates, this study finds that African American children are about 55% more likely to be placed in foster care than white children.

One possible explanation is the fact that there are essentially two types of foster children—those who are placed with relatives and those who are placed with strangers. During the past 15 years, it has become more likely that African American children will be placed with relatives. When the analysis was done separately for kin and nonkin placements, as shown in Table 10-4, it found that the race effect is substantially stronger for transitions to kinship placements. Table 10-4 shows that African American children are 2.13 times as likely to be placed with relatives as white children, whereas they are only 28% more likely than white children to be placed with nonrelatives. The authors believe that the remaining difference between the likelihood of African American children and white children being placed in nonkin foster care placements may be largely due to other characteristics of mothers (such as mother's substance abuse problem) and characteristics of caseworkers who play a key role in making placement decisions in child welfare. We hope to address these possible explanations in future analyses as the data become available.

Conclusion

This chapter attempts to explain to the greatest degree possible the very apparent observations that a disproportionate number of African American children are entering foster care relative to white children. Although this study has not explained all of the race effect seen when not controlling for other factors, it has made progress. A great deal is explained when we split apart entry into kinship care versus all other forms of foster

Table 10-4: Estimated Conditional Risk Ratios: Movement from AFDC/TANF to Foster Care Placements by First Foster Care Placement Type—1991–1998 AFDC/TANF Entry Cohorts in Illinois

Variable	Kinship Care Placement	Significance	Nonkinship Care Placement	Significance
Entry to AFDC/TANF Year				
1991	1.00		1.00	
1992	0.99		1.01	
1993	0.88		0.98	
1994	0.68	*	0.98	
1995	0.79		1.04	
1996	0.62	*	1.09	
1997	0.71		1.01	
1998	0.53		1.23	
Race/Ethnicity				
White	1.00		1.00	
African American	2.13	*	1.28	*
Hispanic	0.49	*	0.49	*
Other	1.14		1.37	
Gender				
Male	1.00		1.00	
Female	1.05		0.96	
Age of Child				
Birth to 4	1.00		1.00	
5–9	0.72		0.33	*
10–14	0.49	*	0.90	
15–17	0.32		0.59	
Region				
Rest of state	1.00		1.00	
Chicago	1.30	*	0.59	*
Being on AFDC/TANF[a]				
No	1.00		1.00	
Yes	1.92	*	1.93	*
Community Poverty				
Less than 10%	1.00		1.00	
10% to less than 20%	0.89		1.45	*
20% to less than 30%	0.81		1.35	*
30% and higher	0.81		1.58	*
Mother's Education				
No high school	1.00		1.00	
High school graduate	0.47	*	0.52	*
Mother's Work Experience				
None	1.00		1.00	
Had some experience	0.94		0.90	
Mother's Age at First Birth				
20 and older	1.00		1.00	
Younger than 20	1.01		0.97	
-2 log likelihood	15,303.79		20,425.72	
df	22		22	

Note: Aid to Families with Dependent Children = AFDC; Temporary Assistance to Needy Families = TANF. Baseline levels are indicated as risk ratio of 1.

[a] The variable *Being on AFDC/TANF* is specified as time-varying covariate.

* $p < .05$.

care. The findings that African American children are much more likely to be placed with kin are consistent with what researchers know about the culture and traditional family structure of African American families. The findings for the transition of nonkinship care show a much smaller race effect. Other characteristics of the families and neighborhoods account for much of the effect seen in models with fewer descriptors. Being on AFDC or TANF, community poverty, and the mother's highest level of education explain a great deal of differences between African American children and children of other races.

References

Goerge, R. M., & Lee, B. J. (1997). Abuse and neglect of the children, kids having kids: Economic cost and social consequences of teen pregnancy. In R. A. Maynard (Ed.), *Kids having kids: Economic cost and social consequences of teen pregnancy.* Washington, DC: Urban Institute Press.

Goerge, R. M., Lee, B. J., Reidy, M., Bilaver, L., Needell, B., Brookhart, A., et al. (2000). Dynamics of children's movement among the AFDC, Medicaid, and foster care programs prior to welfare reform: 1995–1996. Retrieved from http://apse.hhs.gov/hsp/movement00/execsum.htm.

Goerge, R. M., Van Voorhis, J., & Lee, B. J. (1994). Illinois's longitudinal and relational child and family research database. *Social Science Computer Review, 12,* 351–365.

Jaro, M. A. (1989). Advances in record-linkage methodology as applied to matching the 1985 census of Tampa, Florida. *Journal of the American Statistical Association, 84*(406), 414–420.

Newcombe, H. B. (1988). *Handbook of record linkage: Methods for health and statistical studies, administration, and business.* Oxford, UK : Oxford University Press.

Winkler, W. E. (1988). Using the EM algorithm for weight computation in the Fellegi-Sunter model of record linkage. *American Statistical Association: Proceedings of the Section Survey Research Methods,* 667–671.

CHAPTER 11

The Role of Race in Foster Care Placements

Robert B. Hill

One of the most consistent findings in child welfare research is the overrepresentation of African American children in the child welfare system. Although African American children comprise about one-fifth of all children younger than 18 in the nation, they account for more than two-fifths of the children in foster care. Although Hispanic children have sizable numbers in the foster care population, they tend to be represented in proportion to their size in the total population. Why then are African American children overrepresented?

One set of explanations attributes this overrepresentation to racial bias or insensitivity at various stages of the decisionmaking processes in child welfare. African Americans are more likely to be reported to child protection agencies for child maltreatment than whites. Cases involving African Americans are more likely to be referred, investigated, and substantiated than cases involving white families. The combined effects of these three factors are said to contribute to the overrepresentation of African Americans (Billingsley & Giovannoni, 1972; Courtney et al., 1996; Hampton, 1986; Holton, 1990; Stehno, 1982).

Another set of explanations attributes this overrepresentation to class bias. Low-income or poor families are more likely to be reported, investigated, or substantiated than middle- and upper-income families. Because African Americans are more highly concentrated among low-income families, it is their class status—not their race—that contributes to their overrepresentation in the child welfare system (Gelles, 1982; Pelton, 1978).

A third set of explanations describes this overrepresentation as appropriate, because African Americans are said to have higher rates of child maltreatment than whites and to be more tolerant of abuse than whites. Indeed, a number of studies have found higher rates of child abuse and neglect among African Americans than whites (Cappelleri, Eckenrode, & Powers, 1993; Gil, 1970; Jason, Andereck, Marks, & Tyler, 1982; Spearly & Lauderdale, 1983). Yet such findings are strongly contradicted by most national surveys (Gelles & Straus, 1979; Sedlak & Broadhurst, 1996). All three waves of the National Incidence Study (NIS; 1979, 1986, and 1993) reported no overall differences in child maltreatment between African Americans and whites (Sedlak & Broadhurst 1996). Moreover, several studies have found that African Americans have less tolerant attitudes about child abuse and neglect than whites (Giovannoni & Becerra, 1979; Rose & Meezan, 1996).

This chapter will attempt to identify the factors that are strongly correlated with the placement of children in foster care. It will address three questions:

- To what extent is race a strong predictor of placement?
- What are the other strong predictors of placement in foster care?
- Does race continue to have effects on placement when combined with other strong predictors?

In short, this chapter will examine the independent contribution of race as a predictor of the placement of children in the foster care system when combined with other child, family, or case history characteristics.

Before focusing on the findings, however, it is important to place this analysis in the broader context of the child welfare system and the institutional processes that affect the placement of African American children in foster care. Thus, this chapter begins with a brief review of research on the role of race at various stages of the child welfare decisionmaking processes. It proceeds to review studies that have focused on race and other significant variables affecting foster care placement. Then it will present the data analysis, and finally, the authors will discuss findings and their research implications.

Institutional Processes

To what extent does the research literature support the popular belief that there are class and racial differences at various stages of the decisionmaking processes? Several studies found that child maltreatment is reported more for low-income than middle- and upper-income families (Gelles, 1982; O'Toole, Turbett, & Nalepka, 1983). Research has revealed that doctors are more likely to diagnose physical injuries among poor families as abuse, but as accidents among affluent families (Katz, Hampton, Newberger, Bowles, & Snyder, 1986; McPherson & Garcia, 1983).

Similarly, some researchers have concluded that child maltreatment is reported more for African Americans than for whites. For example, Hampton and Newberger (1985) found that hospitals overreported abuse and neglect among African American families and underreported it among white families. Of the number of children who met the NIS definition of experiencing child abuse or neglect, three-fourths of African American families were reported for maltreatment by the hospitals, compared with 60% of white families. Moreover, several studies revealed that African American women who are pregnant are more likely to be reported for substance abuse than pregnant white women (Chasnoff, Landress, & Barrett, 1990; Neuspiel, Zingman, Templeton, DiStabile, & Druckers, 1993). On the other hand, many studies do not find strong racial differentials in the reporting of child maltreatment. These studies have concluded that the strongest predictors of reporting are the severity of injury, cases with prior reports, and a history of family problems (Hampton, 1987; Newberger, Reed, Daniel, Hyde, & Kotelchurch, 1977; Spearly & Lauderdale, 1983; Wolock, Sherman, Feldman, & Metzger, 2001).

Are there racial differentials in referrals and investigation? First, it is important to underscore the fact that sizable numbers of cases reported for child maltreatment are not referred for investigation. A nationwide survey of child welfare agencies revealed that workers screened out about one-third (36%) of the cases reported to child protection agencies in 1996 (Tumin & Green, 2000). Similarly, caseworkers only investigated 3 out of 10 maltreatment reports in NIS-3 (Sedlak & Broadhurst, 1996).

An in-depth longitudinal study of child maltreatment reports in New Jersey found that African American and white families had similar rates of investigation (20% and 23%, respectively; Wolock et al., 2001). Although a reanalysis of NIS-3 did not find that race had main effects, it found strong interactions between race and the severity and type of maltreatment on the probability of investigation (Sedlack & Schultz, Chapter 5, this volume). For example, the NIS-3 reanalysis found higher rates of investigation (a) among African American than among white children who were emotionally maltreated or physically neglected, and (b) among African American than among white children whose parents were substance abusers.

What are the patterns of substantiation of a finding of abuse or neglect? Only a fraction of child abuse reports are substantiated. According to the national survey conducted by Tumin and Green (2000), workers substantiated two-fifths (38%) of the cases investigated for child maltreatment in 1996. This study also found that workers substantiated one-fourth (27%) of all reports for child abuse and neglect in 1996. The New Jersey study of child maltreatment also found that workers substantiated about one-fourth of the reports in 1997 and 1998 (Wolock et al., 2001).

In an Illinois study, Rolock and Testa (Chapter 6, this volume) found that children in African American families were more likely to have a substantiated report of abuse or neglect regardless of the race of the investigator, and white investigators were more likely to indicate a report, regardless of family. Apart from these main effects, the authors found no evidence that investigators are racially biased against families of the opposite race (Rolock & Testa, Chapter 6, this volume).

Are there racial differentials in substantiation? A comprehensive review (Zuravin, Orme, & Hegar, 1995) of studies of the substantiation of child maltreatment reports identified four key predictors: status of reporter, prior reports of maltreatment, race or ethnicity of victim or family, and type of maltreatment. Substantiation was more likely when professionals made the reports, when there had been prior reports of abuse or neglect, when the report was for physical abuse rather than neglect, or when the victim or family was a person of color (i.e., African American or Hispanic). This review also found that workers had greater confidence in substantiating a report when it was a professional reporter, a severe injury or allegation, a male perpetrator, or the victim or family was African American (Zuravin et al., 1995). Moreover, although most risk assessment studies reveal greater substantiation for African Americans than for whites, they have found similar recurrence rates of substantiation among different racial groups (Baird, Ereth, & Wagner, 1999; Eckenrode, Powers, Doris, Munsch, & Bolger, 1988).

On the other hand, the New Jersey study of child maltreatment did not find racial differences in substantiation rates. When researchers included race and ethnicity in regression models to estimate the probability of substantiation, they had no significant effects (Wolock et al., 2001); however, the study revealed three strong predictors of substantiation: parental substance abuse, the number of children, and family. In summary, although many studies suggest substantiation rates are higher among African Americans than whites, contradictory evidence exists in other studies regarding different racial standards at various stages of the decisionmaking processes in the child welfare system.

Predictors of Placement

To what extent is race one of the correlates of placement in foster care? This section will review four studies of predictors of foster care placement that employed rigorous statistical techniques (Katz et al., 1986; Lindsay, 1991; Runyan, Gould, Trost, & Loda, 1981; Zuravin & DePanfilis, 1997). The first study involved a secondary analysis of the 1977 National Survey of Social Services to Children and Families (Lindsay, 1991). Lindsay (1991) conducted a discriminant analysis that distinguished between children who were placed in foster care and those who received in-home support services at various ages.

One strong predictor of placement in foster care was whether the children were referred for neglect or abuse. Interestingly, this study found that children referred for neglect were more likely to be placed in foster care, whereas children referred for abuse were more likely to receive in-home services. The strongest predictor of foster care placement, regardless of the age of the child, however, was the adequacy of the family's income: Families without adequate income from either the government or their wages were most likely to have their children removed. In addition, race was not a predictor of foster care placement in this study.

The second study of factors that predict foster care placement was based on statewide cases that had been substantiated for child maltreatment in North Carolina (Runyan et al., 1981). The researchers placed a number of factors into logistic regression models to identify the most important correlates. Some of the most important predictors were whether the parents had a substance abuse problem, the severity of injury to the child, and the source of referral. Caseworkers were more likely to remove children in cases that were referred by the police or the courts than children referred by other sources. Moreover, this study did not find social class (i.e., income or education) or race to be a significant predictor of foster care placement.

The third study attempted to identify predictors of foster care placement based on an examination of the records of 185 children in a public hospital in Boston, Massachusetts, suspected to be abused or neglected (Katz et al., 1986). Based on a log-linear regression analysis, one of the strongest predictors was a three-way interaction among class (i.e., Medicaid eligible), presence of physical injury, and discharge disposition. Families that were eligible for Medicaid were more likely than affluent families to have their children removed in cases of physical injury and less likely to have their children removed in cases of nonphysical injuries. On the other hand, neither social class nor race or ethnicity had independent effects on foster care placement.

Zuravin and DePanfilis (1997) conducted the fourth study of predictors of foster care placement, which was based on cases that workers substantiated for child abuse or neglect in a large city in the mid-Atlantic region. The authors included various factors in a series of logistic regression models that predicted the probability of foster care placement. The strongest predictors were a prior substantiated report, parental substance abuse problems, parental mental health problems, and parental developmental problems. But neither social class (i.e., Aid to Families with Dependent Children [AFDC] status) nor race was a significant predictor of foster care placement when combined with the other factors in the final model.

What conclusions can we draw from these studies? First, it is interesting to note that social class did not have independent effects on foster care placement in three of the four studies. This might be due to the constricted class variation of their study group (children who had been suspected or substantiated for abuse or neglect), which would have an overrepresentation of low-income families. This selection criterion would exclude children in foster care who had not been suspected or substantiated for child maltreatment, which would encompass a wider spectrum of social classes. Second, restricting analyses to substantiated cases might also explain in part the lack of significance of race as a predictor of foster care placement, as bias might occur prior to substantiation; however, the first study by Lindsay (1991), which was based on a wider pool of families (those receiving child welfare services), also did not find race to be a significant predictor. Third, it is also interesting to note that reasons for placement, whether abuse or neglect, were not strong predictors in most of the studies. And fourth, the two most common predictors of foster care placement were a parental substance abuse problem and the severity of injury.

Method

This study, which proposes to identify the correlates of foster care placement, is based on a nationally representative sample of cases and a much broader pool of children and families than only those who have been reported or substantiated for abuse or neglect. More specifically, the study is a secondary analysis of the 1994 National Study of Protective, Preventive and Reunification Services Delivered to Children and Their Families (NSPPRS). An objective of NSPPRS, which Westat conducted, was to document the number and characteristics of children and families who received in-home or out-of-home child welfare services between March 1, 1993, and March 1, 1994. This analysis will focus on the nationally representative sample of 2,109 children who received child welfare services in-home or out-of-home during that period.

NSPPRS has a longitudinal component, because it obtains outcome data on the segment of children who were discharged during the six-month period after February 28, 1994. This analysis, however, will focus on NSPPRS's cross-sectional aspects, which suffer from the limitations of most point-in-time surveys: It overrepresents cases that remain in care for longer periods of time. On the other hand, a unique advantage of NSPPRS is that the survey was able to include many other variables that are usually not found in studies based solely on administrative records, because it is based on interviews with caseworkers who provided information for specific children and families. Because of the small sample size of Hispanics in this survey, this analysis was restricted to comparisons between African Americans and whites.

Logistic regression models are the primary methods of analysis in this study. Most of the study variables were used in other studies of correlates of foster care placement. The independent variables fall into three groups: children's characteristics, family characteristics, and case history characteristics. Children's characteristics include race, age at entry, disability status, and child problems. Family characteristics include caregiver education, employment status, substance abuse problem, single mother, AFDC status, and Medicaid recipient. Case history characteristics include whether an abuse allegation exists, whether a neglect allegation exists, and whether the family had prior reports. The specific codes for the independent and dependent variables are described in Appendix 11-A.

Which of these variables are strong or weak predictors of foster care placement? The researchers ran the 13 variables separately in logistic regressions as single-factor predictors of foster care placement. Table 11-1 presents the rankings of those predictors by size of the variance (100 X pseudo R^2).[1] Of the variables, 10 had significant relationships with placement in foster care: caregiver substance abuse problem, race, child disability, child problems, abuse allegation, Medicaid recipient, caregiver education, employment status, age entered system, and single-mother household. On the other hand, three variables were not significantly related to foster care placement: whether the child was referred because of a neglect allegation, whether the child's household received AFDC, and whether the family had a prior case.

To examine the degree to which some variables might be highly correlated with one another, the researchers ran a correlation matrix. To minimize multicollinearity, they decided to drop child problems from the analysis because of its high correlation with child disability and child's race. Similarly, they dropped caregiver education because of its high correlation with caregiver employment status and substance abuse problem. They dropped neglect allegation because of its strong correlation with abuse allegation and child disability. In addition, the study excluded two variables (AFDC status and prior case) from the logistic modeling because of their insignificant bivariate relationships with foster care placement and their high correlation with a number of other variables.

Best-Fitting Regression Model

To determine the best-fitting logistic regression model, the researchers entered the remaining eight variables in a stepwise hierarchical sequence from stronger to weaker predictors. Table 11-2 presents the resulting eight models. Model 5 is composed of the best top-ranking five variables (race, substance abuse problem, child disability, abuse allegation, and Medicaid recipient), accounting for 19.6% of foster care placement. The researchers entered the remaining three variables (not employed, age of entry, and single-mother household) sequentially in Models 6 through 8. Yet none of these three variables continued to be a significant predictor of foster care placement when combined with the other variables. Because Model 5 was the only model in which all of the predictors were

[1] Size of the variance (100 X pseudo R^2) measures do not relate to goodness of fit as R^2 measures do, but rather attempt to measure the strength of the association between variables.

Table 11-1: Single-Factor Predictors of Foster Care Placement

Predictor	**Estimate**	***p* Value**	**(100)pseudo R^2**	***F* Value**
Caregiver substance abuse problem	1.37	.00*	6.8%	86.61
Child's race	1.18	.00*	5.6%	32.78
Child disability	1.09	.00*	5.0%	50.73
Child problems	0.37	.00*	4.5%	70.46
Abuse allegation	-1.00	.00*	3.7%	33.92
Medicaid	0.77	.00*	2.3%	15.37
Not high school graduate	0.57	.01*	1.4%	6.95
Not employed	0.54	.01*	1.1%	7.42
Age entered system	-0.04	.04*	0.6%	4.72
Single mother	-0.32	.01*	0.4%	9.01
Neglect allegation	0.28	.10	0.3%	2.94
Aid to Families with Dependent Children status	0.18	.44	0.1%	0.63
Had prior case	0.07	.69	0.0%	0.17

Note: Pseudo R^2 measures do not relate to goodness of fit as R^2 measures do, but rather attempt to measure the strength of the association between variables.
*Statistically significant relationship at $p \leq .05$.

Table 11-2: Steps to Obtain Best-Fitting Model for Predicting Foster Care Placement

	Model							
Predictor	1	2	3	4	5	6	7	8
Intercept	-0.93 (.00)*	-1.39 (.00)*	-2.08 (.00)*	-0.26 (.13)	-0.64 (.01)*	-1.97 (.00)*	-2.19 (.00)*	-2.20 (.00)*
Race (African American = 1)	1.18 (.00)*	0.79 (.00)*	1.00 (.00)*	0.72 (.01)*	0.68 (.02)*	0.43 (.18)	0.51 (.08)	0.51 (.09)
Substance abuse problem	—	1.10 (.00)*	1.21 (.00)*	1.10 (.00)*	1.00 (.00)*	0.96 (.00)*	1.00 (.00)*	1.00 (.00)*
Child disability	—	—	1.41 (.00)*	-1.57 (.00)*	-1.69 (.00)*	1.39 (.00)*	1.33 (.00)*	1.33 (.00)*
Abuse allegation	—	—	—	-1.00 (.00)*	-0.83 (.01)*	-0.52 (.08)	-0.53 (.08)	-0.53 (.08)
Has Medicaid	—	—	—	—	0.60 (.03)*	0.78 (.01)*	0.81 (.00)*	0.81 (.00)
Not employed						-0.47 (.13)	-0.42 (.16)	-0.42 (.16)
Age of entry						—	0.03 (.28)	0.03 (.28)
Single mother						—	—	0.01 (.94)
(100)pseudo R^2	5.6%	8.1%	15.1%	17.8%	19.6%	14.3%	14.1%	14.1%
F Value	32.78 (.00)*	30.44 (.00)*	39.50 (.00)*	21.46 (.00)*	20.00 (.00)*	11.59 (.00)*	9.40 (.00)*	7.90 (.00)*

Note: Pseudo R^2 measures do not relate to goodness of fit as R^2 measures do, but rather attempt to measure the strength of the association between variables.
* Statistically significant relationship at $p < .05$.

Table 11-3: Probabilities of Foster Care Placement by Scenario and Race

Scenario	Substance Abuse Problem	Abuse Allegation	Disability	Medicaid	Foster Care Probability[a]	
					White	African American
1[b]	No	No	No	No	4%	7%
2	No	No	No	Yes	7%	13%
3	No	Yes	No	No	9%	16%
4	Yes	No	No	No	10%	19%
5	No	Yes	No	Yes	15%	26%
6	Yes	No	No	Yes	17%	29%
7[b]	No	No	Yes	No	19%	31%
8	Yes	Yes	No	No	21%	34%
9	No	No	Yes	Yes	30%	45%
10[b]	Yes	Yes	No	Yes	33%	49%
11	No	Yes	Yes	No	35%	51%
12	Yes	No	Yes	No	38%	55%
13	No	Yes	Yes	Yes	49%	65%
14	Yes	No	Yes	Yes	53%	69%
15	Yes	Yes	Yes	No	59%	74%
16[b]	Yes	Yes	Yes	Yes	72%	84%

[a] Calculated as 100 X probability.
[b] Figure 11-1 depicts these four scenarios.

able to continue to maintain a significant relationship with placement in foster care in combination with one another, the researchers considered it the best-fitting model for predicting the likelihood of children being placed in foster care. Although they examined the effects of various race interaction terms on the predictors of the best-fitting model, none of these terms had a significant effect on foster care placement when combined with the other predictors.

Probabilities of Foster Care Placement

The method used in the reanalysis of the NIS-2 data was the basis for determining the probabilities of foster care placement for various subgroups of children (Sedlak, 1993). Table 11-3 presents the probabilities of foster care placement for African American and white children for 16 scenarios that refer to various combinations of four variables: substance abuse problem, abuse allegation, child disability, and Medicaid recipient.

The highest probability of foster care placement for African American (84%) and white (72%) children appear in Scenario 16: a group of children with disabilities, who were placed for an abuse allegation, whose caregiver had a substance abuse problem, and whose household received Medicaid. On the other hand, the lowest probability of foster care placement for African American (7%) and white (4%) children was Scenario 1: children

Figure 11-1: Probability of Foster Care Placement by Race and Scenario

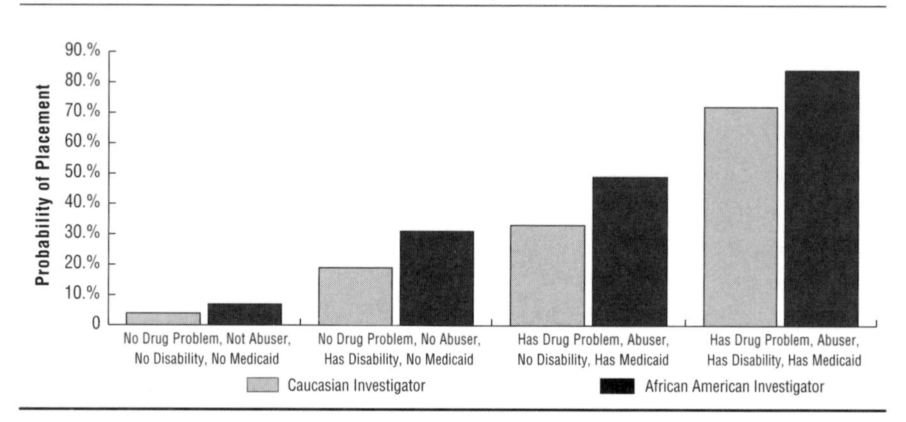

with no disabilities, who were not placed for an abuse allegation, whose caregiver did not have a substance abuse problem, and whose household did not receive Medicaid.

An intermediate probability for African Americans (49%) and whites (33%) for foster care placement is Scenario 10: children with no disabilities, but whose caregiver had a substance abuse problem, who were placed for an abuse allegation, and who received Medicaid. Somewhat lower probabilities of foster care placement for African Americans (31%) and whites (19%) appear in Scenario 7. To depict these results visually, the comparative probabilities of foster care placement for African American and white children appear in the graph in Figure 11-1 for four scenarios: 1, 7, 10, and 16. Figure 11-1 underscores the combination of race and other factors as important determinants of placement into foster care.

Discussion

This analysis revealed that race continues to be an important factor in the child welfare system: African American children are more likely to be placed in foster care than white children with comparable characteristics. Moreover, race continues to have strong independent effects on placement in combination with other predictors, however, a caregiver substance abuse problem, abuse allegations, child disability, and Medicaid receipt are also important factors in the placement of children into the foster care system.

A review of prior studies revealed that a parental substance abuse problem was a frequent predictor of foster care placement (Runyan et al., 1981; Zuravin & DePanfilis, 1997). This analysis also found a parental substance abuse problem to be an important correlate. Children whose parents had problems with substance abuse were more likely to be placed in foster care than those children whose parents did not have substance abuse problems. Clearly, the presence or absence of a substance abuse problem is an important determinant in the decision to place children in foster care. In addition, severity of injury was a common predictor of foster care placement in prior studies. This analysis found the presence of a disability for the child to be an important correlate. Children with disabilities were more likely to be placed in foster care than children without disabilities.

This analysis also found a class variable, whether families receive Medicaid, to be an important predictor of foster care placement. This finding concurs with the results of the analysis by Lindsay (1991), which was the only one of the four studies reviewed that was based on a national sample. The three other studies did not find social class to have independent effects as a predictor of foster care placement, however, Katz et al. (1986) did find that Medicaid eligibility had a significant interaction with severity of injury and discharge disposition. This agreement regarding the importance of social class as a predictor of foster care placement between the two national surveys could be a result of the fact that they incorporated a broader cross-section of families than only substantiated cases.

The review also found that the reason for placement (i.e., abuse or neglect) was not a strong predictor in most prior studies. Nevertheless, the analysis found that an abuse allegation was a strong negative predictor of foster care placement. Thus, this finding concurs with the study by Lindsay (1991), which found that abuse allegation was associated with in-home services, whereas neglect allegation was associated with placement in foster care. In this analysis, neglect allegation had a positive bivariate correlation with foster care placement, but was not significantly related. In short, although removal for abuse *was* a predictor of foster care placement, removal for neglect *was not.*

These findings reveal that although race continues to have important main effects on foster care placement, other attributes of the child (whether the child had a disability), family (whether the caregiver had a substance abuse problem or received Medicaid), or the child's case history (whether the child has a previous or current abuse allegation) are also very important predictors of foster care placement. Children who are disabled and whose caregivers have substance abuse problems, have abuse allegations, and receive Medicaid are more likely to be placed in foster care than children without any of those problems, regardless of their race.

These results suggest that child welfare workers give careful consideration to other than racial factors in deciding whether to place a child into foster care: whether there is an abuse allegation against the parent, whether the child has a disability, whether the caregiver has a substance abuse problem, and whether the family receives Medicaid. Nevertheless, when these variables are held constant, African American children are still more likely than white children to be placed into foster care.

It is also important to note that the five predictors in this study only explained about 20% of the variance of foster care placement. Clearly, social workers give priority to factors related to the remaining 80%, which this analysis did not identify. More studies are needed to identify the correlates in the missing four-fifths of the variance. Research is vitally needed to disentangle the complex effects of race, class, and culture on the probability of foster care placement. Additional studies are also needed to systematically determine how child welfare workers at various stages of the child welfare system take varied child, family, and case-history characteristics into account when determining the types of services white children and children of color receive.

Appendix 11-A: Coding of Study Variables

Independent Variables

Child Characteristics

Race: African American = 1; white = 0
Age entered system: continuous variable
Child problems: continuous variable (ranged from 0–16 problems)
Child disability status: with disability = 1; no disability = 0

Family Characteristics

Parental education: less than high school = 1; high school or more = 0
Parental employment: not employed = 1; employed = 0
Parent substance abuse problem: has problem = 1; has no problem = 0
Parent single mother: is a single mom = 1; is not a single mom = 0
Medicaid recipient: Medicaid recipient = 1; not a Medicaid recipient = 0
Aid to Families with Dependent Children (AFDC) status: received AFDC = 1; did not receive AFDC = 0

Case History Characteristics

Reasons for Placement[1]: only abuse allegation = 1; no abuse allegation = 0; only neglect allegation = 1; no neglect allegation = 0
Prior Case: had a prior case of in-home or out-of-home services = 1; did not have a prior case of services = 0

Dependent Variable

Foster care placement: placed in foster care = 1; not placed in foster care = 0

[1] The variable *only abuse allegation* applies only to allegations that include sexual abuse, physical abuse, and emotional abuse; it excludes any neglect allegations. The variable *only neglect allegation* applies only to allegations that include physical neglect and emotional neglect; it excludes any abuse allegations.

References

Baird, C., Ereth, J., & Wagner, D. (1999, June). *Research-based risk assessment: Adding equity to CPD decision-making*. Madison, WI: Children's Research Center.

Billingsley, A., & Giovannoni, J. (1972). *Children of the storm*. New York: Harcourt, Brace and Jovanovich.

Cappelleri, J., Eckenrode, J., & Powers, J. (1993). The epidemiology of child abuse: Findings from the Second National Incidence and Prevalence Study of Child Abuse and Neglect. *American Journal of Public Health, 83*, 1622–1624.

Chasnoff, I., Landress, H., & Barrett, M. (1990). The prevalence of illicit-drug or alcohol use during pregnancy and discrepancies in mandatory reporting in Pinellas County, Florida. *New England Journal of Medicine, 322*(17), 1202–1206.

Courtney, M., Barth, R., Berrick, J., Brooks, D., Needell, B., & Park, L. (1996). Race and child welfare services: Past research and future directions. *Child Welfare, 75*, 99–137.

Eckenrode, J., Powers, J., Doris, J., Munsch, J., & Bolger, N. (1988). Substantiation of child abuse and neglect reports. *Journal of Consulting and Clinical Psychology, 56*, 9–16.

Gelles, R. (1982). Child abuse and family violence: Implications for medical professionals. In E. Newberger (Ed.), Child abuse (pp. 25–41). Boston: Little, Brown.

Gelles, R., & Straus, M. (1979). Determinants of violence in the family. In W. R. Burr, R. Hill, F. Nye, & I. Reiss (Eds.), *Contemporary theories about the family* (Vol. 1, pp. 549–581). New York: Free Press.

Gil, D. (1970). *Violence against children in the United States*. Cambridge, MA: Harvard University Press.

Giovannoni, J., & Becerra, R. (1979). *Defining child abuse*. New York: Free Press.

Hampton, R. L. (1986). Race, ethnicity and child maltreatment. In Robert Staples (Ed.), *The African American family* (pp. 172–185). Belmont, CA: Wadsworth.

Hampton, R. L. (1987). Race, class and child maltreatment. *Journal of Comparative Family Studies, 18*, 113–126.

Hampton, R. L., & Newberger, E. (1985). Child abuse incidence and reporting by hospitals: Significance of severity, class and race. *American Journal of Public Health, 75*(1), 56–60.

Holton, J. K. (1990). *African American families and child abuse prevention: An African-American perspective and approach*. Chicago: National Committee to Prevent Child Abuse.

Jason, J., Andereck, N., Marks, J., & Tyler, C., Jr. (1982). Child abuse in Georgia: A method to evaluate risk factors and reporting bias. *American Journal of Public Health, 72*, 1353–1358.

Katz, M., Hampton, R., Newberger, E., Bowles, R., & Snyder, J. (1986). Returning children home: Clinical decision making in cases of child abuse and neglect. *American Journal of Orthopsychiatry, 56*, 253–262.

Lindsay, D. (1991). Factors affecting the foster care placement decision: An analysis of national survey data. *American Journal of Orthopsychiatry, 6*, 272–281.

McPherson, K., & Garcia, L. (1983). Effects of social class and familiarity on pediatricians' responses to child abuse. *Child Welfare, 62*, 387–393.

Neuspiel, D., Zingman, T., Templeton, V., DiStabile, P., & Drucker, E. (1993). Custody of cocaine-exposed newborns: Determinants of discharge decisions. *American Journal of Public Health, 83*, 1726–1729.

Newberger, E., Reed, R., Daniel, J., Hyde, J., Kotelchurch, M. (1977). Pediatric social illness: Toward an ecologic classification. *Pediatrics, 60*, 178–185.

O'Toole, R., Turbett, P., & Nalepka, C. (1983). Theories, professional knowledge and diagnosis of child abuse. In D. Finkelhor, R. Gelles, G. Hotaling, & M. Straus, (Eds.), *The dark side of families: Current family violence research* (pp. 349–362). Beverly Hills, CA: Sage.

Pelton, L. (1978). Child abuse and neglect: The myth of classlessness. *American Journal of Orthopsychiatry, 48,* 608–617.

Rose, S., & Meezan, W. (1996). Variations in perceptions of child neglect. *Child Welfare, 75,* 139–160.

Runyan, D., Gould, C., Trost, D., & Loda, F. (1981). Determinants of foster care placement for the maltreated child. *American Journal of Public Health, 71,* 706–711.

Sedlak, A. (1993). *Study of high risk child abuse and neglect groups, NIS-2 reanalysis: Report to Congress* (Appendix C). Washington, DC: U.S. Department of Health and Human Services.

Sedlak, A., & Broadhurst, D. (1996). *Executive summary of the Third National Incidence Study of Child Abuse and Neglect.* Washington, DC: U.S. Department of Heath and Human Services.

Spearly, J., & Lauderdale, M. (1983). Community characteristics and ethnicity in the prediction of child maltreatment rates. *Child Abuse and Neglect, 7,* 91–103.

Stehno, S. (1982). Differential treatment of minority children. *Social Work, 27*(1), 39–45.

Tumin, K., & Green, R. (2000). *The decision to investigate: Understanding state child welfare screening policies and practices* (Urban Institute Report Series A, No. 38). Washington, DC: Urban Institute.

Wolock, I., Sherman, P., Feldman, L., & Metzger, B. (2001). Child abuse and neglect referral patterns: A longitudinal study. *Children and Youth Services Review, 23*(1), 21–47.

Zuravin, S., & DePanfilis, D. (1997). Factors affecting foster care placement of children receiving child protective services. *Social Work Research, 21*(1), 34–42.

Zuravin, S., Orme, J., & Hegar, R. (1995). Disposition of child physical abuse reports: Review of the literature and test of a predictive model. *Children and Youth Services Review, 17,* 547–566.

CHAPTER 12

The Effect of Race on Reunification from Substitute Care in Illinois

Robert M. Goerge and Lucy Mackey Bilaver

Background

The goal of this study is to better understand, in a quantitative manner, the reunification of children in Illinois, with a particular focus on understanding why African American children reunify with their families more slowly than white children. This phenomenon has been a fact in Illinois for many years, and researchers have undertaken a significant effort to better understand the reasons for it. Although this chapter does not definitively explain why this is the case, the authors believe it makes some suggestions about the causes of this disparity. In addition, they present data on the likelihood of children of Hispanic and other racial and ethnic groups achieving reunification.

The authors conducted multivariate modeling of reunification to better understand what characteristics of children, families, services, and neighborhoods reduce the magnitude of the race effect when it is the only explanatory variable. The primary question to be addressed is: What are the factors that affect the likelihood of reunification of African American children with their parents? To explore this question, the researchers contrasted the reunification of African American children with children of other races and ethnicities. They approached this question by modeling the race effects and adding explanatory variables. In this way, they analyzed the effect that additional covariates have on the magnitude of the race effect. Not only does this analysis attempt to understand the effect of covariates used in previous studies, it also includes new covariates and relies on more precise statistical methods.

Policy Changes

There have been some major policy and program changes that were intended to change the achievement of permanence for children in foster care. The federal Adoption and Safe Families Act (ASFA) was intended to provide procedures and incentives to move children who were unlikely to be reunified more quickly toward adoption. Also, in Illinois, the Subsidized Guardianship Program helps children who were languishing in foster care, very often with relatives, move out of foster care into a more permanent placement. Because African American children have traditionally spent longer periods of time in foster care, the authors believe that these children might be more affected by these two major changes.

Literature Review

The latest report of the Multistate Foster Care Data Archive included a multivariate analysis of the discharge of nearly 500,000 children who entered foster care from 1988 to 1998 in 11 states—Alabama, California, Illinois, Iowa, Maryland, Michigan, New Jersey, New York, North Carolina, Ohio, and Wisconsin (Wulczyn, Brunner, & Goerge, 2000). In each of these states, African American children were discharged from foster care more slowly than white or Hispanic children when controlling for year of entry, region, gender, age at entry, and type of foster care. The effect ranged from 33% slower than white children in Illinois to only 4% slower in New Jersey. Across all of these states combined, African American children were discharged 19% slower than white children.

Although discharge includes children who were adopted or discharged for other reasons, reunification represents about 50% of all discharges, and the researchers expect that these race effects would be quite similar if they only analyzed reunification. Other research also points to race being a major factor in reunification (Courtney, 1994; Goerge, 1990; Wells & Guo, 1999). In a study of reunification of children placed in care in Illinois between 1977 and 1986, Goerge (1990) detected effects of race in the spell-level analysis, whereas race effects were not present in the placement-level models. When the authors replicated the study for the 1987 through 1996 cohorts, race effects became statistically significant in both the placement- and spell-level analyses.

Data

The data used for this analysis come from the Integrated Database on Child and Family Services in Illinois. The primary data source is the Illinois Department of Children and Family Services Child Abuse and Neglect Tracking System and Child and Youth Services

Information System. The population of interest included all children age 17 or younger who entered an out-of-home placement between January 1, 1990, and March 31, 2000.

The authors excluded adoption assistance cases that resulted in out-of-home placement. This population included 80,770 children who had 86,866 spells in out-of-home care during the observation period. For the multivariate models, the authors sampled 10% of those who had nonmissing values of all independent variables (they excluded 6,263 spells due to missing information). The final sample for the Illinois model included 8,065 spells representing 7,333 children. For modeling Cook County cases separately, the researchers drew a random sample of 10% of Cook County cases (4,724 children).

This analysis explored the explanatory power of variables at several levels, including the community, the individual, and the case. At the community level, the multivariate models included community characteristics measured at the ZIP code of the child's birthfamily's address. In particular, the models include an indicator of whether a child came from a ZIP code with a 40% or greater rate of child poverty.

In addition to individual demographic characteristics such as race, age, and gender used in previous studies, the researchers included an indicator of disability status. Although this indicator is not a verified measure of a child's disability status, they believe that it reflects the severity of the disability and its effect on serving the child.

The reason for entry is the particular abuse and neglect allegation that led to the out-of-home placement. Allegation-specific indicators included sexual abuse, physical abuse, substance-exposed infant (SEI), lack of supervision, substantial risk of harm, and other abuse and neglect.

Among time-varying covariates, the researchers included an indicator of placement in the home of the relative. The indicator is equal to one when the child is placed with a relative and zero otherwise. Similarly, they constructed a time-varying indicator to mark time when the child was under the case management of a private agency. The multivariate models also included a time-varying control for the permanency goal status. The permanency goal status is one if the child had a permanency goal of reunification and zero otherwise.

Method

The statistical approach used to identify what child, case, neighborhood, and administrative practices affect how quickly a child is reunified with his or her parents is based on a multilevel hazard model (see Lillard, 1993; Lillard & Panis, 1998). The authors used aML software to estimated the multilevel hazard models. Their intention was to extend the failure-time hazard framework to a multilevel context. The model is multilevel because it uses data at the community (defined at the ZIP code level), child, and out-of-home spell level. In addition, changes in characteristics such as placement types, policy changes, and permanency goal adjustments represent a fourth level.

The hazard rate is the measure that is most relevant to the outcome the authors wished to study. The hazard rate describes the probability that a child returns to the home of the parent at a time *t*, given that he or she has not returned home before *t*. The dependent variable is the log hazard of reunification at time *t* for a child with community characteristics (*c*), child characteristics (*k*), spell characteristics (*s*), and interval characteristics (time-varying covariates [*i*]). Unlike Cox proportional hazard models, the baseline duration dependence is specified in the models used in this analysis. The baseline duration dependence is a piecewise-linear spline (also known as generalized Gompertz). The model that was estimated can be described as follows:

$$\ln h^{1st}_{\mathrm{cksi}}(t \mid \mathrm{X}, \varepsilon) = \alpha_0 + \alpha_1' \mathrm{A}_{\mathrm{cksi}}(t) + \alpha_2' \mathrm{X}_{\mathrm{c}} + \alpha_3' \mathrm{X}_{\mathrm{ck}} + \alpha_4' \mathrm{X}_{\mathrm{cks}} + \alpha_5' \mathrm{X}_{\mathrm{cksi}}(t) + \varepsilon \quad (1)$$

The second term in the equation represents the baseline duration dependence. The next four terms represent the proportional effects of covariates. The final term represents the effects of unmeasured factors at the community, child, and spell levels.

Results

Table 12-1 presents the descriptive statistics for the sample that was modeled. Of the children in the sample, 35% resided in communities with 40% or greater concentrations of child poverty at the time of foster care placement. The majority (71%) of the children in the sample are African American, 23% are white, and 6% are Hispanic. More than half were younger than age 4 at the time of placement into foster care. Fifteen percent had disabilities. Among the spell-level variables, two-thirds of the sample consisted of Cook County cases (64%). The type of abuse or neglect experienced prior to out-of-home placement revealed that more than half of the children in the sample entered care after substantiated lack-of-supervision or substantial-risk-of-harm allegations. Twelve percent entered as SEIs, and only 3% entered after substantiated sexual abuse.

When examining these distributions by race, several of the characteristics vary considerably. The percentage of children coming from communities with 40% or greater child poverty was much higher for African American and Hispanic children than for white and other children. Nearly half of the African American children (46%) and one-quarter of Hispanic children (26%) came from such communities. Age distribution of children in the sample also varied across the race groups. Of the African American chil-

Table 12-1: Descriptive Statistics for Children in 10% Sample by Race

Variable	Total	African American	White	Hispanic	Other
Community-Level					
Child originates from ZIP code with ≥40% child poverty	35	46	5	26	6
Child-Level					
White	23	—	100	—	—
African American	71	100	—	—	—
Hispanic	6	—	—	100	—
Other race/ethnicity	1	—	—	—	100
Male	51	50	53	51	54
Female	49	50	47	49	46
Presence of disability	15	12	22	13	19
Infant	27	30	20	23	33
Ages 1–3	25	25	25	26	30
Ages 4–6	19	18	18	22	21
Ages 7–9	15	15	17	17	7
Ages 10–12	14	12	19	11	8
Age 13 or older	0	0	1	0	1
Spell-Level[a]					
Cook County case	64	77	23	78	32
Non–Cook County case	36	23	77	22	68
Entered 1990–1991	15	16	16	13	10
Entered 1992–1993	23	24	23	20	17
Entered 1994–1995	27	29	23	30	23
Entered 1996–1997	18	18	19	20	30
Entered 1998–2000	16	14	19	17	20
Sexual abuse	3	2	6	5	1
Physical abuse	7	5	10	10	12
Substance-exposed infant	12	14	5	6	7
Lack of supervision	31	32	29	25	25
Substantial risk of harm	22	20	26	27	29
Other abuse or neglect	10	9	12	11	8
No linked abuse or neglect	17	18	12	16	18
One out-of-home spell	91	93	87	93	90
More than one out-of-home spell	9	7	13	7	10
Time-Varying Covariates[a]					
Ever in relative care	65	72	48	59	40
Ever served by private agency	58	66	34	60	40
Ever had permanency goal of reunification	81	79	85	79	79

[a] Percentages describe the sample during the first spell only.

dren, 30% entered care entered as infants, compared with 20% of white children, 23% of Hispanic children, and 33% of children of other races. The concentration of African American and Hispanic children coming from Cook County mirrored the percentages coming from poor communities. Seventy-seven percent of African American children and 78% of Hispanic children were served in Cook County. A final factor that varied substantially across the race groups was the use of relative care placements. Of African American children, 72% had been placed with a relative during their foster care placement spell, whereas only 48% of white children, 59% of Hispanic children, and 40% of children of other races had a similar experience.

Multivariate, Multilevel Results

Table 12-2 presents the results of six nested specifications of the model (Models 1–6). In the first specification, the researchers included race in addition to the baseline duration dependencies. Both African American and Hispanic children are much less likely to be reunified when controlling for time in care.

The second specification includes an indicator for Cook County cases. Including this characteristic in the model highlights the race effects dramatically. The magnitude of the race effect for African American children is reduced by 50%, and the race effect for Hispanic children is no longer statistically significant. This suggests that part of the reason that African American children are reunified at a slower rate than other children is that characteristics of Cook County, in which the largest proportion of African American children live, cause slower reunification.

The remaining model specifications do not seem to affect the race effect. Of particular note is the fact that the addition of covariates for age, type of placement, and poverty failed to change the magnitude of the race effect. The authors expected the effect to be diminished by the addition of these covariates because each disproportionately affects African American children. The fact that the race effect did not change suggests that it reflects characteristics unrelated to the independent effects of age at placement, type of placement, and poverty on the time to reunification.

Interaction Effects

With the available covariates, the authors found that African American children have a hazard of reunification two-thirds (.65) that of white children when controlling for other covariates. Although this is a valid estimate across Illinois, significant interaction effects may differentially affect African American children. The researchers used region and cohort interaction effects with all of the variables in the model by running separate

Table 12-2A: Estimated Parameters for Multilevel Model of Reunification in Illinois

Covariates	**Model 1**	**Model 2**	**Model 3**	**Model 4**	**Model 5**	**Model 6**
Duration 0–2 months	-0.0269***	-0.0267***	-0.0266***	-0.0259***	-0.0259***	-0.0266***
Duration 2–6 months	-0.0023***	-0.0022***	-0.0022***	-0.0021**	-0.0021**	-0.0021**
Duration 6–18 months	-0.0010***	-0.0009***	-0.0009***	-0.0008***	-0.0008***	-0.0004
Duration 18–24 months	-0.0010**	-0.0008*	-0.0008*	-0.0008	-0.0008	0.0005
Duration >24 months	-0.0005***	-0.0004***	-0.0005***	-0.0004***	-0.0004***	-0.0002***
Constant	-5.2509***	-5.1163***	-5.0251***	-4.7067***	-4.6939***	-5.6056***
African American	-0.9854***	-0.5149***	-0.4637***	-0.4815***	-0.4440***	-0.4305***
Hispanic	-0.5473***	-0.0398	-0.0104	-0.0535	-0.0421	-0.0595
Other	-0.2480*	-0.2005	-0.1123	-0.1320	-0.1367	-0.0903
Cook County		-0.9549***	-0.9346***	-0.9586***	-0.9381***	-0.8914***
Male			-0.0299	0.0178	0.0155	0.0209
Infant			-0.4669***	-0.4785***	-0.4786***	-0.4156***
Age 4–6			0.0990*	0.1597***	0.1575***	0.1770***
Age 7–9			0.1085*	0.2090***	0.2084***	0.2070***
Age 10–12			0.2417***	0.3506***	0.3485***	0.3830***
Age ≥13			0.2495	0.5489	0.5388	0.5422
Entered care 1992–1993			-0.1836***	-0.1269**	-0.1324**	-0.1052
Entered care 1994–1995			-0.1393**	-0.0879	-0.0955	-0.0610
Entered care 1996–1997			-0.0630	-0.0421	-0.0503	-0.0154
Entered care 1998–2000			-0.1325**	-0.1448*	-0.1538*	-0.1857**
In relative care				-0.3230***	-0.3234***	-0.3232***
Sexual abuse				-0.1414	-0.1436	-0.1923*
Physical abuse				0.1678**	0.1691**	0.0920
Substance-exposed infant				-0.2184*	-0.2195*	-0.1803
Lack of supervision				-0.0822	-0.0824	-0.1246*
Substantial risk of harm				-0.0083	-0.0092	-0.0517
Other abuse or neglect				-0.1777**	-0.1739**	-0.2206**
Private agency case management				-0.0165	-0.0152	0.0095
Presence of disability				-0.8830***	-0.8862***	-0.8618***
Number of spells				-0.0905*	-0.0914*	-0.0105
Child originates from ZIP code with 50% or greater child poverty					-0.1350***	-0.1145**
Child had a permanency goal of reunification						0.9118***
ln-L	-24,927.79	-24,693.09	-24,614.52	-24,467.95	-24,464.22	24,305.63

$^*p < .1$. $^{**}p < .05$. $^{***}p < .01$.

Table 12-2B: Estimated Parameters for Multilevel Model of Reunification in Illinois by Risk Ratio

Covariates	Model 1	Model 2	Model 3	Model 4	Model 5	Model 6
Duration 0–2 months	0.97***	0.97***	0.97***	0.97***	0.97***	0.97***
Duration 2–6 months	1.00***	1.00***	1.00***	1.00**	1.00**	1.00**
Duration 6–18 months	1.00***	1.00***	1.00***	1.00***	1.00***	1.00
Duration 18–24 months	1.00**	1.00*	1.00*	1.00	1.00	1.00
Duration >24 months	1.00***	1.00***	1.00***	1.00***	1.00***	1.00***
Constant	0.01***	0.01***	0.01***	0.01***	0.01***	0.00***
African American	0.37***	0.60***	0.63***	0.62***	0.64***	0.65***
Hispanic	0.58***	0.96	0.99	0.95	0.96	0.94
Other	0.78*	0.82	0.89	0.88	0.87	0.91
Cook County		0.38***	0.39***	0.38***	0.39***	0.41***
Male			0.97	1.02	1.02	1.02
Infant			0.63***	0.62***	0.62***	0.66***
Age 4–6			1.10*	1.17***	1.17***	1.19***
Age 7–9			1.11*	1.23***	1.23***	1.23***
Age 10–12			1.27***	1.42***	1.42***	1.47***
Age ≥13			1.28	1.73	1.71	1.72
Entered care 1992–1993			0.83***	0.88**	0.88**	0.90
Entered care 1994–1995			0.87**	0.92	0.91	0.94
Entered care 1996–1997			0.94	0.96	0.95	0.98
Entered care 1998–2000			0.88**	0.87*	0.86*	0.83**
In relative care				0.72***	0.72***	0.72***
Sexual abuse				0.87	0.87	0.83*
Physical abuse				1.18**	1.18**	1.10
Substance-exposed infant				0.80*	0.80*	0.84
Lack of supervision				0.92	0.92	0.88*
Substantial risk of harm				0.99	0.99	0.95
Other abuse or neglect				0.84**	0.84**	0.80**
Private agency case management				0.98	0.98	1.01
Presence of disability				0.41***	0.41***	0.42***
Number of spells				0.91*	0.91*	0.99
Child originates from ZIP code with 50% or greater child poverty					0.87***	0.89**
Child had a permanency goal of reunification						2.49***

$^{*}p < .1$. $^{**}p < .05$. $^{***}p < .01$.

models by region and cohort. Table 12-3 presents the effect of race among children from Cook County cases only. The relative risk of reunification for African American children compared with white children is nearly identical in the Cook County and Illinois models in the final model specification. Of course, because Cook County children are reunified more slowly than children in the balance of the state, African American children in Cook County are reunified more slowly than African American children in the balance of the state.

The effect of race did change significantly across time. Table 12-4 presents the estimated effects of race in the final model specification by entry cohort. The cohort models are based on the entire set of cases falling in the study population. For spells beginning during 1990 and 1991, African American children were 26% less likely to be reunified than white children during the same time period. Between 1992 and 1997, the likelihood of reunification among African American children decreased with coefficients of .64 to .69 that of white children controlling for other covariates. Among children entering care during 1998 to 2000, the likelihood increased once again to levels equal to those of the 1990–1991 cohort. In time period, African American children remained 21% less likely to reunify than white children. As was the case in the Illinois model, the addition of the Cook County indicator in each of the cohort models explained the largest amount of the African American effect in Illinois.

There was strong evidence of a changing effect of race over time for Hispanic children. The models for 1990 to 1991 and 1992 to 1993 reveal effects similar to those observed in the Illinois model. In the final model specification, the researchers saw evidence that Hispanic and white children have similar hazards of reunification when controlling for other covariates; however, the picture changes dramatically from 1994 to 1995. Hispanic children entering during these two years were significantly less likely to be reunified than white children. In the final model specification, they remain 18% less likely to be reunified. Although each of the coefficients remain negative for Hispanic children entering between 1996 and 1997, most estimates are not statistically significant. From 1998 to 2000, the hazard of reunification among Hispanic children once again equaled that of white children in the state and represented a significant increase in the hazard over the 1996–1997 cohort when controlling for other covariates. Across each of the cohorts, no evidence existed that the relative risk of reunification among children of primarily Asian, Native American, and mixed racial groups (which consist of biracial children as well as children in other racial groups) differed from that of white children.

Given that the full model suggested some significant interaction effects between race and other key covariates, the researchers also estimated the models for each racial and

Table 12-3: Estimated Parameters for Multilevel Model of Reunification in Cook County by Risk Ratio

Covariate	Model 1	Model 2	Model 3	Model 4	Model 5
Duration 0–2 months	0.96***	0.96***	0.96***	0.96***	0.96***
Duration 2–6 months	1.00	1.00	1.00	1.00	1.00
Duration 6–18 months	1.00	1.00	1.00	1.00	1.00
Duration 18–24 months	1.00	1.00	1.00	1.00	1.00***
Duration >24 months	1.00***	1.00***	1.00*	1.00*	1.00
Constant	0.00***	0.00***	0.00***	0.00***	0.00***
African American	0.56***	0.59***	0.61***	0.64***	0.65***
Hispanic	1.19	1.11	1.06	1.07	1.03
Other	1.12	1.07	1.00	0.99	1.04
Male		0.97	0.99	0.98	0.98
Infant		0.55***	0.58***	0.58***	0.67**
Age 4–6		1.11	1.13	1.14	1.19
Age 7–9		1.08	1.14	1.14	1.19
Age 10–12		1.19	1.28*	1.28	1.46**
Age ≥13		0.62	0.61	0.62	0.78
Entered care 1992–1993		0.80**	0.81*	0.81	0.85
Entered care 1994–1995		1.12	1.13	1.13	1.23
Entered care 1996–1997		1.40**	1.38*	1.38*	1.48**
Entered care 1998–2000		1.54***	1.44**	1.42*	1.27
In relative care			0.72***	0.71***	0.71***
Sexual abuse			1.11	1.10	0.94
Physical abuse			0.96	0.96	0.84
Substance-exposed infant			0.70	0.70	0.75
Lack of supervision			0.82	0.82	0.77
Substantial risk of harm			1.06	1.06	0.96
Other abuse or neglect			0.91	0.92	0.84
Private agency case management			0.96	0.96	1.00
Presence of disability			0.42***	0.42***	0.43***
Number of spells			1.21	1.20	1.25
Child originates from ZIP code with ≥50% child poverty				0.87	0.86
Child had a permanency goal of reunification					3.91***
ln-L	-11,529.07	-11,465.49	-11,413.42	-11,410.80	11,239.93

*$p < .1$. **$p < .05$. ***$p < .01$.

Table 12-4: Estimated Race Effects for Multilevel Model of Reunification by Cohort

Covariates	Cohort	Final Model Parameter Estimate	*p*	Risk Ratio
Black	1990–1991	-.2993	***	0.74
	1992–1993	-.4552	***	0.63
	1994–1995	-.3678	***	0.69
	1996–1997	-.3908	***	0.68
	1998–2000	-.2401	***	0.79
Hispanic	1990–1991	.0843		1.09
	1992–1993	.0434		1.04
	1994–1995	-.2052	***	0.81
	1996–1997	-.1359	*	0.87
	1998–2000	.0686		1.07
Other	1990–1991	.0724		1.08
	1992–1993	-.1350		0.87
	1994–1995	.0778		1.08
	1996–1997	-.1394		0.87
	1998–2000	-.1263		0.88

*$p < .1$. ***$p < .01$.

ethnic group separately. The results in Table 12-5 reveal the known factors that affect the likelihood of reunification in each group. The table shows the final model specification for each race category. Across all of the race groups, certain factors are common. In all groups, coming from Cook County, being placed with a relative, having a disability, or entering between 1998 and 2000 reduces the likelihood of reunification relative to the children in the comparison categories. Having a permanency goal of reunification increased the likelihood of reunification for all of the race groups.

Discussion

For foster children in Illinois during the 1990s, race is a strong predictor of the likelihood of reunification. This analysis illustrates that when race is the only predictor of reunification, a significant proportion of the effect reflects differences in the regional distribution of children by race. Specifically, the likelihood of reunification changes significantly for African American and Hispanic children when controlling for where the child lived at the time of placement. After controlling for Cook County, however, only African American children have a statistically significant different likelihood of reunification compared with white children. Not only does the effect remain statistically significant, surprisingly, it does not change with the addition to the model of other characteristics of children, their parents, and services that the authors believed would lower

Table 12-5: Estimated Parameters for Multilevel Model of Reunification by Race by Risk Ratio

Covariates	African American	Hispanic	Other Race/Ethnicity	White
Duration 0–2 months	0.97***	0.98***	0.97***	0.98***
Duration 2–6 months	1.00	0.99***	1.00	1.00***
Duration 6–18 months	1.00	1.00	1.00	1.00***
Duration 18–24 months	1.00	1.00	1.00	1.00***
Duration >24 months	1.00	1.00***	1.00***	1.00***
Constant	0.00***	0.00***	0.01***	0.01***
Cook County	0.39***	0.51***	0.47***	0.43***
Male	1.01	1.06	1.04	1.09***
Infant	0.56***	0.85	0.55***	0.60***
Age 4–6	1.01	1.03	1.24	1.11***
Age 7–9	1.18	1.24**	1.26	1.24***
Age 10–12	1.28**	1.39***	1.43**	1.40***
Age ≥13	0.95	1.61	2.01**	1.71***
Entered care 1992–1993	0.85	0.70***	0.83	0.86***
Entered care 1994–1995	0.96	0.79***	0.91	0.82***
Entered care 1996–1997	1.09	0.84**	0.88	0.87***
Entered care 1998–2000	0.82*	0.78***	0.85	0.75***
In relative care	0.66***	0.86***	0.73***	0.91***
Sexual abuse	1.01	1.46***	1.00	0.79***
Physical abuse	1.27*	1.13	1.54***	1.13***
Substance-exposed infant	0.91	0.48***	0.81	0.86*
Lack of supervision	0.86*	0.88	0.88	0.91***
Substantial risk of harm	1.03	1.14	1.05	1.01
Other abuse or neglect	0.77***	0.72***	0.82	0.88***
Private agency case management	1.05	0.92	0.84*	0.90***
Presence of disability	0.41***	0.39***	0.52***	0.44***
Number of spells	1.06	0.82***	0.74**	0.91***
Child originates from ZIP code with 50% or greater child poverty	0.94	1.09	0.57***	0.70***
Child had a permanency goal of reunification	2.79***	1.63***	1.64***	1.27***
ln-L	14,154.75	13,913.96	-4,947.75	-76,612.90

*$p < .1$. **$p < .05$. ***$p < .01$.

the likelihood of reunification and disproportionately affect African American children. For example, children living in relative care placement reunify more slowly than children in other living arrangements. From this analysis, the effect appears independent of race, meaning that the African American effect in the model without a control for HMR placement does not reflect the characteristic that children placed with relatives reunify more slowly. The same lack of relationship to race is true for the effect of age at first placement and poverty.

The question remains, What does the differential likelihood of reunification between African American and white children reflect? Although the authors have pursued with one statistical approach, the inclusion of variables that might explain the differential, they have not exhausted that strategy. Another approach is to capture these effects through inclusion of more characteristics of the birthparents. In particular, the authors believe that the educational level and earnings history of the parents could strengthen the current analysis. These measures would capture the important human capital dimension of the parents. Another birthparent characteristic is the amount of visitation that occurs while the child is in substitute care. As demonstrated by Davis, Landsverk, Newton, and Ganger (1996), parental visitation at the level recommended by the court was associated with a greater likelihood of reunification. Although administrative databases do not identify these data, they are a key measure that could explain part of the remaining effect of race.

This study also finds that the effects of race are independent of some factors while dependent on others. The model including a sample of Cook County children showed an African American race effect remarkably similar to that found in the model for the entire state. This finding suggests that there are some characteristics of African American children in all areas of the state that explain the longer times to reunification and provide more support for the inclusion of parental characteristics. This study also finds a relationship between the race effects and time during some years of the study period. This finding supports the idea that there are effects of practice, policy, or other variables that this analysis leaves uncontrolled. Researchers must continue to study why children of different racial and ethnic backgrounds vary in their likelihood of reunification (and other child welfare outcomes) during specific time periods, in specific communities, and under different policy and practice models.

References

Courtney, M. E. (1994). Factors associated with the reunification of foster children with their families. *Social Service Review, 68*, 81–108.

Davis, I., Landsverk, J., Newton, R., & Ganger, W. (1996). Parental visiting and foster care reunification. *Child and Youth Services Review, 18*, 363–382.

Goerge, R. (1990). The reunification process in substitute care. *Social Service Review, 64*, 422–457.

Lillard, L. A. (1993). Simultaneous equations for hazards: Marital duration and fertility timing. *Journal of Econometrics, 56*(1–2), 189–217.

Lillard, L. A., & Panis, C. W. A. (1998, April). *Multiprocess multilevel modeling*. Paper presented at PAA Meeting in Chicago.

Wells, K., & Guo, S. Y. (1999). Reunification and reentry of foster children. *Child and Youth Services Review, 21*, 273–294.

Wulczyn, F., Brunner, K., & Goerge, R. (2000). *An update from the Multistate Foster Care Data Archive: Foster case dynamics 1983–1998.* Chicago: Chapin Hall Center for Children at the University of Chicago.

CHAPTER 13

The Role of Race in Parental Reunification

Robert B. Hill

Reuniting children in foster care with their families has been a primary goal of public and private child welfare services for many years. In fact, a major objective of the landmark Adoption Assistance and Child Welfare Act of 1980 was to institute timelines to expedite children's discharge from foster care, and, to the extent possible, facilitate a timely return to their families. Moreover, the Adoption and Safe Families Act of 1997 (ASFA) allows states to use federal funds to provide reunification services for the first 15 months after a child enters foster care.

ASFA, however, also reduces from 18 to 12 months the length of time that a child may remain in foster care without a permanency hearing, and it requires states to file for termination of the rights of parents of children who have spent 15 of the most recent 22 months in foster care. These shortened time frames present special challenges for efforts to reunite children with parents who may have serious problems, such as drug addiction, alcoholism, or child abuse (Courtney, 1995; Goerge & Lee, Chapter 10, this volume; Hohman & Butt, 2001).

Such reduced timelines may have special implications for children of color, because many child welfare studies have identified racial differentials among children in out-of-home care. They have documented the fact that African American children are more likely than white children to be placed in foster care, to be placed in kinship care, and to remain in care for longer time periods (Courtney et al., 1996; Goerge & Lee, Chapter 10, this volume; McMurty & Lie, 1992; U.S. Children's Bureau, 1997).

Several studies have also found racial patterns in parental reunification (Courtney, 1994; Goerge & Bilaver, Chapter 12, this volume; McMurty & Lie, 1992; Wells & Guo, 1999). For example, workers reunify white children more quickly and at higher rates than African American children. What are the reasons for the lower reunification rates of African American children? To what extent are they due to the greater economic deprivation and associated social problems among African American families relative to white families? Alternatively, are these lower rates a result of racial insensitivity? That is, does the foster care system treat African American families with the same characteristics and problems as white families differently? This study will address the role of race in reunification patterns.

Prior Research

This review focuses on five reunification studies (Barth et al., 1986; Courtney, 1994; Goerge, 1990; McMurty & Lie, 1992; Wells & Guo, 1999). The author selected these studies because: (a) reunification was a major dependent variable, (b) race was an important independent variable, (c) they had adequate size samples of African Americans, and (d) they employed rigorous multivariate statistical techniques. Four studies used event history or hazard rates analyses that focused on reunification patterns for first-time cohorts of children based on administrative records (Courtney, 1994; Goerge, 1990; McMurty & Lie, 1992; Wells & Guo, 1999).

The study by Goerge (1990) tracked a statewide sample of children in Illinois who entered foster care for the first time from 1977 to 1984. He employed proportional hazards analysis to describe the declining probability of reunification the longer a child remained in foster care. Interestingly, his analysis did not find lower reunification rates for African Americans than whites, nor that race alone had any independent or main effects on reunification rates. Goerge did find interactions between race and region. For example, African American children in Cook County had a lower probability of reunification than non–African American children in Cook County. He also found that children who were not placed with relatives had higher reunification rates than children placed with relatives.

Courtney (1994) also used the proportional-hazard regression model to track the experiences of a cohort of children who entered foster care for the first time between January 1988 and May 1991. His analysis revealed that less than half of the children entering foster care for the first time would be reunified with their families within three years. Among children reunified with their families, about half went home within six months and about 70% returned within one year. Thus, Courtney concluded the probability of reunification is greatest immediately following placement. His analysis also revealed important differences in reunification patterns between children placed with relatives and those placed with nonrelatives. About half of the children placed with nonrelatives during the first six months of the study were reunified, compared with only 36% of those placed with relatives; however, the differences declined between the two groups for children who had been in care for more than six months. As a result of these deviations from the proportional-hazards framework, Courtney stratified his sample into relatives' and nonrelatives' placement types.

Courtney (1994) found racial differentials in reunification. Whether the children were placed with relatives or not, African American children were reunified at about half the rate of white children, regardless of age. Further analyses revealed that these differences were due in part to the lower reunification rates of African American children who were infants or older youth than the rates of white children who were infants or older youth. In fact, race and age interactions revealed that among children placed with nonrelatives, African American children between the ages of 1 and 12 years old had similar reunification rates as comparable-age white children. Yet he found no similar race and age interactions between African Americans and whites among children placed with relatives.

Wells and Guo (1999) conducted a longitudinal study of children who entered the foster care system for the first time in Cuyahoga County, Ohio, between January 1, 1992, and December 31, 1993. Their study used administrative records for more than four years and three months from January 1, 1992, through March 31, 1996. They examined rates of reunification 24 months after each child's first entry into foster care. Wells and Guo employed proportional hazards regression models to conduct event-history analysis of rates of reunification and reentry. The researchers found racial differentials in reunification: African American children had lower rates of reunification than white children. They also found an interaction between race and age of entry. Workers reunified African American infants at slower rates than non–African American infants; however, these differentials declined as the children got older, such that by age 13, no differences existed in reunification rates between the racial groups. Interestingly, the researchers did not find different reunification rates between children placed with relatives and nonrelatives.

McMurty and Lie (1992), who conducted a study of children entering foster care in Arizona, found lower rates of reunification among African American children than white children. Barth and colleagues (1986) conducted a stepwise discriminant analysis of the discharge status of children who had been placed in foster care for physical abuse in San Mateo County, California. Among the study sample of 101 children who had been discharged between 1980 and 1984, 80 were reunified and 21 had other permanent out-of-home placements (including adoption, placement with kin, guardianship, and emancipation). Barth et al. found that African American children were less likely to be reunified than white children.

Four of the five studies found lower rates of reunification for African American than white children (Barth et al., 1986; Courtney, 1994; McMurty & Lie, 1992; Wells & Guo, 1999). Two studies found interactions between race and age of entry, that is, racial differentials in reunification rates at younger ages, which declined as the children grew older (Courtney, 1994; Wells & Guo, 1999). Two studies found lower reunification rates among children who were placed with relatives than among those placed with nonrelatives (Courtney, 1994; Goerge, 1990).

The study reported in this chapter seeks to answer the question, Is race a strong predictor of reunification when combined with other important child, family, or case history characteristics? Related questions are (a) What other child, family, or case history characteristics are also strong predictors of reunification? and (b) Are the main effects of race reduced when controlling for other important predictors?

Method

The data for this study came from the 1994 National Study of Protective, Preventive and Reunification Services Delivered to Children and Their Families (NSPPRS). An objective of NSPPRS, which Westat conducted, was to document the number and characteristics of children and families who received various in-home or out-of-home child welfare services between March 1, 1993, and March 1, 1994, based on a national sample of 2,109 children. This chapter will focus on the subsample of 1,034 children who had foster care experiences (i.e., who were placed in foster care) during the study period.

This chapter's primary analysis methods are logistic regression models. Other reunification studies used many of the study variables. The independent variables fall into three groups: children's characteristics, family characteristics, and case history characteristics. Children's characteristics include race, gender, age at entry, and disability status. Family characteristics include social class index (combining parent's education and employment status) and whether the parent lacks job skills, has substance abuse problems, is a single mother, or receives Aid to Families with Dependent Children (AFDC). Case history characteristics include reason for placement (only abuse allegation and only neglect allegation), placement type (relative or nonrelative), and services provided to the caregiver. The study asked caseworkers whether the caregivers received any of the following services: parent training (at home or in classes); household management; homemaker services; day care; respite care; emergency financial aid; family planning; legal services; schooling; employment training; health care; mental health treatment, outpatient or inpatient; substance abuse treatment, outpatient or inpatient; self-help groups; housing; housing payment; temporary shelter; and transportation. The dependent variable in this analysis is parental reunification (that is, the proportion of children who were reunified versus those who were discharged for other reasons or are still in care). The specific codes for the independent and dependent variables are described in Appendix 13-A.

Findings

The data in Table 13-1 reveal that workers reunified 34% of white children, compared with only 9% of African American children. Thus, white children are four times more likely than African American children to be reunified. To identify the independent variables that were strong predictors of reunification, the researcher ran logistic regressions separately with single factors. Table 13-2 presents the rankings of 15 variables by size of R^2. Eleven variables have significant bivariate relationships with reunification: race, services provided to caregivers, age of entry, parental job skills, socioeconomic status (SES), parental employment status, parental substance abuse problem, child placed because of neglect allegation, child placed because of abuse allegation, parental education, and relative caregiver.

These findings reveal that reunification rates were higher among parental caregivers who received services, who had job skills, who had no substance abuse problem, who had completed high school, and who were currently working. Moreover, white and older children had higher reunification rates than African American and younger children. In addition, children with relative caregivers had lower reunification rates than children with nonrelatives. Yet it should be noted that abuse and neglect allegations had opposite relationships with reunification. Children with abuse allegations were more likely to be reunified, whereas children with neglect allegations were less likely to be reunified. On the other hand, four variables were not significantly related to reunification: child disability, child's gender, if parent was a single mother, and whether the child's parental household received AFDC. Thus, the researcher decided to drop these four variables from any further analysis.

To examine the possible presence of multicollinearity, the author examined correlations between the nine variables that were significantly related to reunification (Table 13-3). He did not include parental education and employment status because they com-

Table 13-1: Reunification by Race

	White	African American	Total
Weighted *N*	277,858	303,840	581,698
Total percentage	100	100	100
Reunified	34	9	21
Not reunified[a]	66	91	79

Note: $p = .00$.

[a] *Not reunified* includes children discharged for reasons other than reunification and those children who are still in care.

Table 13-2: Single-Factor Predictors of Reunification

Predictors	Estimates	*p* Value	$(100)R^2$	*F* Value
Race	-1.61	.00*	9.2%	22.98
No caregiver services	-1.36	.00*	6.4%	19.97
Age at entry	0.11	.00*	5.5%	24.81
Lack of job skills	-1.35	.00*	5.2%	23.22
Low socioeconomic status	-1.27	.00*	4.9%	16.74
Not employed	-0.99	.00*	3.5%	11.60
Substance abuser	-0.91	.00*	3.2%	11.32
Neglect allegation	-0.98	.01*	2.8%	9.43
Abuse allegation	0.90	.00*	2.7%	9.95
Low education	-0.63	.03*	1.6%	5.01
Kin caregiver	-0.68	.03*	1.2%	5.14
Child disability	-0.15	.64	0.1%	.23
Child gender	-0.09	.65	0.0%	.21
Single mother	0.14	.48	0.0%	.52
Aid to Families with Dependent Children recipient	0.09	.73	0.0%	.13

*Statistically significant relationships at $p \leq .05$.

Table 13-3: Correlations of Estimates

	No Services	Entry Age	Lack Skills	Substance Abuser	Neglect Allegation	Abuse Allegation	Kin Caregiver	Low Socioeconomic Status
Race	-.12	.38	.18	-.36	.19	.39	.53	.01
No services		-.15	.21	.05	-.16	-.16	.05	.21
Age of entry			.11	.15	-.11	-.04	-.25	.08
Lack job skills				.30	-.06	.23	-.14	-.28
Substance abuser					.04	.15	-.08	-.61
Neglect allegation						.53	.01	-.37
Abuse allegation							-.34	-.27
Kin caregiver								-.06

prised the SES index. The strongest correlations were found between substance abuse problems and SES (-.61), between abuse and neglect allegations (.53), and between race and placement with kin (-.53). To minimize collinearity problems, the author excluded abuse allegation from the initial analyses of the best-fitting models for predicting reunification and retained neglect. Despite the high correlations between relative placement and race and between SES and substance abuse problems, the author decided to retain them to assess their effects on the best-fitting models, because they were important predictors of reunification in prior studies.

Best-Fitting Regression Model

To identify possible interaction effects among the stronger predictors, the researcher examined several regression models (such as Race X Entry Age, Race X Services, Race X Job Skills, Race X Substance Abuse Problem, Race X Kinship Placement, Substance Abuse X Services, etc.). None of the interaction terms, however, maintained significance in combination with the remaining variables. In some cases, the addition of interaction terms reduced the size of the R^2. Thus, the researcher decided to focus on regression models that excluded interactions.

To determine the best-fitting logistic regression model, the author entered the top-ranking eight variables in a stepwise sequence from stronger to weaker predictors. Table 13-4 presents the resulting eight models. The researcher entered the top-ranking five variables (race, age at entry, job skills, caregiver services, and substance abuse problem) sequentially in Models 1 through 5. As each variable was entered, the others continued to be significant predictors of reunification. In Model 5, their combined effects accounted for a 20.5% variance in reunification, with an F value of 15.45.

When the researcher added neglect allegation in Model 6, however, it was not significantly related to reunification, whereas four of the five other predictors continued to be significant predictors. Similarly, when kin caregiver was added in Model 7, it was no longer significantly related to reunification, whereas all five of the other variables were significant predictors. It is interesting that the strong correlation between race and parental reunification was not reduced when relative placement was added to the model. Finally, when the researcher added SES in Model 8, it was no longer significantly related to reunification, whereas four of the five other variables continued to be significant predictors, nor does the addition of SES reduce the influence of race.

Because time in foster care, abuse allegation, and caregiver's education were important predictors in past studies, the author ran additional regression models separately for each of these three variables. Moreover, he also included a broader definition of ne-

Table 13-4: Best-Fitting Models for Predicting Reunification

Predictor	Model 1	2	3	4	5	6	7	8
Intercept	-.69 (.00)*	-.32 (.07)	-1.05 (.00)*	-.55 (.06)	-.33 (.33)	-.18 (.69)	-.22 (.64)	-.33 (.53)
Race	-1.61 (.00)*	-1.54 (.00)*	-1.50 (.00)*	-1.57 (.00)*	-1.46 (.00)*	-1.47 (.00)*	-1.49 (.00)*	- .93 (.05)*
No services	—	-1.06 (.00)*	-1.07 (.00)*	-.97 (.01)*	-1.04 (.00)*	-1.04 (.01)*	-1.08 (.01)*	- .99 (.01)*
Age at entry	—	—	.09 (.00)*	.08 (.00)*	.08 (.01)*	.08 (.02)*	.09 (.02)*	.11 (.01)*
No job skills	—	—	—	-1.40 (.00)*	-1.36 (.00)*	-1.36 (.00)*	-1.36 (.00)*	-1.07 (.01)*
Substance abuse problem					-.48 (.04)*	-.46 (.10)	-.46 (.00)*	-.04 (.92)
Neglect allegation					—	-.33 (.39)	-.27 (.47)	.04 (.93)
Kin caregiver					—	—	.10 (.79)	.18 (.66)
Low socioeconomic status					—	—	—	-.78 (.09)
(100)R^2	9.2%	12.7%	16.8%	20.1%	20.5%	22.4%	22.1%	19.8%
F value	22.8 (.00)*	28.12 (.00)*	21.28 (.00)*	15.78 (.00)*	15.45 (.00)*	18.77 (.00)*	14.77 (.00)*	7.08 (.00)*

*Statistically significant relationships at $p \leq .05$.

glect (including physical, emotional, medical, abandonment, lack of supervision, and failure to thrive) in a separate regression model; however, none of these additional variables continued to be significantly related to reunification when combined with the other five predictors. Because Model 5 was the only model in which all of the predictors were able to maintain a significant relationship with reunification in combination with one another, it is considered to be the best-fitting model for predicting parental reunification.

Probabilities of Reunification

The author derived probabilities of reunification for subgroups of children who entered foster care at the average age of 7 based on the parameters of the best-fitting model. Using the methodology employed in the reanalysis of National Incidence Study–2 data (Sedlak, 1993), the author derived probabilities of reunification for eight scenarios that involve combinations of caregiver services, job skills, and substance abuse problems (see Table 13-5). The highest probabilities of reunification were represented in Scenario 8. It included children whose parental caregivers had job skills, received services, and had no substance abuse problem. For this scenario, the probability of reunification was 56% for white children, compared with only 23% for African American children.

Scenario 6 represents intermediate probabilities. It included children whose parental caregivers had job skills and had no substance abuse problem, but received no services. For

Table 13-5: Probabilities of Reunification for Children Entering Foster Care at Age 7 by Scenario and Race

Scenario	Job Skills	Caregiver Services	Substance Abuse Problem	Probability of Reunification[a]	
				African American	White
1	No	No	Yes	2%	7%
2	No	No	No	3%	10%
3	No	Yes	Yes	4%	17%
4	Yes	No	Yes	6%	22%
5	No	Yes	No	7%	24%
6	Yes	No	No	9%	31%
7	Yes	Yes	Yes	15%	44%
8	Yes	Yes	No	23%	56%

[a] Calculated as 100 X Probability.

this scenario, white children had a probability of reunification that was three times higher than African American children (31% vs. 9%). Other intermediate probabilities appear in Scenario 4. It included children whose parental caregivers had job skills, but also had substance abuse problems and received no services. In this scenario, whites had a probability of reunification that was about four times higher than African Americans (22% vs. 6%). Scenario 1 included the group of children with the lowest probabilities of reunification. These children had parental caregivers who had no job skills, received no services, and had substance abuse problems. In this scenario, the probability of reunification among white children was 7%, compared with only 2% for African American children.

To depict visually the various probabilities of reunification by race, the authors created Figure 13-1, which compares Scenarios 1, 4, 6, and 8. It reveals that the probability of reunification increases as the parental caregivers' characteristics become more advantaged. Yet it also reveals that even when the parents of African American children have the same desirable (or undesirable) characteristics as white parents, white children are still three or more times more likely to be reunified than African American children. Moreover, the probability of reunification for African Americans with the more desirable characteristics in Scenario 8 (23%) is about the same as it is for whites in Scenario 4 (22%), in which parents have substance abuse problems, received no services, but have job skills. Clearly, race continues to be a strong predictor of reunification in each of the scenarios.

Discussion

Although this study is based on cross-sectional data, it is interesting to note that many of the findings are consistent with those from several longitudinal studies. This is espe-

Figure 13-1: Probability of Reunification for Children Entering Foster Care at Age 7 by Race and Scenario

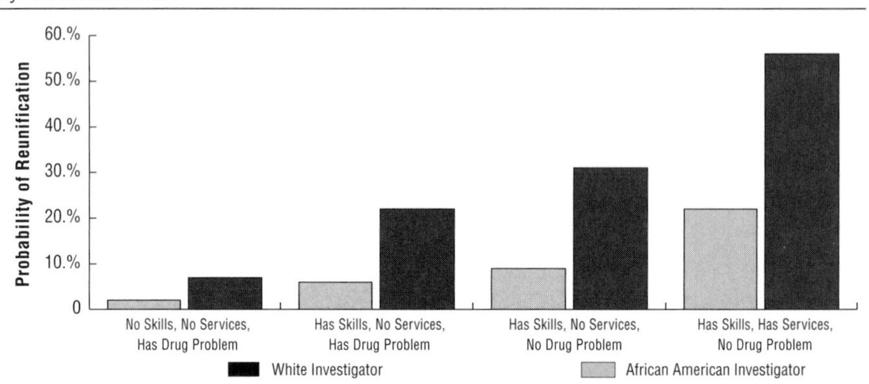

cially the case when some of the bivariate relationships with reunification are compared with those of prior research. First, the analysis found race to be significantly related to reunification: White children are more likely to be reunified than African American children. This finding agrees with those of Barth et al. (1986), Courtney (1994), Wells and Guo (1999), and McMurty and Lie (1992). In addition, although Goerge (1990) found no direct racial differences, he obtained interactions between race and region. For example, African Americans in Cook County had lower reunification probabilities than non–African Americans in Cook County.

Second, this study found relative placement to be inversely related to reunification. Children who were placed with relatives were less likely to be reunified than children placed with nonrelatives. These findings agree with those of Goerge (1990) and Courtney (1994), however, Wells and Guo (1999) did not find relative placement to be related to reunification. Moreover, this study did not find relative placement to be significantly related to reunification when combined with race and the other predictors in the regression models. Thus, the higher relative placement rate of African American children does not explain the lower reunification rates relative to white children.

Third, this study found age of entry to be significantly related to reunification. Rates of reunification rose directly with increases in the age that the children entered foster care. Several studies also found lower reunification rates among infants and young children than older children (Courtney, 1994; Goerge, 1990). Moreover, Courtney (1994) found large racial differences in reunification between African Americans and whites at young ages, but declining racial differentials as the age of the children increased. Although Wells and Guo (1999) found no significant relationship between age of entry and reunification, they found a positive relationship between the interaction term African American X Age of Entry and reunification.

Fourth, although this study found reasons for placement to be significantly related to reunification, other studies differed widely in this regard. For example, Goerge (1990) found neglected children to have higher reunification rates than abused children, however, Wells and Guo (1999) found that children placed for abuse had higher rates of reunification than those placed for neglect or dependency. Courtney (1994) found that children placed for sexual abuse with nonrelatives had higher reunification rates than those placed for neglect. He also found no significant relationships between any of the reasons for placement and reunification among children placed with relatives. In addition, this study found that abuse and neglect allegations were both significantly correlated with reunification, but in opposite directions. Children with abuse allegations were more likely to be reunified, whereas children with neglect allegations were less likely to be reunified, however, neither reason for placement continued to be significantly related to reunification when combined with other predictors in the regression models.

On the other hand, studies by Courtney (1994) and Wells and Guo (1999) found that children with health problems were reunified more slowly than children without any health problems. This chapter's analysis did not show that child disability or health problems were significantly related to reunification. Nor did this study find, as did Courtney (1994), that AFDC status was significantly related to reunification. Yet the analysis conducted in this study did find that two other measures of SES (parental education and employment status) were positively related to reunification. Children whose parental caregivers had completed high school or were currently employed were more likely to be reunified than children whose parental caregivers were high school dropouts or were not employed.

The study reported in this chapter reveals that race is a strong predictor of reunification when combined with other important child, family, or case history characteristics. This study also reveals four important predictors of reunification in addition to race. These are the age of the child at entry into care, caregiver job skills, caregiver substance abuse problem, and caregiver services. Finally, this study found that controlling for the other essential predictors does not reduce the independent effects of race. In sum, race plays a major role in the reunification of children in addition to other child, family, and case history characteristics.

Implications

The overriding goal of foster care workers is to reunify children with their parents. Yet many studies have found that disproportionate numbers of children who are reunified return to the foster care system (Courtney, 1994; Frame, Berrick, & Brodowski, 2000; Goerge, 1990; Wells & Guo, 1999). Workers want to avoid returning children to unsafe and unstable environments. This study found the following five variables to be strong predictors of parental reunification: race of child, age of entry, caregiver job skills, caregiver substance abuse problem, and caregiver services. These finding have implications for workers.

Clearly, the lack of job skills of parental caregivers is a barrier to reunification. This suggests the need for more targeted efforts to connect parents of children in foster care with employability opportunities in the public or private sectors. Such opportunities might include completing a general equivalency diploma, work-readiness sessions, work experience, on-the-job training, apprenticeships, subsidized jobs, or unsubsidized work. Similarly, more substance abuse treatment programs should be targeted to the parents of children in foster care to facilitate the children's return home. Unfortunately, because most drug abuse treatment programs have been designed for men, more gender-specific programs that include such services as child care, coping with spousal abuse, family planning, and other women's health issues are needed for female caregivers.

This study also found that children whose parents received services were more likely to be reunified than those whose parents received no services. It is not enough to merely provide more services. Parents need specific services that are tailored to their needs. Because many of these caregivers have multiple problems, such as inadequate parenting skills, substance abuse problems, mental health problems, and shelter needs, an array of services should be provided, however, more knowledge is needed to determine the mix of specific services that are most effective for various types of parental caregivers. Are different services needed for caregivers of different races? Social work professionals might consider addressing such questions as, What efforts are made to avoid equating the poverty of clients with dysfunction, abuse, or neglect? How often do we assess clients' assets and strengths? Do we appreciate diverse cultural beliefs and child-rearing practices? To what extent do considerations of race, ethnicity, or poverty influence reunification decisions?

ASFA presents new challenges to the social work profession. It allows states to use federal funds to provide family reunification services for the first 15 months after a child enters foster care. It also reduces the time a child may remain in foster care without a permanency hearing. This shortened timeline is consistent with a number of studies that suggest the greatest opportunities for reunification are within one year after the child enters foster care. Many years ago, Maas and Engler (1959) argued that the chances for reunification drop sharply after 18 months. Indeed, many studies provide strong support for the reduced timetable recommended by Maas and Engler (Courtney, 1994; Goerge, 1990; Wells & Guo, 1999).

ASFA, however, also requires states to file for the termination of the rights of parents of children who have spent 15 of the most recent 22 months in foster care. This shortened timeline may hinder the efforts of workers who are trying to return children to parents with prolonged conditions, especially alcohol and drug abuse. As Hohman and Butt (2001) pointed out, because clients recovering from substance abuse addiction must go through various complex and prolonged stages, including relapses, most drug programs cannot treat the addicts effectively in less than 24 months. It is important to realize that after recovery from addiction is stabilized, additional time is needed to enhance parenting capabilities, job skills, and employment stability. The widespread proliferation of crack cocaine among mothers in low-income communities requires policies that balance the need to quickly place children in safe and supportive environments with providing adequate time for successful drug rehabilitation.

This analysis suggests a number of future directions in research on race and reunification. First, as Courtney and colleagues (1996) concluded in their comprehensive review of the literature, it is important to acknowledge the role of race and ethnicity in future child welfare research:

> We encountered many studies in which these factors were not mentioned as variables, although the sample size and location of the study would have lent themselves to such analysis. The failure or unwillingness to at least acknowledge the relationships among race, child welfare services, and child welfare outcomes may only serve to invite uninformed speculation about the reasons for these relationships. Whenever methodologically possible, child welfare researchers should include race as an explanatory factor in research designs and consider their theoretical justification for doing so (i.e., why does the researcher think that race might play a role?). (p. 127)

Second, a need exists for reunification studies that not only include adequate sample sizes of African Americans, but of Hispanics, Native Americans, and Asian and Pacific Islanders as well. Although many studies have obtained similar results for whites and Hispanics, little is known about reunification rates for Native Americans or Asians, because they are most often excluded due to their small sample sizes.

Third, the literature needs more longitudinal studies that are based on both administrative records and surveys that track cohorts of children over time to better understand the dynamics of reunification patterns among racial and ethnic groups. Such longitudinal studies should be conducted statewide and nationally. National studies would help distinguish findings about reunification that can be generalized across the country from those that are specific to states or local areas.

Fourth, additional research is needed on the type of services that are most appropriate for enhancing reunification among parental caregivers of different racial and ethnic groups (Maluccio, Fein, & Davis, 1994). This analysis found lower reunification rates among families that received fewer services. Reviews of child welfare research revealed that families of color are less likely to receive services than white families (Courtney et al., 1996). Researchers should conduct more studies to determine the mix of services that are most effective in facilitating reunification among specific kinds of caregivers.

Fifth, more research is needed that continues to include common measures from prior studies to more adequately examine their separate and combined effects on reunification. Such an approach might resolve contradictory findings related to the importance of kinship placement, SES, child disability, age of entry, and reasons for placement as predictors of reunification.

Appendix 13-A

Independent Variables

Child Characteristics

Race: African American = 1; white = 0
Gender: male = 1; female = 0
Age of entry: Continuous variable (average age of entry was 7 years old)
Child disability status: with disability = 1; no disability = 0

Family Characteristics[1]

Parent job skills: lacks job skills = 1; has job skills = 0
Parent substance abuse problem: has problem = 1; has no problem = 0
Parent single mother: is a single mom = 1; is not a single mom = 0
Parent social class: finished high school and employed = 0; all other combinations = 1 (social class index comprises only parental education and employment status)

Case History Characteristics

Reasons for placement[2]: only abuse allegation = 1; no abuse allegation = 0; only neglect allegation = 1; no neglect allegation = 0
Type of placement: with relatives = 1; with nonrelatives = 0
Parental caregiver services: no services received = 1; some services received = 0

Dependent Variable

Parental reunification: reunified = 1; other discharges and still in care = 0

[1] The index excluded the variable *AFDC recipient* because it was not correlated with the other two measures of socioeconomic status.

[2] The variable *only abuse allegation* applies only to allegations that include sexual abuse, physical abuse, and emotional abuse; it excludes any neglect allegations. The variable *only neglect allegation* applies only to allegations that include physical neglect and emotional neglect; it excludes any abuse allegations.

References

Barth, R., Snowden, L., Ten Broeck, E., Clancey, T., Jordan,C., & Barusch, A. (1986). Contributors to reunification or permanent out-of-home care for physically abused children. *Journal of Social Service Research, 9*(2/3), 31–45.

Courtney, M. E. (1994). Factors associated with the reunification of foster children with their families. *Social Service Review, 68*, 81–108.

Courtney, M. E. (1995). Reentry to foster care of children returned to their families. *Social Service Review, 69*, 226–241.

Courtney, M. E., Barth, R., Berrick, J., Brooks, D., Needell, B., & Park, L. (1996). Race and child welfare services: Past research and future directions. *Child Welfare, 75*, 99–137.

Frame, L., Berrick, J. D., & Brodowski, M. L. (2000). Understanding reentry to out-of home for reunified infants. *Child Welfare, 79*, 339–369.

Goerge, R. M. (1990). The reunification process in substitute care. *Social Service Review, 64*, 422–457.

Hohman, M. M., & Butt, R. L. (2001). How soon is too soon? Addiction recovery and family reunification. *Child Welfare, 80*, 53–67.

Maas, H., & Engler, R., Jr. (1959). *Children in need of parents*. New York: Columbia University Press.

Maluccio, A. N., Fein, E., & Davis, I. (1994). Family reunification: Research findings, issues and directions. *Child Welfare, 73*, 489–504.

McMurty, S., & Lie, G.-Y. (1992). Differential exit rate of minority children in foster care. *Social Work Research and Abstracts, 28*(1), 42–48.

Sedlak, A. (1993). *Study of high risk child abuse and neglect groups, NIS-2 reanalysis: Report to Congress* (Appendix C). Washington, DC: U.S. Department of Health and Human Services.

U.S. Children's Bureau. (1997). *National Study of Protective, Preventive and Reunification Services delivered to children and their families*. Washington, DC: U.S. Government Printing Office.

Wells, K., & Guo, S. (1999). Reunification and reentry of foster children. *Children and Youth Services Review, 21*, 273–294.

CHAPTER 14

The Changing Significance of Race and Kinship for Achieving Permanence for Foster Children

Mark F. Testa

Much of the literature and research on the topics of race and permanence has historically focused on the problems of finding legally permanent homes for children of color (primarily African American; Bartholet, 1999; Billingsley & Giovannoni, 1972; Wilson, 1991). The overrepresentation of African American children in public foster care and on lists of children awaiting adoption has prompted researchers and policymakers to search for underlying causes and propose alternative solutions. A consensus has gradually emerged in federal policymaking circles that defines the problem primarily in terms of an undersupply of African American homes that are interested in adoption and the persistence of barriers to transracial adoption, which prevent authorities from tapping into the oversupply of non–African American homes that are presumably willing to adopt.

This particular formulation of the problem and solution resulted in the passage of the Multiethnic Placement Act of 1994, which prohibits the use of race, color, or national origin to delay or deny children's placement in racially or ethnically diverse foster and adoptive homes, and the Adoption and Safe Families Act of 1997, which requires that children be placed for adoption if they remain in nonrelated foster care for longer than 15 out of 22 months. It is still too early to judge whether these federal initiatives have increased transracial adoptions. Although the jury is out on the effectiveness of these

Author's Note: Portions of this chapter appeared previously in: Testa, M. (2001). Kinship care and permanency. *Journal of Social Service Research, 28*(1), pp. 25–43.

laws, new evidence is quickly emerging that safe and permanent homes are successfully being found for African American children by building on the cultural traditions of informal adoption and kinship care among African Americans.

The purpose of this study is to report on recent developments in finding permanent homes for African American children in Illinois. Since 1995, the Illinois Department of Children and Family Services (IDCFS) has been engaged in a massive reorganization of its kinship care policies and contractual-services system to promote the achievement of safe and permanent homes for children in long-term kinship care. This chapter uses the term *permanence* to refer to those substitute care arrangements that are recognized as legally binding, such as adoption and private guardianship. Under this definition, the care of children by kin that occurs outside of these formal categories would not be considered "permanent," although the underlying social relationship may be quite stable.

This study draws on administrative data from IDCFS to examine the achievement of legal permanence for African American and white foster children in Chicago and suburban Cook County, Illinois. The researcher extracted case histories from the administrative database of kinship and nonrelated foster placements that began in Cook County between July 1, 1990, and June 30, 1997. He then tracked these placements longitudinally until adoption, guardianship, placement disruption, or June 30, 2000, whichever came first.

Background

In his landmark study *Informal Adoption Among Black Families*, Robert Hill (1977) documented the central importance of informal adoption and kinship care for the protection and care of African American children. The custom of informal adoption and kinship care has historical roots in African American adaptations to slavery and job migration patterns, which disproportionately deprived African American children of regular parental care. Grandparents, aunts, uncles, or other extended and fictive kin would take over childrearing responsibilities until the parents were able to resume custody or the children reached adulthood. This tradition continued in the urban North where informal adoption helped compensate for the discriminatory withholding of voluntary and statutory child welfare services from African American neighborhoods (Billingsley & Giovannoni, 1972).

In the 1970s, private agencies, the courts, and public departments began turning their attention to the problem of the "left-out" child. The growth of child protective services brought hundreds of thousands of new cases that had gone undetected in the past to the attention of child welfare authorities. Courts demanded that religiously affiliated child welfare agencies eliminate restrictions on the social origins of children they could serve. Private agencies targeted communities of color for the recruitment of foster homes. To accommodate the growing demand for child placement services in African American communities, public officials increasingly turned to relatives to enforce their new and expansive child protective powers.

Since the mid-1980s, placement with relatives has accelerated into the fastest growing component of public foster care in the United States (Testa, Shook, Cohen, & Woods, 1996). As of 1998, an estimated 30% of foster children were placed formally with kin (U.S. Department of Health and Human Services, 2000). With the growth of kinship foster care, a new problem was identified as contributing to the overrepresentation of African American children in the child welfare system. Researchers were documenting that kinship foster placements tended to last longer and children to remain longer in care than children in nonrelated foster placements (Iglehart, 1994; Scannapieco, Hegar, & McAlpine, 1997; Wulczyn & Goerge, 1992). This was partly related to the fact that children in kinship foster care were less likely than children in nonrelated foster care to exit the child welfare system through the established legal channels of reunification and adoption (Berrick, Barth, & Needell, 1994; Testa, 1997; Thornton, 1991). As a consequence, the active caseloads of public child welfare departments steadily swelled as more and more children accumulated in long-term kinship care.

Early investigations into the problem of long-term kinship care purported to find that most caregivers were resistant to the idea of adopting their own kin because their attachment was already sealed by blood ties (Thornton, 1991). Others posited that cultural traditions worked against the formalization of kinship bonds through adoption (Burnette, 1997). Still others warned that risks were inherent in kinship foster care, particularly with respect to intergenerational family dysfunction and dangerous neighborhoods, which made extended families poor prospects for permanent homes (Bartholet, 1999). Although some kinship homes are definitely unsuitable and some of the appropriate homes remain steadfastly against the idea of adopting their own kin, more recent research and focus groups with kin caregivers are finding evidence of a much greater potential for safety and permanence among kin than previous literature has suggested (Testa, Cohen, & Smith, 2003).

The reluctance that some relatives feel about adoption does not mean that they are unwilling to assume legal responsibility for raising their grandchildren, nieces, and nephews to adulthood. Research shows that most are prepared to look after their kin until the children are fully grown (Gleeson, 1999; Testa et al., 1996). Instead of pressuring these kin to adopt, however, the preference is for a legal permanency option that transfers legal responsibility without disrupting customary kinship norms and severing the natural bonds that connect children to their birthparents and siblings.

Subsidized guardianship is a permanency option that is responsive to many of the reservations that some families harbor about adopting their own kin (Leashore, 1984/1985; Williams, 1991). Unlike adoption, the transfer of the guardianship of a child from the birthparent to another adult does not require the surrender or termination of parental rights. Birthparents may retain certain residual rights and obligations, such the rights to visit and consent to adoption as well as the obligation for child support, but the primary rights of care, custody, and control of the child are assigned to the guardian. The guardian can exercise these rights until the child attains majority age or a court vacates guardianship.

A major obstacle to the use of private guardianship as a permanency option, however, is the loss of federal reimbursement when a foster child is discharged from public custody. Unlike subsidized adoption, which is reimbursable under Title IV-E of the Social Security Act, governments must fund subsidized guardianship with either state dollars or Temporary Assistance to Needy Families (TANF) grants, the latter of which is usually only one-half to one-third of the amount relatives are able to receive as licensed foster parents.

Under federal waiver provisions, eight states, including Illinois, have now been approved for subsidized guardianship demonstrations so they are able to use Title IV-E dollars to increase private guardianship subsidies, if they choose, up to the level of foster boarding payments, so that families do not incur any loss in maintenance payments. These eight states are finally in a position to test whether the historic difference in the rates of permanence among African American and white children reflect an essentialist bias against the formalization of kinship bonds or the lack of supplementary permanency options that are in keeping with the cultural traditions and preferences of African American families and communities. The next section discusses the data and methods used to evaluate these alternative hypotheses.

Data and Method

The author drew the data for this study from the IDCFS Integrated Database, which the Chapin Hall Center for Children designed and maintained for IDCFS. It is a longitudinal, relational database on children and families that relies on probabilistic record linkage techniques to match child records across IDCFS administrative files. For the present study, the researcher extracted administrative case records from the Integrated Database on the universe of 21,674 kinship and nonrelated foster placements that began every other year in Cook County, Illinois, between July 1, 1990, and June 30, 1997. These placements were then tracked longitudinally with administrative data until case resolution, placement disruption, or June 30, 2000, whichever came first.

Because placement data are linked to billing records, the information on placement sequence, duration, type of care, and placement outcome is the most valid and reliable information in the data system. Other computerized data on child needs, behavior, and well-being tend to be less reliable, so the researcher only extracted demographic information on the gender, race, and age of the child.

Table 14-1 presents the percentages, means, and standard deviations of the variables used in the analyses of entry cohorts. The gender, age, and first placement distributions are similar by race of the child. Although the gender and age distributions are similar for kin and nonkin placements, a substantial difference exists in the percentage of kin placements that were first placements compared with nonkin placements. This difference reflects, in part, the greater instability of nonkin placements. Approximately 70% of nonkin placements terminated in re-placement, compared with 41% of kin placements. The difference also shows up in the much shorter mean length of nonkin placements than kin placements.

Table 14-1 also contains evidence of differences in permanency rates of adoption and guardianship that run contrary to the usual assumption that race and kinship are obstacles to finding legally permanent homes for African American children. Analysis of permanency rates poses special challenges that are best handled by proportional hazards analysis. *Proportional hazards analysis* is a statistical method for studying the occurrence and timing of events, such as adoption, foster placement disruption, or any other dependent variable, that changes from one status to another (Allison, 1995). The dependent variable is an unobserved variable, commonly called a *hazard* or *transition rate*, that measures the probability that an event will occur at a particular time given that it has not yet occurred. This method offers advantages over other approaches, such as linear regression, because it can accommodate the analysis of case histories that have not been observed long enough for the event of interest to have occurred. This problem of so-called "censored observations" is quite common in social services research because a remainder of cases are usually still active or in the process of some change occurring. Simply discarding these censored observations introduces unknown biases, which is best avoided by conducting a proportional hazards analysis.

The name *proportional hazards analysis* refers to the assumption that the hazard rate of an event's occurrence for a baseline group is proportionally related to the rate in its comparison group. In other words, the hazard's rates are in constant proportion to one another over time. It is not uncommon for the proportionality assumption to be met at

Table 14-1: Percentages and Means (Standard Deviations) for Children

Variables	Race of Child		Placement	
	White	African American	Nonkin	Kin
N	1,491	20,183	3,998	17,676
Female	50.4%	51.2%	49.9%	51.4%
First placement	47.0%	57.0%	22.0%	63.0%
Age at placement	6.311(5.168)	5.565(4.941)	4.746(4.610)	5.814(5.016)
Days of care	865(951)	1,127(1035)	530(850)	1,240(1,024)
Care episodes	1.044(0.232)	1.050(0.242)	1.023(0.175)	1.056(0.254)
Adopted	16.7%	18.7%	9.4%	20.6%
Guardianship	2.2%	5.9%	0.4%	6.8%
Returned to parent	19.8%	11.0%	6.8%	12.7%
Still in foster home	3.6%	5.9%	2.9%	6.4%
Re-placed	42.8%	46.2%	70.4%	40.5%
With kin	15.1%	22.4%	20.8%	22.1%
With nonkin	19.7%	17.1%	41.9%	11.8%
Other	8.0%	6.7%	7.7%	6.6%
Other closing	1.8%	1.0%	0.1%	1.3%
Reached age 18	3.0%	4.7%	1.9%	5.2%
Group care	7.6%	4.0%	6.5%	3.7%
Ran away	1.9%	2.1%	1.4%	2.2%
Detention	0.6%	0.5%	0.2%	0.6%

Note: All placement data are as of June 2000.

the early stages of observation but later to be violated when a social process has had sufficient time to unfold. In such instances, it is recommended that a nonproportional hazards model be fitted to the data, in which an interaction term between the group variable and some function of the survival time variable is included as a predictor (Allison, 1995). Even when the proportionality assumption is unmet, it is sometimes useful to suppress intentionally the interaction with time. The effect that is then estimated can be interpreted as a sort of "average" effect over the range of times observed in the data.

Findings

The researcher fitted separate hazards models to placement data for the four cohorts of children who were taken into Illinois state custody during FYs 1991, 1993, 1995, and 1997, respectively. These entry cohorts were tracked for legal permanence through June

2000. Because the cumulative hazard curves for kin and nonkin were inconsistent with the assumption of proportionality, the model includes kinship and cohort-time interaction terms that allow for the hazard functions to vary with placement duration.

Adoption and Guardianship

The researcher fitted hazards models to examine whether African American children are at a disadvantage with respect to permanence and the extent to which kin placements are convertible into legally permanent homes. He obtained the estimates from the complete census of kinship and foster care placements made during this period, so statistical significance is reported only for purposes of evaluating substantive importance. Subtracting 100% from the exponentiation of the hazards coefficient ($= e^b - 1$) yields a readily interpretable measure.

The kinship effects displayed in Table 14-2 and 14-3 show that African American children who were taken into state custody in FY 1991 were 44% less likely to be adopted or taken into guardianship than white children. Similarly, kinship care is less likely at the early stages of placement to result in legal permanence compared with nonrelated foster care. Both results replicate past research that show that African Americans and children in kinship care are at a disadvantage with respect to achieving permanence (Berrick et al., 1994; Testa, 1997; Thornton, 1991).

A major qualification to these findings, however, is picked up by the kinship-time interaction term. It shows the kinship disadvantage gradually diminishes over time. The point at which the kinship advantage shrinks to zero can be estimated by setting the main kinship effect equal to the kinship-time interaction and solving for year. For FY 1991 cohorts, the kinship disadvantage vanishes approximately 6.6 years after the children were placed (see Table 14-3). Similar calculations can be done for later cohorts. Solving for the year variable in the kinship-time interaction yields a successively smaller estimate for each subsequent cohort: It takes successively fewer years for the kinship difference to vanish compared with earlier cohorts. As a result, the overall kin effect "averaged" over the range of observed placement durations steadily dwindles from -42.7% for the FY 1991 cohort to -2.2% for the FY 1995 cohort before turning into a 57.3% advantage for the FY 1997 cohort.

In other words, whereas children who entered kinship foster care in the early 1990s were 43% *less* likely than children in nonrelated foster care to find permanent homes with their caregivers, children who entered kinship foster care in FY 1977 were 57% *more* likely to be adopted or taken into private guardianship by their caregiver. Over this same period, the "zero-order" or crude race effect diminished from a -50.2% permanency disadvantage to a -15.8% disadvantage.

Table 14-2: Proportional Hazards Models for Legal Permanence: Coefficient Estimates

Variables	Entry Cohort							
	FY 1991		FY 1993		FY 1995		FY 1997	
	b	e^b-1	b	e^b-1	b	e^b-1	b	e^b-1
African American (vs. white)	-0.586	-44%	-0.517	-40%	0.169	ns	-0.194	ns
Kin (vs. Nonkin)	-2.534	-92%	-3.131	-96%	2.009	-87%	-1.229	-71%
Kin X Duration (in years)	0.381	46%	0.582	79%	0.521	68%	0.603	83%
Female (vs. male)	0.102	ns	0.057	ns	0.014	ns	0.089	ns
Age at placement	-0.109	-10%	-0.044	-4%	-0.041	-4%	-0.041	-4%
First (vs. second) placement	-0.047	ns	0.080	ns	-0.019	ns	-0.057	ns

Note: ns = not statistically significant at the .05 level.

Table 14-3: Proportional Hazards Models for Legal Permanence: and Effect Estimates

Variables	Cohort			
	FY 1991	FY 1993	FY 1995	FY 1997
N of children	4,867	5,320	7,427	4,060
N of episodes	5,139	5,629	7,795	4,191
N of adoptions	725	1,036	1,562	700
N of guardianships	164	315	546	190
Percent censored	82.7%	76.0%	73.0%	78.8%
Crude race effect	-50.2%	-44.8%	-15.6%	-15.8%
Estimates years in which kinship difference vanishes[a]	6.6	5.4	3.9	2.0
Average kin effect	-42.7%	-27.7%	-2.2%	57.3%

[a] Years = kin main effect/Kin X Duration interaction effect.

Permanency Initiatives

The changing significance of race and kinship for legal permanence in Illinois can be tied to several policy initiatives that the state launched in the late 1990s. Adding each time estimate of the vanishing point to the corresponding cohort year predicts approximately the same convergence period for all four cohorts: July 1, 1997, through June 30, 1999. This corresponds to the period when Illinois implemented three major policy initiatives to boost permanency rates: (1) the Illinois Subsidized Guardianship Waiver Demonstration implemented on May 11, 1997, which provides subsidies to families who assume private guardianship of foster children; (2) the performance contracting payment system implemented for Cook County home-of-relative programs on July 1, 1997, which rewards agencies for the attainment of permanency goals; and (3) a package of state legislative reforms (dubbed the "Permanency Initiative") implemented on October 1, 1997, in Cook County, which shortened the judicial timeline for finalizing permanency plans.

All three initiatives helped reinforce the achievement of permanence for children in kinship care. As Leashore (1984/1985) predicted, the availability of subsidized guardianship established a supplementary permanency option that was more in keeping with the custom of informal adoption that has long been established in the African American community. In discussing this new option, relatives confronted their own biases and misunderstandings and, as Hill (1977) predicted, chose to convert their informal adoptions into formal adoptions in far greater numbers than most people would have guessed. Similarly, performance contracting helped neutralize worker biases against kinship adoptions and eliminate financial disincentives to the agencies' bottom lines. Finally, the courts were given a clear signal and mandate that legal permanence, not long-term foster care, was in the best interests of children and families.

Discussion and Conclusion

The findings of this study run contrary to the usual assumption that race and kinship are obstacles to finding permanent homes for African American children. By restructuring its permanency options in ways that build on the strengths of extended families and cultural traditions of informal adoption among African Americans, Illinois was able to diminish the magnitude of the racial disparity in adoption and guardianship and turn kinship into a positive advantage for the timely achievement of permanence.

This study's findings on the conversion of relative placements into adoptive and guardianship homes point to limitations of essentialist interpretations of past racial differences in adoption rates. Recent trends in Illinois suggest a much greater potential for formal adoption by kin than prior literature suggested. Between FY 1995 and FY 1999, annual adoptions of Illinois children out of foster care increased from 1,640 to 7,315 children (IDCFS, 2000). Kin accounted for 43% of adoptions in FY 1995 and 58% of adoptions in FY 1999. Illinois' implementation of its three permanency initiatives in 1997 helped dispel many of the myths harbored by kin about adoption, such as the lack of ongoing subsidies, the need to alter birth certificates, or prohibitions on birthparents ever visiting the child. Once these misunderstandings were cleared up, relatives were far more willing to consider adoption than previously thought likely (Testa et al., 1996).

Now, with the availability of subsidized guardianship under federal waiver authority in Illinois, a far more complicated issue is coming to the fore: Who should have the final say about what form of permanence is in the best interests of the child? After the misinformation and myths are cleared away, a layer of resistance to kinship adoption still remains that is not so easily dismissed. Some relatives prefer to leave the rights of the birthparents undisturbed and to become the child's legal guardian instead. Even when parental rights are terminated, some relatives prefer to remain the child's custodian as grandmother, aunt, or cousin, rather then become the child's adoptive parent. Still other families are willing as the legal guardian to assume some additional financial burden beyond the subsidy, but they are reluctant to assume the full child support obligation as an adoptive family. Should such family preferences be honored by child welfare agencies and the courts?

The inferences one can draw about the comparative advantages of adoption, guardianship, or long-term foster care are greatly limited in this study. Survey data that Westat, Inc. (2003) collected on a probability sample of 2,263 adult and 1,211 child participants in the Illinois Subsidized Guardianship Waiver Demonstration capture a much richer set of behavioral, attitudinal, and well-being information on children in both kin and nonkin homes than are available in the Illinois computerized database. Analyses of these data suggest that little is to be gained for either the child or family by postponing guardianship in the hope of convincing kin to make the more legally binding commitment of adoption (Testa, 1997). On various measures of the quality of permanence—intent, continuity, belonging, and respect—children in subsidized guardianship arrangements fared about the same as or better than children in adoptive homes. Furthermore, no relevant differences existed in child safety or well-being to suggest that adoption should be preferred strongly over guardianship, once the family's wishes are taken into account (Testa, Cohen, & Smith, 2003).

Empirical findings from the full five years of the Illinois demonstration show convincingly that subsidized guardianship improves permanency performance (Westat, 2003). Extrapolating from the Illinois experience suggests that kinship care is a vast and largely untapped resource for securing legally permanent homes for foster children in other states as well. Making subsidized guardianship a provision of the Social Security Act in addition to subsidized adoption would greatly expand the options for ensuring that every foster child is afforded the opportunity to find a permanent home with his or her extended family.

A culturally sensitive policy that respects the wishes of family in converting stable kinship attachments into legally permanent ties offers a workable solution to the historical problem of finding permanent homes for children of color. By interweaving principles of legal permanence with the particular interests of the family, new forms of practice and policy can emerge that can integrate and strengthen the values of kinship bonds, community attachment, and legal permanence to safeguard the best interests of children of all races.

References

Allison, P. (1995). *Survival analysis using the SAS® system: A practical guide.* Gary, NC: SAS Institute.

Bartholet, E. (1999). *Nobody's children: Abuse and neglect, foster drift, and the adoption alternative.* Boston: Beacon Press.

Berrick, J. D., Barth R., & Needell, B. (1994). A comparison of kinship foster homes and foster family homes: Implications for kinship foster care as family preservation. *Children and Youth Services Review, 16*(1/2), 33–64.

Billingsley, A., & Giovannoni, J. M. (1972). *Children of the storm.* New York: Harcourt, Brace, Jovanovich.

Burnette, D. (1997). Grandparents raising grandchildren in the inner city. *Families in Society: The Journal of Contemporary Human Services, 78*, 489–501.

Gleeson, J. P. (1999). Kinship care as a child welfare service. In R. L. Hegar & M. Scannapieco (Eds.), *Kinship foster care: Policy, practice, and research* (pp. 28–53). New York: Oxford University Press.

Hill, R. B. (1977). *Informal adoption among black families.* Washington, DC: National Urban League.

Iglehart, A. P. (1994). Kinship foster care: Placement, service, and outcome issues. *Children and Youth Services Review, 16*, 107–122.

Illinois Department of Children and Family Services. (2000). *A program and budget briefing FY01.* Springfield, IL: Author.

Leashore, B. R. (1984/1985). Demystifying legal guardianship: An unexplored option for dependent children. *Journal of Family Law, 23*, 391–400.

Scannapieco, M., Hegar, R., & McAlpine, C. (1997). Kinship care and foster care: A comparison of characteristics and outcomes. *Families and Society, 78*, 480–488.

Testa, M. (1997). Kinship foster care in Illinois. In J. D. Berrick, R. Barth, & N. Gilbert (Eds.), *Child welfare research review* (Vol. 2, pp. 101–129). New York: Columbia University Press.

Testa, M., Cohen, L., & Smith, G. (2003). *Illinois subsidized guardianship waiver demonstration: Final evaluation report.* Springfield, IL: Department of Children and Family Services.

Testa, M. F., Shook, K. L., Cohen, L. S., & Woods, M. G. (1996). Permanency planning options for children in formal kinship care. *Child Welfare, 75*, 451–470.

Thornton, J. L. (1991). Permanency planning for children in kinship foster homes. *Child Welfare, 70*, 593–601.

U.S. Department of Health and Human Services, Children's Bureau. (2000). *Report to Congress on kinship care.* Washington, DC: Author.

Westat, Inc. (2003). *Evaluation of the Illinois subsidized guardianship waiver demonstration, final report.* Rockville, MD: Author.

Williams, C. C. (1991). Expanding the options in the quest for permanence. In J. E. Everett, S. S. Chipungu, & B. R. Leashore (Eds.), *Child welfare: An Africentric perspective* (pp. 266–289). New Brunswick, NJ: Rutgers University Press.

Wilson, M. N. (1991). The context of the African American family. In J. E. Everett, S. S. Chipungu, & B. R. Leashore, (Eds.), *Child welfare: An Africentric perspective* (pp. 85–118). New Brunswick, NJ: Rutgers University Press.

Wulczyn, F., & Goerge, R. M. (1992). Foster care in New York and Illinois: The challenge of rapid change. *Social Service Review, 66*, 278–294.

About the Editors and the Authors

Editors

Dennette M. Derezotes, MSW, LCSW, is an Assistant Director for the Children and Family Research Center, School of Social Work, University of Illinois at Urbana-Champaign. She has more than 20 years of child welfare experience working with children and families in direct care, therapeutic services, administration, training, program development and evaluation, community advocacy and collaboration, and case consultation with the Illinois Department of Children and Family Services, as well as private agencies throughout Illinois. In her current position, she focuses on evaluation of the effectiveness of services and the translation of these activities into a format useful to individuals in the practice community as well as the relationships between researchers, policymakers, and practitioners. Ms. Derezotes is the project director for the Race Matters Consortium, a national, multisystem initiative to prevent and reduce racial and ethnic disproportionality in the child welfare system.

John Poertner, DSW, is Professor Emeritus at the School of Social Work, University of Illinois at Urbana-Champaign. Dr. Poertner has studied and written on public child welfare issues for 25 years. While at the University of Illinois, Dr. Poertner was responsible for developing and reporting on outcomes for children who were the responsibility of the Illinois Department of Children and Family Services until 2002. He has also served on the faculty of the School of Social Welfare at the University of Kansas.

Mark F. Testa, PhD, is an Associate Professor in the School of Social Work at the University of Illinois at Urbana-Champaign, Director of the Children and Family Research Center, and Principal Investigator for Fostering Results, a two-year public education campaign funded by The Pew Charitable Trusts to improve federal financing and accountability in foster care. He formerly served as Research Director for the Illinois Department of Children and Family Services, where his research was instrumental in policy innovations leading to better services for children and families. Dr. Testa has been recognized nationally and locally for his work in child welfare, including the Adoption 2002 Excellence Award for Applied Scholarship and Research and the 2004 Blue Bow Award for significant contributions for the prevention of child abuse. Recent publications include: "The Risk of Subsequent Maltreatment Allegations in Families with Substance-Exposed Infants," *Child Abuse and Neglect* (2002); "Subsidized Guardianship: Testing an Idea Whose Time Has Finally Come," *Social Work Research* (2002); and "When Children Cannot Return Home: Adoption and Guardianship," *The Future of Children* (2004).

Authors

Christopher Baird, MA, is the Executive Vice President of the National Council on Crime and Delinquency (NCCD) and has directed the Midwest Office in Madison, Wisconsin, since 1985. He has designed risk assessment, classification, and case management systems for child welfare, adult probation and parole, and juvenile justice systems. He developed and managed the National Institute of Corrections Model Probation and Parole program, which was implemented in 31 state agencies and hundreds of county probation departments throughout the United States. Mr. Baird served as principal investigator on two grants from the National Institute of Justice, including a comprehensive evaluation of the Florida Community Control Program. From 1990 through 1997, he directed NCCD's Children's Research Center, which developed risk assessment and structured decisionmaking systems for child protective services (CPS) for more than 50 state and county agencies in the United States and Australia. He and colleagues wrote a comprehensive evaluation of structured decisionmaking in Michigan assessing its effect on subsequent abuse and neglect. He directed and authored a national study funded by the Office of Child Abuse and Neglect that compared CPS risk assessment systems in four jurisdictions. He is currently conducting research for the Casey Foundation's workforce initiative.

Mr. Baird has authored numerous journal articles and other publications on research, program development, and management issues in child welfare, juvenile justice, and corrections. In 1992, he received the University of Cincinnati Award from the American Probation and Parole Association for outstanding research contributions to the field. In

2001, he and his colleague Dennis Wagner received the Pro Humanitate Literacy Award for "The Relative Validity of Actuarial and Consensus-Based Risk Assessment Systems" from the North American Resource Center for Child Welfare. His educational background includes a master's degree in economics.

Richard P. Barth, PhD, MSW, is the Frank A. Daniels Distinguished Professor in the School of Social Work at the University of North Carolina, Chapel Hill. He is author or coauthor of 12 books on child welfare services. He has been a Fulbright Scholar, recipient of the Presidential Award for Excellence in Research from the National Association of Social Workers, and winner of the Frank Breul Prize from the University of Chicago.

Lucy Mackey Bilaver, MA, is a Senior Research Associate at the Chapin Hall Center for Children at the University of Chicago. She serves as Project Director of the Quick Response Project, an effort to perform timely statistical analysis of linked administrative data on child abuse and neglect and foster care at the request of policymakers and administrators from the Illinois Department of Children and Family Services. Her research interests include the health of children in foster care, outcome indictors for children in foster care, and children with disabilities.

Robert M. Goerge, PhD, is a Chapin Hall Research Fellow. Robert Goerge is an internationally recognized expert in policy and program assessment of child and family human services and systems, with particular emphasis on the management and analysis of large administrative datasets. Dr. Goerge has conducted extensive research over nearly two decades involving adolescent child-bearing, child welfare, Medicaid, multiple service use, monitoring well-being in youth populations, and many other topics. He was coeditor of *State of the Child in Illinois: 2001*, a comprehensive examination of the status of Illinois's children.

Dr. Goerge is the Principal Investigator of a four-state study of program participation—encompassing income maintenance, Medicaid, and child welfare systems—that was designed to help assess the effect of welfare reform on children. He is currently involved with two studies that examine federal food and nutrition programs—one for the U.S. Department of Agriculture and the other for the Brookings Institution. He heads an examination of an Illinois program that investigates abusive head trauma incidents involving cases brought to Chicago-area hospital emergency rooms. Dr. Goerge is also Principal Investigator of the Integrated Database on Child and Family Programs in Illinois (IDB) project. IDB, a longitudinal database on children's service receipt, provides a comprehensive picture of a child's contact over time with publicly provided or financed service programs in Illinois. Dr. Goerge has published both on the substantive topics of his research and on the application of computer technology to human services policy research. Before he began his academic career, Dr. Goerge was a house parent in a group home for juveniles. He has been a Chapin Hall staff member since 1986 and holds an appointment as a University of Chicago Research Associate (Associate Professor).

Brian M. Gryzlak, MSW, MA in sociology, has worked on research projects assessing the effect of welfare reform on recipients, as well as how state and local income-maintenance programs and local social services provision have evolved in the Temporary Assistance for Needy Families program environment. He has experience working with maltreated youth in a residential treatment center and most recently was employed as a case manager serving the elderly. He currently holds a research assistant position in the Department of Epidemiology at the University of Iowa, Ames.

Gardenia Harris, PhD, MSW, teaches social welfare policy and field practicum courses as an Assistant Professor at Illinois State University, Normal. Her research interests include racial disparities in the provision and outcomes of social services, the differential effect of child welfare policies on nonwhite people, the effectiveness of drug treatment courts, and HIV among middle-aged African American women. Ms. Harris began her career working as an in-home family therapist and later served as a manager of an adolescent residential treatment facility. She was subsequently employed as an academic skills counselor at a private college. Ms. Harris received her bachelor's in social work from Iowa State University, Ames, in 1985, her MSW from the University of Iowa in 1988, and her PhD from the University of Illinois at Urbana-Champaign in 1999. Ms. Harris also earned an undergraduate degree in business administration in 1995.

Robert B. Hill, PhD, is a Senior Researcher at Westat, a research firm in Rockville, Maryland. He was formerly Director of the Institute for Urban Research at Morgan State. His research interest is the effect of public policies on African American children and families. He is the author of the "Strengths of African American Families: Twenty-Five Years Later" (R & B Publishers, 1997).

Michelle A. Johnson, MSW, is a doctoral student at the School of Social Welfare, University of California, Berkeley. She has worked in residential care with foster youth and coordinated child abuse prevention programs in Illinois. After completing her MSW at the University of Illinois, Urbana-Champaign, she worked as a community planner for child welfare services for Hawaii. Her research interests focus on how neighborhood factors mediate social, health, and welfare outcomes among children and families. She is currently a Fellow at the Center for the Development of Peace and Well-Being, Institute for Human Development, University of California, Berkeley.

Will Johnson, PhD, is Director, Office of Evaluation and Research, Alameda County Social Services Agency, Oakland, California, and Adjunct Professor of Public Administration, California State University, Hayward.

Bong Joo Lee, PhD, is Associate Professor at Department of Social Welfare, Seoul National University, Korea, and Faculty Associate at Chapin Hall Center for Children at the University of Chicago. He also holds an appointment as a University of Chicago Research Associate (Associate Professor). Dr. Lee holds a PhD in social policy from the University of Chicago and has held an Assistant Professorship at Boston University School of Social Work. His research focuses on child poverty, child welfare, and social service reform issues. His recent work includes using multivariate methods to examine the effects of early child-bearing and neighborhood poverty on abuse and neglect of children; an examination of food stamp and Women, Infants, and Children utilization patterns before and after welfare reform; and a study of employment outcomes of welfare reform.

Nancy Rolock, MA, has been a Research Specialist at the Children and Family Research Center at the School of Social Work at the University of Illinois at Urbana-Champaign since 1996. Ms. Rolock provides data analysis and evaluation for the office on a variety of topics. Prior to her current position, she directed a national refugee resettlement program, overseeing 30 community-based organizations in their resettlement efforts. Ms. Rolock coauthored an article, "Professional Foster Care: A Future Worth Pursuing?" in *Child Welfare* (1999). Ms. Rolock holds a MA from the University of Chicago, School of Social Service Administration.

Dana Schultz, MPP, is a Senior Policy and Research Analyst at Westat, Rockville, Maryland, with experience in research design, data analysis, and program evaluation. She has worked on several major federal contracts in the areas of child welfare services, child abuse and neglect, missing children, and runaways. Ms. Schultz was the lead analyst for the main National Incidence Study–3 (NIS-3) estimates as well as for the reporting of suspected cases of child maltreatment, and for the NIS-3 CPS Screening Policies study, which summarized the screening policies of CPS agencies. Since the NIS-3, Ms. Schultz has conducted further analyses of the NIS data to look at substance abuse involvement in child maltreatment and risk factors for serious or fatal injuries among maltreated children.

Andrea Sedlak, PhD, is an Associate Director of Human Services Research at Westat, Rockville, Maryland. She received her PhD in social psychology from Rutgers University, New Brunswick, New Jersey, and completed a postdoctoral fellowship in applied social psychology at Yale University, New Haven, Connecticut. She taught at both the graduate and undergraduate levels before joining the research staff at Westat, where she has specialized in research on children, youth, and families, with special focus on troubled, vulnerable, or victimized subpopulations. Dr. Sedlak is currently directing NIS-4, sponsored by the U.S. Department of Health and Human Services. She previously directed both NIS-2 and NIS-3 and several design efforts to enhance the utility and quality of the NIS findings. Under cooperative agreement awards from the Office of Juvenile Justice and

Delinquency Prevention (OJJDP) in the U.S. Department of Justice, she directed Planning for the Survey of Youth in Residential Placement (SYRP) and is currently completing SYRP's first national implementation. She has been a principal investigator on both the first and second National Incidence Studies of Missing, Abducted, Runaway, and Thrownaway Children (NISMART). Her work has also included a study on parental abductions for OJJDP, a study of justice system processing of child abuse and neglect cases for the National Institute of Justice, a national evaluation of runaway and homeless youth for the U.S. Department of Health and Human Services, as well as studies on adoption outcomes, child protective service systems, and domestic violence.

Gail Tittle, MSW, is the Manager of Curriculum Development for the Protective Services Training Institute of Texas at the University of Houston. Prior to this, she was a Research Specialist at the Children and Family Research Center, School of Social Work, University of Illinois at Urbana-Champaign. Gail is currently completing her PhD in social work and has an MSW from the University of Illinois at Urbana-Champaign as well as an MA from the Naval Postgraduate School, Monterey, California; a master's of science from Troy State University, Troy, Alabama; and a bachelor's of science from Texas Wesleyan College, Fort Worth, Texas. Gail also spent 14 years as an Air Force Officer.

Susan J. Wells, PhD, MSW, is the Gamble Skogmo Land Grant Chair in Child Welfare and Youth Policy. She focuses on child welfare practice and policy with special interests in risk assessment and screening, decisionmaking, service coordination, and promoting research-based practice. In collaboration with the Minnesota Department of Human Services (DHS), the Center for Advanced Studies in Child Welfare and the Children, and the Youth and Families Consortium, Dr. Wells developed a child welfare research agenda to help guide policy and practice in Minnesota. She has served as principal investigator on studies of foster care placement stability and reentry into foster care in Hennepin County, Minnesota. Currently, Dr. Wells serves as a consultant on a study for DHS involving racial disparities in out-of-home care and as evaluator on a Minneapolis Foundation educational project, Destination 2010. She is a member of the editorial board of *Children and Youth Services Review* and serves as an expert consultant on a variety of national panels including, for example, the NIS Child Abuse and Neglect Technical Advisory Group. Dr. Wells received her MSW from the State University of New York at Albany, and her doctorate from the University of Southern California, Los Angeles, and was a National Institute of Mental Health postdoctoral fellow at the Johns Hopkins University School of Hygiene and Public Health, Baltimore, Maryland.